SUFFRAGISTS IN AN IMPERIAL AGE

SUFFRAGISTS IN AN IMPERIAL AGE

U.S. Expansion and the Woman Question
1870–1929

ALLISON L. SNEIDER

OXFORD
UNIVERSITY PRESS

2008

OXFORD
UNIVERSITY PRESS

Oxford University Press, Inc., publishes works that further
Oxford University's objective of excellence
in research, scholarship, and education.

Oxford   New York
Auckland   Cape Town   Dar es Salaam   Hong Kong   Karachi
Kuala Lumpur   Madrid   Melbourne   Mexico City   Nairobi
New Delhi   Shanghai   Taipei   Toronto

With offices in
Argentina   Austria   Brazil   Chile   Czech Republic   France   Greece
Guatemala   Hungary   Italy   Japan   Poland   Portugal   Singapore
South Korea   Switzerland   Thailand   Turkey   Ukraine   Vietnam

Published by Oxford University Press, Inc.
198 Madison Avenue, New York, New York 10016

www.oup.com

Oxford is a registered trademark of Oxford University Press

Library of Congress Cataloging-in-Publication Data
Sneider, Allison L.
Suffragists in an imperial age: U.S. expansion and the woman
question, 1870–1929 / Allison L. Sneider.
p.   cm.
Includes bibliographical references.
ISBN 978-0-19-532116-6; ISBN 978-0-19-532117-3 (pbk.)
1. Women—Suffrage—United States—History.   2. Suffragists—United States—History.
3. United States—Territorial expansion—History—19th century.
4. United States—Territorial expansion—History—20th century.   I. Title.
JK1896.S64 2007
324.6'230973—dc22   2007005086

Printed in the United States of America
on acid-free paper

For Steven David Pike and Coco Mae Pike

ACKNOWLEDGMENTS

Books are written in isolation, but like all authors I have been sustained, supported, encouraged, and prodded by family, colleagues, and friends whose generosity and care have contributed in immeasurable ways to making this book possible. The Woodrow W. Wilson Foundation's Charlotte W. Newcombe Dissertation Fellowship, and the Huntington Library's Ernestine Richter Avery Fellowship supported early stages of this research. Paula and Jon Mosle's generous gift to the Rice University School of Humanities offered crucial financial assistance for conducting research during the later stages of this project. Catherine Fitzgerald-Wyatt, Laura Renee Chandler, Gale Kenny, Ann Ziker, and Meg Nunnelly Olsen contributed valuable time, energy, and talent as research assistants when they always had better things to do, and I am extraordinarily grateful for their efforts. Paula Platt and Rachel Zepeda gave generously of their time in more ways then I can count.

Early drafts of this project benefited from the critical gaze of my Philadelphia writing group: Kirsten E. Wood, Jason McGill, and Jennifer Ritterhouse, and the support and encouragement of Sarah Barringer Gordon. Kirsten E. Wood read the manuscript again and again. Her patience is limitless. I have benefited enormously from the comments of Rice colleagues and friends. At different stages Kerry Ward, Ussama Makdisi, Carol Quillen, Elizabeth Long, Rachel Zuckert, Caroline Levander, Alexander Byrd, Lora Wildenthal, and members of the Rice University Feminist Reading Group lent their time and energy and have helped make this a better book than it would have been without their input. Mikas Kalinauskas found a crucial court case at a critical moment and saved the day. Shannon Elizabeth Rhoades always lent me her ear, and one crucial summer, Joyce Appleby lent me her driveway within walking distance of the UCLA library. Phara Charmchi's unwavering commitment made all the difference in the world.

Michael Salman's contributions to this project, both in its formative phases and in later stages, have been invaluable, and I appreciate his enthusiasm and encouragement more than I can say. A year spent with Ann D. Gordon in the editorial offices of the Stanton-Anthony Papers at Rutgers University taught me a great deal about the practice of history without which I would not have been able to research this book. I am especially grateful to Ann for her willingness to share some of her own scholarship in advance of publication and to critique early chapters. Portions of this book were presented at the Berkshire Conference of Women's Historians in 1999 and in 2005; I thank Connie Backhouse and Kathi Kern for their insightful and useful comments.

Lisa Gail Materson's contributions to this project have been boundless. She has edited, critiqued, argued, supported, commiserated, and laughed with me through every word and still claims not to be bored. Thank you.

For the past fifteen years I have been fortunate to participate in an ongoing conversation with Ellen Carol DuBois about the history of the U.S. suffrage movement. This conversation began in the classroom at UCLA when Ellen wondered aloud about why Stanton and Anthony disagreed about the Spanish-American War, but over the years has taken place in airports, at conferences, in her office, in my office, on her back porch, and in her mother's kitchen. Her intellectual generosity has been crucial to this project at every step, and in many ways this book is my latest contribution to this conversation.

Susan Ferber at Oxford University Press is, simply, a heroine. I am also especially indebted to my Oxford readers Louise Newman and Robyn Muncy for their insight, expertise, and timely interventions.

The support of my family has nourished me at every step. Ruthann Sneider is a fellow traveler. If I did not invite my mother to the Berks, I know she would go without me.

I thank my grandparents, Constance and Sumner Stroyman, and Mildred and William Sneider, for their love and generosity, and my extended family Stanley and Priscilla, Marc and Michelle, Arthur and Rebecca, William and Zachary, Matthew and Jacqueline, Carol and Bobby, Arthur, Freddy and Nancy, Jonathan and Ellen and Max, Carol and Lawrie, Daniel and Sarah, Marney and Allan, Michelle and Scott, and Jamie. And above all, my husband, Steven David Pike, who has sustained me through the ups and downs of the creative process.

CONTENTS

SUFFRAGISTS IN AN IMPERIAL AGE

1

U.S. EXPANSION AND THE WOMAN QUESTION, 1870–1929

"We were expansionists in those early days," Henry Brown Blackwell recalled in May 1899, in remarks he wrote for the eightieth birthday celebration of Julia Ward Howe, the Boston suffragist, socialite, and renowned author of "The Battle Hymn of the Republic."[1] Blackwell, co-editor of the Boston suffrage newspaper *Woman's Journal,* had been Howe's collaborator in the struggle for woman suffrage for almost thirty years. His comment referred back to the early 1870s, when he and Howe's husband, the reformer Samuel Gridley Howe, were both investors in the New York–based Samana Bay Company, which leased the Samana peninsula from the Caribbean republic of Santo Domingo from 1872 to 1874.[2] At the time, Blackwell had hoped that the United States would forge a more permanent political relationship with Santo Domingo, and he and Howe, as Blackwell described it, "stood with President Grant for tropical annexation, with the consent of the inhabitants."[3] Blackwell's recollection of his Santo Domingo days was surely provoked by contemporary politics and perhaps intended to underscore the ideological distance he had traveled over the last three decades. In 1899, Blackwell was a vocal critic of the ongoing Philippine-American War and an opponent of U.S. efforts to establish sovereignty over the former Spanish colony by putting down the Filipino resistance movement.[4] Like many suffragists that spring, Blackwell was beginning to think that self-government for women and self-government for the Philippines might be two sides of the same coin.[5]

In 1899 Blackwell may have felt that his location in the antiwar and anti-imperial camp required him to explain away his earlier, expansionist ambitions, but his comments reflected a certain nostalgia for the time he and the Howes had spent together traveling across the "lovely island" of Santo Domingo, visiting the capital, that "picturesque old city founded by Columbus," and enjoying the warm tropical breezes, which were especially welcome after a cold, Boston winter.[6] Indeed, Blackwell's nostalgic vision blended past and present politics. Almost thirty years after President Ulysses S. Grant's treaty of annexation for Santo Domingo failed to pass the Senate, Blackwell maintained that if annexation had succeeded in the 1870s it might have prevented the 1899 Philippine-American War. Like many former advocates of Dominican annexation, Blackwell believed that a U.S. presence in Santo Domingo in the 1870s would have ended slavery in the Spanish colonial Caribbean, and that, as a result, "long frightful years of suffering and bloodshed would have been saved to unhappy Cuba."[7] By this logic, a successful Dominican annexation in the 1870s would have prevented the Spanish-Cuban conflict of the 1890s. It was the 1898 U.S. intervention in this conflict, the U.S victory over Spain, and the decision to maintain control over the Spanish colonial Philippines that led to the 1899 U.S. war of pacification in those islands. To be an anti-imperialist in 1899 did not require Blackwell to renounce his earlier expansionist ambitions as ill-conceived; rather, the Philippine-American War only demonstrated how farsighted his desire for Dominican annexation had been.

Blackwell's engagement with the Dominican annexation project of the 1870s is but one early moment in a much longer narrative of U.S. suffrage and U.S. imperial history that continued through the Spanish-American and Philippine-American wars and well into the twentieth century. During the 1920s, for example, U.S. suffragists, newly enfranchised by the Nineteenth Amendment (1920) to the federal Constitution, successfully lobbied Congress to impose woman suffrage on the U.S. colony of Puerto Rico, against the will of the Puerto Rican legislature.[8] Henry Brown Blackwell and Julia Ward Howe did not live to witness this turn of events, but one wonders how they might have viewed this situation: as an antidemocratic act of colonial rule or a triumph of democratic sisterhood that bridged the boundaries of oceans and crossed the lines of color? In either case, surely Blackwell and Howe would have appreciated the magnitude and the irony of the shift that had occurred in the roughly sixty years between the 1869 formation of two rival U.S. woman suffrage associations that hoped to convince legislators to legalize votes for women, and the 1929 decision by the Puerto Rican legislature to enfranchise women under pressure from the U.S. Congress. In the decades immediately after the Civil War, suffragists had to overcome the larger sense that their measure was "fraught with great danger to the free institutions under which we live, and to the harmony, welfare, and good order of society."[9]

By 1929, votes for women looked likely to become a common feature of the extension of U.S. "imperial democracy" overseas.[10]

U.S. woman suffragists struggled for the vote in an imperial age as Americans looked outward and considered expanding U.S. borders into the Caribbean, Latin America, and even Canada. Yet the history of the postbellum U.S. woman suffrage movement is most often treated as a profoundly, even foundationally, national story.[11] This may be because the organized suffrage movement emerged during Reconstruction, a crucial moment in the formation of the nation-state. During Reconstruction, the passage of two new amendments to the federal Constitution, the Fourteenth (1868) and the Fifteenth (1870), together created a newly national definition of citizenship and enfranchised black men, but not black or white women.[12] From the first, the history of the U.S. woman suffrage movement has been a personal and political history of the responses of woman's rights activists to the passage of these two constitutional amendments. As historians of the early suffrage movement have shown, the founding of the U.S. woman suffrage movement is one of the most complex stories of sex, race, and rights in the nineteenth century.[13] Inseparable from the constitutional history of Reconstruction and the question of political rights for former slaves, the story of woman suffrage is at once a history of women, but also one of racial conflict, states' rights, federal power, and the meaning of citizenship in the new Union.

The history of the U.S. woman suffrage movement is also inseparable from the history of U.S. expansion and the related question of political rights for potential new citizens that expansion inevitably raised. In January 1870, when the newly formed U.S. woman suffrage organizations began petitioning Congress for a sixteenth (woman suffrage) amendment to the federal Constitution, the Forty-first Congress was engaged not only with the nation-building questions surrounding freedmen and secessionist states but also with the expansionist questions raised by the possibility of bringing Santo Domingo into the Union and creating new U.S. citizens in the Caribbean. In 1870, national Reconstruction and Caribbean expansion were both on the national agenda, and U.S. suffragists, like their legislators, were participating in two seemingly distinct, yet overlapping, conversations about citizenship, political capacity, self-government, and national belonging, each of which had its own vocabulary. To use the vocabulary of national Reconstruction was to talk in terms of black and white, of slaves and citizens, and of federal power and states' rights. By contrast, to use the vocabulary of expansion and empire blurred these seemingly coherent categories, replacing black and white with the graded colors of the "Latin races," citizen and slave with the more legally ambiguous terms "ward" and "subject," and the geographic and political entities of state and territory that together made up the United States with the less well-defined geographies of "dependencies" and "possessions." In 1870, U.S. suffragists were much more fluent when they thought about votes for women in the terms of national Reconstruction, of citizenship, of universality, and of constitutional rights. By the end of the nineteenth century, many suffragists were increasingly well versed in the language of empire. In this imperial frame of reference, voting was less a right of citizenship than of civilization, and less defined by universal inclusion than by a shared capacity to exercise the privileges of democracy based on a combination of racial traits and religious commitments.[14]

To think of U.S. suffragists as struggling for the vote in an imperial age and in the context of an expanding national state is not to say that over time all suffragists became imperialists. In Blackwell's case, for example, it could be said that the trajectory went in the opposite direction; in 1899, he was far more critical of U.S. expansionist ambitions than he had been in the 1870s. Rather, it is to suggest that after the Civil War the consolidation of U.S. sovereignty over peoples and territories in the continental West and overseas provided an important political context and intellectual framework for the development of the postbellum U.S. suffrage movement, just as the antislavery movement and political abolition served as an important political context and intellectual framework for the development of the woman's rights movement before the Civil War.[15]

Indeed, it is a central argument of this book that if the United States had not been such an expansive nation after the Civil War suffragists would have had a much harder time raising their question at the national level. One of the enduring puzzles of the U.S. woman suffrage movement is that most U.S. women citizens were granted the vote by federal constitutional amendment at a time when Supreme Court decisions and congressional legislation indicated a national consensus that voting was a state right, and that votes for women should be enacted, if at all, by individual state legislatures.[16] This consensus that the right to vote was properly the subject of state (not national) law reflected a retreat from the national promise to protect black men's voting rights codified during Reconstruction by the Fourteenth and Fifteenth Amendments. In the era of Jim Crow, states were largely left to do as they pleased, and by the turn of the century, state constitutions that disfranchised immigrant and black voters through literacy tests, grandfather clauses, and other means were held to be constitutional.[17] Expansionist ambitions that held that "uncivilized" races were unfit for self-government echoed assumptions about racial difference and racial hierarchy that justified disfranchisement at home. But expansion was an inherently national project, and when legislators discussed the precise ways of governing those at the borders of an expanding Union, they raised questions of self-government, self-sovereignty, and voting rights to the level of national debate. In an age of states' rights and Jim Crow, U.S. expansion in the continental West and overseas was thus crucial to keeping alive a national discussion of the right to vote. As this book demonstrates, over time suffragists would become experts at inserting their question into these national debates.

In 1899, when Henry Brown Blackwell reflected back on Grant's Caribbean ambitions in the 1870s, he used the word "expansionists" to describe those individuals, like himself and Howe, who had supported the annexation of Santo Domingo. Even in 1899, "expansionist" would have had an old-fashioned ring. All around Blackwell, "imperialists" and "anti-imperialists" were daily fighting over the proper disposition of the Philippines and the impact that taking colonies would have on republican institutions within the United States, but Blackwell did not see events in the 1870s through this imperial lens.[18] Rather, he used the term "expansionists" deliberately, as a way of distinguishing U.S. ambitions in the Caribbean in the 1870s from U.S. imperialism in the Caribbean and the Pacific in 1899, and from European imperialism throughout the nineteenth century. In Blackwell's mind, one of the key distinctions between "expansionism" and "imperialism" was consent. As an active and engaged reformer coming of age in the mid–nineteenth century, Blackwell was familiar with the multiple instances of anticolonial rebellion against the rule of European powers across the globe. Although many doubted that Dominican president Buenaventura Báez spoke for the Dominican people when he negotiated a treaty of annexation with the United States, nonetheless, annexation by treaty seemed very different than the rule of force employed by the United States in the Philippines in 1899, or by the Spanish in the Caribbean for centuries. To think of Grant's Caribbean ambitions as "expansionist," as opposed to "imperialist," also located this overseas venture within a tradition of continental expansion that had brought Texas and California, Utah and Oregon, Wyoming and Louisiana into the Union. In this tradition, expansion turned territories into states, and territorial inhabitants into citizens, with all the political privileges of other U.S. citizens.[19]

Blackwell's expansionist model made a simple equation between citizenship and political rights that hid the importance of gender and race to U.S. citizenship and masked a long history of conquest and the rule of force that underlay the history of U.S. expansion. Grant's expansionist ambitions for the Caribbean in 1870, like U.S. expansion across the continental West, were supported by notions of "manifest destiny" that privileged gender, race, and ethnicity as forms of national belonging.[20] As Blackwell told one skeptic of Grant's annexation plans in 1871, "The presence and enterprise of resident white men [in Santo Domingo] is indispensable to Progress."[21] Blackwell's notion that "Progress" in the tropics depended on the presence and enterprise of "white men" is only one of many examples of the ways in which American civilization was equated with manhood and whiteness, with gender and race, rather than with the more abstract principles of freedom and democracy. As a supporter of woman suffrage, Blackwell was well aware that the United States had different categories of citizens with different rights, and that citizenship did not always mean political participation.[22] But in the 1870s, Blackwell shared many of the same assumptions about Anglo-Saxon superiority and the intrinsic benefits of Western civilization that were held by his white European counterparts who were busily elaborating a variety of imperial systems across the globe: the British in India, the French in West Africa, the Dutch in the East Indies.

It would take Blackwell almost thirty years to begin to develop a critique of U.S. imperialism from a woman's rights perspective—that is, one that linked the demand for self-government for women to the right of other peoples to self-determination. During this time, other suffragists would also move back and forth between the language of race and civilization, and that of citizenship and rights to reach different conclusions. In 1899, Carrie Chapman Catt, who succeeded Susan B. Anthony as head of the National American Woman Suffrage Association in 1900, would take up Blackwell's expansionist arguments from the 1870s to make a case that it was the "duty" of U.S. women to help lift the inhabitants of its new island possessions up from "barbarism" to "civilization," a project that would presumably demonstrate the capacity of U.S. women for full citizenship and political rights.[23] In 1899, both imperialist and anti-imperialist visions competed for space on suffrage platforms, with neither clearly in the ascendant. Regardless of where individual suffragists stood on the question of expansion, whether into the Caribbean in the 1870s, across the continental West in the 1880s, or into the Pacific and the Caribbean in 1899 and through the first decades of the twentieth century, the effect of expansion on the U.S. suffrage movement was two-fold: in the first instance it created a political context for a national discussion of woman suffrage in an age of states' rights; in the second, it deepened and complicated the racial divisions always at play in U.S. suffrage politics.

This book brings together a series of events that collectively constitute a history of postbellum suffragism in the context of U.S. empire. It begins with suffragists' intervention in congressional debates over new government for the federal territory of Washington, D.C., in 1870, at the same time that the annexation of Santo Domingo was up for debate. It ends with suffragists' engagement with the question of Puerto Rican woman suffrage in the 1920s.

In between, the question of votes for women became entangled with discussions of Indian citizenship, polygamous women voters in Utah Territory, and statehood for Washington and Wyoming—two western territories where women voted at the end of the Civil War. At the end of the century the taking of colonies and territorial possessions during the Spanish-American War provided a new context for suffragists to push their question, and U.S. suffragists became concerned with the political fate of native women in Hawaii and the Philippines. The chapters that follow examine the different ways that demands for women's ballots have overlapped and inflected parallel debates about political rights, citizenship, and political capacity for other potential new citizens. The focus here is on expansive moments in U.S. history, those moments when national boundaries and borders were redrawn by annexation, treaty, or territorial incorporation. Expansion reconstituted the nation geographically, and, like immigration, culturally, socially, and politically as well. Suffragists quickly realized that expansion effectively opened up space on the congressional calendar for the question of woman suffrage by putting the related question of political rights for potential new citizens (Dominicans, Indians, Mormons, Hawaiians, Filipinos, and Puerto Ricans) on the national agenda.

Tracing how the woman question was framed and reframed in the context of national discussions of citizenship and voting rights for potential new citizens within the District of Columbia, federal territories in the U.S. West, and island territories in the Caribbean and the Pacific highlights the protean nature of the political community that suffragists intended to enter. These varied geographies are held together in a single analytical framework by keeping the focus on national discussions of annexation and expansion. This approach is at once broader and narrower than other histories of U.S. suffragism. Locating suffrage activism in the context of national debates over expanding U.S. borders privileges the emergence of new ideas about race, rights, and the meaning of citizenship, while extending the parameters of U.S. suffrage history both geographically and chronologically. In turn, it de-emphasizes the history of institution building and individual biography. Unlike many histories of suffragism, this is not a narrative of progress that documents the inevitable extension of political rights from propertied white men, to all men, to women. Nor is it a history of declension that tracks the increased use of racist and race-based arguments for white women's ballots within the organized U.S. suffrage movement. Rather, by linking the history of woman suffrage to that of U.S. expansion, this book shows the variety of ways that suffragists brought together arguments about gender, race, and rights over time. In this history individuals wear many different hats, hold divergent and contradictory opinions, and advocate inharmonious policies. These intellectual inconsistencies reveal some of the difficulties of learning to think like imperial citizens and to claim democratic rights in an expanding federal republic that included colonies and dependencies, and that divided sovereignty between the states and the nation.

In chapter 2, suffragists walk onto the national stage in 1870 at their first ever hearing before a joint committee of the House and Senate on the District of Columbia. This introduction to the people and ideas at the forefront of the U.S. suffrage movement after the Civil War shows how the question of votes for women intersected with congressional efforts to reorganize the government of D.C. from a municipality to a federal territory. In 1870, D.C. was the home of some of the nation's first black voters. The debates over turning D.C. into a federal territory demonstrated the complicated ways that black male suffrage, black woman suffrage, and white woman suffrage remained related and overlapping concerns even after black men's formal enfranchisement. In turn, these debates show how votes for women challenged not only a set of gender relations that located women in the private sphere but also a set of federal relations that viewed states, not the national government, as the primary guarantor of a citizen's rights.

Suffragists' D.C. hearing occurred just as administration plans for Dominican annexation made headlines nationally. Within a year suffragists would begin to engage in the debate surrounding U.S territorial expansion into the Caribbean. While not completely unknown, suffragists' engagement with what is generally regarded as a small, quixotic moment in the history of American foreign relations lies buried in the footnotes of biographies of individual reformers.[24] These debates did not become full-fledged in the 1870s because the annexation of Santo Domingo did not occur, but the Santo Domingo episode shows the first glimmerings of how woman's rights activists began to see the question of expanding national borders and the political rights of potential new citizens as related to their own question.

In the 1870s, suffragists began to make claims for women's votes based on their new status as national citizens under the terms of the Fourteenth Amendment. These claims embroiled suffragists in the politics of U.S. federalism—that is, conflicts over the proper balance of state and national authority over the vote. Chapter 3 examines how continental expansion reopened questions of citizenship and suffrage at the national level that suffragists first raised in the early 1870s. More specifically, it shows how congressional debates over territorial statehood and the corollary efforts to resolve the political status of Indians and Mormons raised the woman suffrage question in Congress in the 1880s. Congressional discussions of Indian citizenship and Mormon polygamy focused suffragists' attention on the problems of "uncivilized" voters. To a large extent, however, suffragists sought to lift their question out of the framework of savagery and civilization, and continued to frame women's ballots as a question of national authority over the states.

Chapter 4 moves outside U.S. continental borders and addresses how suffragism was shaped by the U.S. involvement in the Spanish-American and Philippine-American wars. Despite anti-imperialists' assumptions at the time that woman suffragists should be the staunchest critics of antidemocratic efforts to subjugate foreigners and to annex foreign territory, suffragists proved to be complex critics of U.S. imperialism. Viewing overseas expansion in 1898 in much the same way they approached continental expansion in the 1880s, suffragists focused on how congressional control of annexed territories might provide new opportunities to set positive national precedents for women's voting rights. Blending constitutional arguments about national authority over the vote with racial arguments about Filipino and Hawaiian "barbarism," suffragists made claims for women's ballots that linked woman suffrage to the U.S imperial project overseas.

Historians have not considered the federal territory of Washington, D.C., or the federal territories in the nineteenth-century U.S. West as colonies in the European sense of a people and place belonging to, but outside, the nation.[25] This is because territorial status in the United States through the nineteenth century was regarded as a temporary stage on the way to statehood. As a result, the study of western territorial expansion remains largely distinct from the study of U.S. colonialism. Reflecting on the nature of the constitutional relationship between the U.S. government and the inhabitants of the island territories over which it has asserted formal sovereignty, but has not incorporated into the family of states (Puerto Rico, the Northern Mariana Islands, Guam, the U.S. Virgin Islands), the legal scholars Christina Duffy Burnett and Burke Marshall have called U.S. imperialism "empire by deferral."[26] This phrase calls attention to the distinction between incorporated territories whose final status is statehood, and unincorporated territories whose final status is undecided, a distinction that lies at the center of the legal apparatus of U.S. colonial rule. The U.S. territories in the American West were not colonies, but the U.S. colonies of Puerto Rico and the Philippines were (and, in the case of Puerto Rico, still are) federal territories. As such, the determination of whether or not women, or men, should vote in the territories was a decision that rested with the U.S. Congress, unless it chose to cede this decision to local legislative bodies within the territories. To a large extent, suffragists in the early twentieth century approached the problem of votes for women in the "new possessions" of Puerto Rico and the Philippines in much the same way they approached the problem of woman suffrage in D.C. in 1870, and in the western territories

11

in the 1880s, and the strategies that suffragists devised for solving the problem of votes for women in the context of U.S. empire in the first three decades of the twentieth century had roots in these earlier moments.

The 1927 and 1928 congressional debates over extending suffrage to U.S. women citizens in Puerto Rico serves as the final chapter to this study of U.S. expansion and the woman question. Despite their status as U.S. citizens, Puerto Rican women were not enfranchised by the Nineteenth Amendment to the federal constitution. Congressional debates over rewriting the territorial constitutions, or Organic Acts, for Hawaii, Puerto Rico, and the Philippines during the first two decades of the twentieth century contributed to suffragists' hopes for a federal resolution to the suffrage question. In 1917, on the eve of American entry into world war, U.S. suffragists saw votes for women as part of the larger conversations about global democracy, but the question of expanding voting rights for men in the U.S. colonies of Puerto Rico and the Philippines provided a specific political context for women to advance their claims. As they had in the case of D.C. fifty years earlier, suffragists and their congressional allies attached woman suffrage amendments to new governing bills for these U.S. island possessions. This attention to congressional decisions regarding voting rights in U.S. territories overseas brought the status of Puerto Rican women to the attention of U.S. suffragists, and after the passage of the Nineteenth Amendment U.S. suffragists deepened their ties to women in the Puerto Rican suffrage movement. Like U.S. women citizens before them, Puerto Rican women similarly attempted to claim the vote on the basis of their status as national citizens under the law. In so doing, they reopened questions of citizenship, suffrage, and national authority over the vote that most had thought closed during the 1880s, and reengaged the politics of U.S. federalism in a new colonial context.

Since Aileen S. Kraditor's classic study of suffrage ideology between 1870 and 1920 first traced white suffragists' move away from "justice" arguments that were grounded in universal natural rights toward "expediency" arguments, or race-based claims for white women's ballots, scholarly attention has been drawn to the precise ways that woman's rights activists have deployed ideologies of race to reinforce rather than to challenge existing social hierarchies.[27] In light of the fact that "woman suffrage in practice meant primarily suffrage for white women," as Ann Gordon has put it, the historians' goal has been to explain what outside factors were responsible for white woman's rights activists decisions to compromise and narrow their essentially "universalist" and "egalitarian" aims.[28] Answers to this question have taught us much about the racial thinking of individual woman's rights activists and the difficulty of asking male legislators for the vote in a climate of fear over new freedmen and immigrant voters. But Kraditor's "expediency" framework also encouraged historians to describe suffragists' use of racist arguments for white women's ballots as "opportunistic," "strategic," and "tactical," and to view suffrage leaders such as Elizabeth Cady Stanton and Henry Brown Blackwell—who came into the suffrage movement with abolitionist pedigrees and abolitionist sympathies but later championed race-based arguments for white women's ballots—as having undergone a "metamorphosis."[29] Yet neither the classical liberal nor republican traditions on which nineteenth-century U.S. suffragists and abolitionists drew were inconsistent with the belief in natural hierarchies between men and women or between races. To speak in the language of constitutional rights, or of a citizen's right to vote does not preclude the belief that some men and women are more fit to exercise these rights than others.

Louise Newman's recent attention to the importance of civilizing missions as a primary context for the development of women's activism across the nineteenth century makes clear the precise ways in which notions of racial difference and racial hierarchy have been foundational, and not "expedient" necessities, to arguments for white women's empowerment, and as such succeeds in significantly revising Kraditor's long-standing paradigm.[30] In Newman's hands "civilization-work"—that is, "converting 'savages' to Christianity, 'Americanizing' immigrants in settlement houses, 'uplifting' Negroes for the Freedmen's Bureau, and 'bringing civilization' to Indians on reservations"—formed the basis for an activist sisterhood among white women that allowed them to enter the public sphere as allies of white Christian men in the service of progressive reform.[31] U.S. women's civilization work depended not only on exporting Christian spiritual beliefs but also on nineteenth-century gender norms that emphasized the sexual differences between men and women and the importance of distinct female roles in civilized societies. The belief that in primitive societies sexual differences were less highly evolved, and that significant sexual difference was in fact a marker of civilization, reinforced the importance that nineteenth-century white woman's rights activists ascribed to woman's special roles in the work of civilization and helped extend their "rule" in the home into reforming activities in the public sphere. As Newman demonstrates, merging the new nineteenth-century science of evolutionary biology with the benevolent ideology of Christian evangelicalism enabled white women to demonstrate their importance as women to national culture as agents of Anglo-Protestant civilization.

Neither white nor black suffragists stood outside the cultural logic that informed civilizationist discourses across the nineteenth century; in the main, white suffragists accepted the racial hierarchies central to the Anglo-Protestant civilizing mission, while black suffragists sought to claim "civilization" for themselves.[32] But at the end of the Civil War, the demand for woman suffrage was perceived as a challenge to the very gender relations that the advocates of Christian female moral reform were set on bringing to the far reaches of the globe because suffragists, in veteran suffrage leader Elizabeth Cady Stanton's famous phrase, intended to "bury the woman in the citizen." As historians of the postwar Christian women's movements have demonstrated, "churchgoing American women" were not a natural constituency for the suffrage movement because they resisted the challenge that suffragism posed to the prescriptive ideology of "separate spheres" for men and women.[33] Many individual suffragists engaged actively in civilizing projects, and over time many reform-minded Christian women outside the suffrage movement would come to see women's votes as a necessary and useful tool for the fulfillment of their other "womanly" and "Christian" commitments. Nonetheless, arguments for women's empowerment that were founded on women's ability to do the work of civilization and demands for woman suffrage grounded in women's claims for full citizenship did not fit easily together. In 1899, for example, when the Indiana suffragist May Wright Sewall claimed that the "women of the United States were sovereign citizens, even if they didn't have a vote" because they shared in the U.S. civilizing mission as representatives of U.S. womanhood on a global stage, Susan B. Anthony could only wonder if some of her fellow suffragists understood what "true citizenship really means," or if they even wanted the vote.[34]

U.S. suffragism developed in advance of formal empire but within an expanding Union, and the scholarship of historians of gender and empire working in other national contexts provides important models for thinking about how U.S. expansion provided specific political, legal, and constitutional opportunities in which suffragists might transform cultural arguments about white women's empowerment into more specific demands for women's votes. Much of this scholarship has looked outward from the nation, tracking imperialist women and men from the metropole into the colonies, describing the importance of gender to policing the racial boundaries of colonial settlement, and examining how gender has shaped specific colonial encounters.[35] Antoinette Burton, Jane Rendall, Catherine Hall, Patricia Grimshaw, and Ian Fletcher, among others, have built on a central premise of this work—that national and imperial histories are inseparable—to open up the study of suffragism in new ways.[36] Burton, for example, has shown how the issue of licensed prostitution in British colonial India provided British suffragists with a specific political context in which they could engage with the impact of imperial policies for women in the colonies and at home that enabled them to make stronger claims for national representation and formal political participation. British women's ability to construct themselves as both national and imperial citizens depended on the figure of the colonized woman whose need for protection highlighted British women's special abilities, as women, to contribute to the health and vitality of the empire. As Burton demonstrates, a key aspect of British feminists' imperial logic was that woman suffrage would enable British women to carry out more easily the "white woman's burden." In some cases, British feminists came to understand woman suffrage *as* the white woman's burden.[37] As new scholarship on debates over licensed prostitution in the U.S. colonial Philippines has begun to demonstrate, U.S. suffragists often made similar arguments, as in 1902 when women demanded the vote in order to aid President Theodore Roosevelt in preventing state-sanctioned vice in these new U.S. island possessions.[38]

Similarly interested in the "imperial location of western feminism," Jane Rendall, Catherine Hall, and Keith McClelland have turned attention to parliamentary debate in an effort to think about how demands for woman suffrage have intersected the discussion about citizenship, political rights, and national belonging for British subjects in Ireland, Jamaica, and Canada.[39] Hall, McClelland, and Rendall, for example, show how the politics surrounding the British Reform Act of 1867, which significantly reduced property qualifications for the vote and nearly doubled the number of male voters in England, created an opportunity for British suffragists to push their cause when respected radical John Stuart Mill offered an amendment substituting the word "person" for "man."[40] The debates over the British Reform Act took place against the backdrop of violence in the colonies of Jamaica and Ireland, and demands for woman suffrage quickly became part of a larger conversation about the meaning and content of national and imperial citizenship. Voting rights within the United States were largely legislated through state laws, but analogous cases exist. In 1914, for example, the Illinois Republican James Mann attempted to amend the new Philippine government bill to include woman suffrage. Mann's woman suffrage amendment forced Congress to debate votes for women as part of a larger discussion about citizenship and rights in a colonial context, and provides one example of how votes for U.S. women, like votes for their British counterparts, were at once conversations about expanding democracy as well as the meaning of citizenship in the context of empire.

Drawing attention to the complexities faced by metropolitan suffragists when women in the colonies were granted the vote in advance of their imperial sisters, Patricia Grimshaw and Raewyn Dalziel direct the attention of suffrage historians back to the peripheries of imperial systems, to New Zealand and Australia, where women voted in 1893 and 1894, respectively. U.S. historians have paid a great deal of attention to the fact of women's early enfranchise-ment in the territories of the U.S. West, but the story of territorial suffrage into the twentieth century is frequently neglected. For example, although the 1917 Jones Bill for Puerto Rico, which conferred U.S. citizenship on the inhabitants of Puerto Rico, did not grant woman suffrage in that territory as many suffra-gists had hoped, it was a gender-neutral document that allowed Puerto Rico to decide the woman question for itself. This was a privilege that was denied to Hawaii in 1898, despite suffragists' appeals. In 1917 suffragists noted the passage of the Jones Bill with the complaint that votes for women would now come more easily for women living in U.S. possessions than for U.S. women themselves. But the luxury of hindsight indicates that the 1917 Jones Bill must occupy a place alongside individual state suffrage victories on the time line leading up to the passage of the Nineteenth Amendment.

Examining the U.S. suffrage movement in the context of U.S. expansion is part of a larger project of mapping how and in what ways Americans did and did not come to think of themselves as imperial citizens. This project encompasses a wide range of scholarship that includes Kristin Hoganson's investigation of the "manly ideals" that pushed the nation into an imperial war with Spain at the end of the nineteenth century, Mary Renda's study of the "paternal" culture of U.S. empire during the U.S. occupation of Haiti from 1915 though 1940, and Laura Briggs's investigation of the regulation of prostitution in U.S. colonial Puerto Rico during the first decades of the twentieth century.[41] At the most fundamental level the work of these scholars demonstrates the importance of gender and race to how Americans explained to themselves dynamics of power and relationships of rule that could not be explained constitutionally, at least at first.[42] As Hoganson, Renda, and Briggs show, interrogating the gendered metaphors of colonial rule is crucial to understanding how language and culture structured relationships between U.S. soldiers and other representatives of U.S. authority to individual men and women in Haiti, the Philippines, and Puerto Rico, and between U.S. men and women at home.

This book is less concerned with the gendered metaphors of imperial rule than with the related question of how expansion and empire provided political opportunities for U.S. suffragists to raise their question to the level of national debate. This orientation is not designed as a critique of studies that address the cultural work that has sustained U.S. imperial projects, and the importance of imperialist discourse to arguments for female emancipation. Rather, it seeks to include suffragists' efforts to seize the legal and constitutional opportuni-ties presented by U.S. expansion within this frame, and to investigate how debates about voting rights and equal citizenship for women also constituted debates about the boundaries of the nation and the power of the state. Thinking about the relationship between laws about women and the power of the state has been at the heart of projects on women and gender in the United States for the last decade, from Ellen Carol DuBois's investigation of the judicial responses to suffragists' efforts to extend the promises of the Fourteenth and Fifteenth Amendments to women, through Sarah Barringer Gordon's study of antipolygamy legislation in the nineteenth century, to Nancy Cott's recent investigation of the legal history of marriage and national sovereignty.[43] In this scholarship, laws about women expose tensions in American federal relations, between states' rights and national power. Suffragists' efforts to get the vote in an age of empire brought these dilemmas in federal relations to an international stage and in the process demonstrated the importance of expanding U.S. borders to the success of the U.S. suffrage movement at home.

2

✳

RECONSTRUCTION AND ANNEXATION

Suffragists in Washington, D.C., and Santo Domingo, 1870–1875

On January 10, 1870, just three months before the ratification of the Fifteenth Amendment prohibited states from disfranchising male citizens on the basis of race, Republican president and former Union general Ulysses S. Grant presented the U.S. Senate with a treaty of annexation for what was officially the Dominican Republic, but was more popularly known as Santo Domingo.[1] Located just southeast of Cuba, on the eastern half of Hispaniola—an island it shared with the free black republic of Haiti—Santo Domingo was only six or seven days by ship from the harbor of New York. Santo Domingo had been a center of Spanish imperialism in the Caribbean since Columbus first established the colony of Isabella on its northern coast in 1493.

President Grant's expansionist ambitions deeply divided the post–Civil War Republican Party.[2] The Massachusetts Republican senator Charles Sumner, who served as chairman of the Senate Foreign Relations Committee and was famous for his unswerving dedication to the Radical Republican Reconstruction program of black suffrage and civil rights, was a staunch opponent of Grant's plans for annexation and a very public critic of the president and his policies.[3] Already deeply suspicious of Grant's commitment to enforcing the Fifteenth Amendment and to protecting the rights of black citizens within U.S. borders, Sumner viewed the president's plan to annex Santo Domingo's Creole population of mixed Spanish and African descent as potentially disastrous for the Dominicans and their Haitian neighbors. "*Ulysses Grant* and all his friends [a]re strong for annexation; While *Sumner* swears the thing's a fraud, [a]nd ruin to the nation," ran a poem in one Washington daily.[4] The Republican infighting inspired by Sumner and his allies treated newspaper-reading Americans to a frequently bitter public debate over the boundaries of the nation, the capacity of Dominicans for self-government, and the meaning of democracy in a multiracial United States.

In 1870, the advocates of votes for women were also beginning to inspire public debate over the rights of citizenship, the capacity of women for self-government, and the meaning of democracy in a political system that largely excluded women from formal participation. On January 22, less than two weeks after the announcement of Grant's treaty, suffragists had their first ever hearing before a joint congressional committee of the House and Senate. A woman suffrage amendment to the bill creating a new government for Washington, D.C., provided the first opportunity for suffragists to press their claims on a national stage after the Civil War.[5] Like annexation, the question of woman suffrage divided the post–Civil War Republican Party, the home of suffragists' most important allies.[6]

In January 1870, it was not immediately clear how the "Santo Domingo question" and the "woman question" would intersect. At first glance, these two issues—the physical boundaries of national territory, and the gendered boundaries of political space—could not have seemed more separate. Over the next several years, however, suffragists and annexationists, activists who supported both causes, and politicians who supported neither, continued to cross paths and to confront each other in Congress and the press. These disputes between long-standing friends and alliances between strange political bedfellows began to indicate the first outlines of a relationship between questions of citizenship and political rights for U.S. women, and questions of citizenship and political rights for other potential new citizens on the borders of an expanding national state.

Henry Brown Blackwell and the former abolitionist Frederick Douglass were the two U.S. suffragists who became most directly involved in the Santo Domingo question. Blackwell visited the island as a correspondent for the farming magazine *Hearth and Home*, and Douglass was sent to Santo Domingo as part of an official government commission of inquiry. Both men became ardent supporters of annexation and in different ways attempted to link their support for annexation to their woman suffrage commitments. In the 1870s, the links suffragists like Blackwell and Douglass made between votes for women and U.S. expansion were partial, fledgling, and attenuated. Discussions of self-government for women and self-government for Santo Domingo overlapped, but what is so striking about the parallel development of these

FIGURE 2.1. MAP OF SANTO DOMINGO AND HAITI THAT SHOWS THE
EASTERN COAST OF THE UNITED STATES, CIRCA 1870

debates is how difficult it was for women's rights activists in 1870 to frame the question of woman suffrage in colonial or anticolonial terms. By 1899 woman's rights activists would be quick to think through the debate over U.S. expansion into the Caribbean and the Pacific in terms of women's own claims to self-government, but in the 1870s, suffragists did not, or could not, articulate this connection with any degree of analytic rigor. That is, they did not develop strong anticolonial arguments that grounded an opposition to annexation in women's own claims for the right of self-government. Nor did they develop a coherent "imperial suffragism" that linked votes for women to women's ability to partner men in the project of "civilizing" the Caribbean, although they sometimes came very close to doing so.

Tracing suffragists' engagement with the Republican annexation project of the 1870s, then, is an exercise in sighting the very first instances of a complex set of ideas that would not become full-blown until the end of the century but that would link woman suffrage to the project of expanding U.S. borders. Examining this early moment, however, makes it possible to isolate how suffragists began to seize the opportunities presented by national debates over the government of federal territory to raise the woman question in Congress.

WOMAN SUFFRAGE AND RECONSTRUCTION: WASHINGTON, D.C., 1870

On January 22, 1870, members of the Senate, the House, and the press packed a committee room at the Capitol building to observe the spectacle of suffrage activists presenting their arguments for woman suffrage under the new District government at a joint hearing of the House and Senate Committees on the District of Columbia.[7] The veteran woman suffrage activist Elizabeth Cady Stanton stood at one end of the committee room's long center table; the Republican senator Charles Sumner, the renowned advocate of freedmen's civil and political rights, sat at the room's opposite end. Suffrage movement sympathizers took pains to describe the gravity of the occasion that brought "these two veterans in the cause of freedom" face-to-face, noting the cool light of the winter morning, the bare walls of the committee room, and the plain style of Stanton's dress that "held the mind strictly to the simple facts" and lent this meeting its "moral significance."[8] Afterward Stanton would complain to her cousin, the abolitionist reformer Gerrit Smith, about the *Tribune's* foolish decision to send "a girl of 18 whose mind is full of beaux to report such a moment!!!"[9]

Congress's decision to reorganize the government of D.C. provided the first congressional forum for woman's rights activists to make their case for women's ballots since the end of the Civil War. Stanton was joined in the committee room that Saturday morning by a lively and diverse bunch of long-time veterans from the antebellum struggle for abolition and woman's rights. Among them was Stanton's friend and collaborator, forty-nine-year-old Susan B. Anthony. The two had worked together since antislavery days, when Stanton was a young mother with a growing family. Other reform veterans who made the trip to Washington included Paulina Wright Davis, the organizer of the first National Woman's Rights Convention in 1850, and the Connecticut suffragist Isabella Beecher Hooker. Hooker's famous siblings included the novelist Harriet Beecher Stowe, the author of *Uncle Tom's Cabin*, and the educator Catharine Beecher, whose writings on women's domestic calling were widely read. Olympia Brown, the first woman Universalist minister in the United States, and Josephine Griffing, a D.C. resident and freedmen's aid advocate, also joined the group. Together these activists introduced in 1870 a style and rhythm of organizing that would remain in place for years to come: May meetings in New York City, January hearings in Washington, D.C., and months of touring and lecturing across the country in between.[10]

Notably absent from the D.C. committee hearings that January were the husband-and-wife team of Lucy Stone and Henry Brown Blackwell. In 1868 Stone and Blackwell, like Stanton and Anthony, had been members of the American Equal Rights Association (AERA), a postbellum reform coalition of antislavery and woman's rights activists who had worked for universal suffrage since May 1866. Before the Civil War, Stone had been an extraordinary orator on the antislavery and woman's rights circuits, with audiences often numbering in the thousands. In the 1850s, Blackwell devoted his energies to business and journalism, but became, with Stone, a partner in the struggle for woman's rights.

Even in its barest outlines, understanding how the AERA came together in May 1866, and the reasons behind its demise in May 1870, requires jumping headfirst into a sea of Fourteenth and Fifteenth Amendment legal scholarship that explores how these amendments together created a constitutional revolution that fundamentally revised the relationship between the federal government and the states.[11] The split within the AERA began with the first discussions over the terms of the Fourteenth Amendment (1868), which promised equality before the law to all national citizens. The amendment's first clause declared that, "all persons born or naturalized in the United States, and subject to the jurisdiction thereof, are citizens of the United States."[12] This one amendment overturned nearly a century of state and federal law that had made it legally impossible for black men and women to become citizens in most states. Emancipation without citizenship would have left former slaves in a legally ambiguous and personally precarious position. In this respect, many AERA members supported the Fourteenth Amendment because it continued the emancipatory work set in motion three years earlier when the Thirteenth Amendment (1865) abolished slavery.

Even as the Fourteenth Amendment's first clause created a newly national definition of citizenship, and prohibited states from abridging the privileges and immunities of national citizens, its second clause spelled out the precise reduction in congressional representation a state could expect if it denied male citizens the right to vote.[13] There was no penalty for denying women this same right. Advocates of black enfranchisement, regardless of where they stood on the question of woman suffrage, were concerned by the weak protections of male voting rights offered by the Fourteenth Amendment. The amendment's second clause at once established a right to vote but also set precise penalties for states that denied this right to their citizens. So, too, the amendment left ambiguous whether or not the right to vote was a fundamental privilege and immunity of citizenship. Despite these concerns over voting rights, many AERA members lent their support to the Fourteenth Amendment because it established the citizenship of newly emancipated slaves.

For Elizabeth Cady Stanton the issue was less that the Fourteenth Amendment offered only limited and weak protections of men's right to vote, but that these protections, however weak, applied only to men. The Fourteenth Amendment was incompatible with a commitment to universal equal rights for men and women, Stanton argued, because its piecemeal approach gave black men the privileges of citizenship before women, white or black, and created the legal foundation for an "aristocracy of sex."[14] Many of those who followed Stanton and Anthony to D.C. in 1870 stood similarly opposed to the Fourteenth Amendment precisely because its second clause put the word "male" in the Constitution for the first time.

Frederick Douglass was at the center of these arguments that splintered advocates of universal suffrage, divided the suffrage movement, and entangled it, despite itself, in racial politics. With Stone and Blackwell, Douglass was convinced that in the immediate aftermath of the Civil War, freedmen's political rights had to take precedence over votes for women. In the midst of these debates over the Fourteenth Amendment, Stone, Blackwell, and Douglass began to distance themselves from Stanton and Anthony. In February 1869, this distance was widened when Congress passed the Fifteenth Amendment (ratified in 1870). The Fifteenth Amendment rectified the Fourteenth Amendment's weak protection of freedmen's voting rights by prohibiting disfranchisement on the basis of "race, color, or previous condition of servitude" and by providing for federal action to enforce this ban.[15] By failing to include "sex" in its list of special prohibitions, however, it left in place the sexual discrimina-tions that had been newly embedded in the Constitution by the Fourteenth Amendment. Stanton's vocal opposition to the Fifteenth Amendment was often expressed in language that was hostile to black voting rights and contrib-uted to polarization within the AERA. AERA members who believed, along with Douglass, that "if the elective franchise is not extended to the negro, he dies" could hardly be expected to sympathize with Stanton's protest that "'a man's government' is worse than 'a white man's government,'" or even to speak alongside her on the same platform.[16]

In May 1869, Stanton, Anthony, and other like-minded suffragists came together in New York City to found the National Woman Suffrage Associa-tion (NWSA), the first national organization dedicated exclusively to votes for women. Six months later Stone and Blackwell, "the Boston clique," as Anthony put it, founded the rival national American Woman Suffrage Asso-ciation (AWSA) and completed the rift between leaders in Boston and New York that would last for twenty years. Under the editorial stewardship of Stone and Blackwell—and with the financial and editorial support of Julia Ward Howe, among others—the *Woman's Journal* made its debut as the offi-cial newspaper of the AWSA on January 8, 1870.[17] "The Woman's Journal is here—just as nice & prim as you please," Anthony wrote to Isabella Hooker a few days before leaving New York for D.C., and "not a mention of the National W.S.A. or The Revolution."[18] This was exactly two years to the day from the first publication of Stanton and Anthony's *Revolution*.[19] Stone and Blackwell, on the one hand, and Stanton and Anthony, on the other, had initially divided over policy, but personal animosities quickly magnified their differences.

Despite this rivalry, the existence of two national suffrage organizations was a fair indication that in 1870 the U.S. woman suffrage movement was vibrant. Indeed, in January 1870 suffrage activists across the states had good reason to hope that legislation authorizing votes for women might occur in the not-too-distant future. After all, the 1868 passage of the Fourteenth Amendment made citizens and potential voters of 13 million freedmen across the South and North, and in the spring of 1869 Wyoming Territory became the first U.S. territory to give full voting rights to women. Utah Territory looked likely to follow suit in the coming year. If this were not enough to give woman's rights activists some hope that their enfranchisement lay just around the corner, the Fifteenth Amendment, passed in 1869 and on its way to being ratified, signaled the Republican Party's commitment to using the federal courts to protect freedmen's right to vote against state action. Although votes for women were not included in these constitutional amendments, the American electorate was rapidly expanding, and it did seem as if the time was finally at hand for a national discussion of the woman question.

When suffragists arrived in Washington in the winter of 1870, the structure of the government of D.C. was on the congressional agenda. Since the Civil War, the nation's capital had become the site of a tremendous influx of black refugees fleeing from the racial violence and economic depravations in the South. Between 1860 and 1870, the black population of D.C. grew from just over 10,000 to roughly 35,000, making the capital one of the largest urban black communities in the nation and one of the fastest growing cities overall.[20] Article 1, Section 8 of the U.S. Constitution gave exclusive legislative control of D.C. to the federal government, which made voting rights in the nation's capital entirely dependent on Congress. In 1867, despite local disapproval and presidential veto, Congress had opened voting in D.C.'s municipal government to black men.[21] At a time when black men could vote in only six other states in the Union, black men's ability to participate fully in D.C. government was a controversial affair with national significance.[22]

In 1870, even those who supported black suffrage in D.C. and nationally were concerned with the inability of the existing municipal government to handle effectively the variety of issues confronting this rapidly expanding post-war city. Congress was forever being sidetracked from national affairs by local D.C. issues.[23] Proposed instead was a territorial form of government, with a governor and upper house appointed by the president and a lower house elected by the residents—much like the territorial form used in the West to govern the territories of Washington, Utah, and Wyoming.[24] In the American imagination, territories represented possibility; as potential new states, they were the future of the nation, both geographically and socially. Wyoming Territory's decision to grant suffrage to women in 1869 was just one example of what was possible for women in those locales where the weight of custom was not heavy.[25]

Suffragists were drawn to the idea of pursuing votes for women in D.C. not only because such a victory might usher in a future of women's political equality, as it had for freedmen, but also because past congressional efforts to reorganize D.C. government had already raised the woman question to the level of national debate. During the 1866 Senate discussion of black male suffrage in D.C., just prior to black men's 1867 enfranchisement, Democratic senator Edgar Cowan of Pennsylvania proposed to strike out "male" as well as "color" and "race" from the qualifications for electors and sparked the first debate over votes for women in the U.S. Senate.[26] Cowan was neither a champion of woman's rights nor of voting rights for black men. Rather, as he told his fellow senators, "If the franchise is to be widened, if more people are to be admitted to the exercise of it," he would much prefer "to allow females to participate than I would negroes."[27] A *New York Tribune* editorial speculated that Cowan's interest in votes for women "subjects him to the suspicion of being considerably more anxious to embarrass the bill for enfranchising the blacks, than to amend it by conferring upon women the enjoyment of the same right."[28] Regardless of Cowan's intentions, his proposed amendment to the District government bill engendered three days of Senate debate before it was defeated thirty-seven to nine.[29]

Restructuring the government of D.C. thus opened a political space for the woman question in 1866, and it seemed likely to do so again in 1870. Yet not every suffragist gathered in D.C. that winter was convinced that the reasons behind the establishment of a new D.C. government were sound. Some advocates of black voting rights worried that the reconstitution of D.C.'s government from a municipality to a territory would serve as a means to undermine an important example of vibrant black democracy. In 1866, the abolitionist and woman's rights advocate Frederick Douglass traveled to D.C. to speak out for black enfranchisement in the District just as Congress took up the debate.[30] By 1870, Douglass was himself a D.C. resident and editor of the *New Era*, D.C.'s paper of record for the black community.

Douglass's *New Era* opposed the reorganization of D.C. government and viewed the effort to rescind municipal government in the District as a plot to disfranchise black Americans. As one *New Era* editorial explained, "[In] plain Anglo-Saxon, the old fogies are opposed to negro suffrage; and as they cannot withdraw it, they seek to diminish, if not destroy, the opportunities for its exercise." The *New Era* was particularly concerned with the problem of permanent territorial status. Unlike the western territories, which were expected to come into the Union as new states, Congress's control over D.C. extended in perpetuity, and writers in the *New Era* warned their readers that "Here, in the very sight and hearing of a Republican Congress—on ground made historical as the birthplace of emancipation and equal suffrage—it is proposed to erect a government independent of suffrage and derogatory to citizenship." For many of D.C.'s black voters, a municipal government elected by the people and answerable to Congress was a special and exemplary status that had the weight of congressional approval behind it. In contrast, a territorial government that was appointed by Congress would mark D.C.'s black inhabitants as less fit and less ready for self-government. Territories were considered an appropriate "stepping stone to State organization," but as a permanent form, *New Era* writers deemed them "both unrepublican and irresponsible."[31]

The *New Era* did not couch its opposition to a territorial government in the language of anticolonialism—its journalists could not know at that time that permanent territorial status would become one of the primary structural forms of U.S. colonial rule. However, the *New Era* did show clearly what was at stake: a national capital inhabited by some of the nation's first black voters, who might now be moved even further outside the regular workings of American democracy.

Stanton and Anthony, among others who attended the D.C. committee hearings in 1870, viewed the situation differently than writers in Douglass's *New Era*. They focused instead on the possibilities that any changes in the government of D.C. might hold for woman's rights. Many D.C. suffragists believed that because woman suffrage in the District, like black male suffrage before it, would have the force of congressional approval, it would be a far more significant achievement than votes for women in any other municipality, territory, or state in the Union. Stanton shared the *New Era*'s concerns that the proposal to abolish municipal government, and to reduce D.C. "to a mere territory" was "clearly retrogressive legislation; as in the former, the chief magistrate is elected by the people and in the latter appointed by the President."[32] Regardless, her priority was women's enfranchisement, and she thought that Congress's "primal duty is to extend to the women of the District the right of suffrage ... whether their government shall be republican with a Representative in Congress, municipal officers, or territorial with a Governor appointed by the President."[33] The suffrage activist Olympia Brown convinced herself that because black suffrage in the District was already firmly established, the proposed changes in D.C.'s governing structure would not pose a serious threat to black male voting rights. At a meeting of the Universal Franchise Association, a local organization of District suffragists, Brown asserted that "there was no question of negro suffrage now in the District, and she hoped no abatement of interest [in the suffrage question] would manifest itself until woman is placed on an equal footing with man before the law."[34]

In a political situation in which black suffrage and woman suffrage were frequently counterposed, the specific claims of black women could be easily lost. An anonymous writer in the *New Era,* who signed her letter "A Colored Woman" reminded readers that both black men and black women had long been staunch supporters of woman's rights, and that the opposition between black suffrage and woman suffrage was inherently false. She recalled the emotions she had felt more than twenty years earlier when she had watched a colored man escort the white suffragists Ernestine Rose and Antoinette Brown as they presented a woman's rights petition to the New York state legislature: "I felt proud that, although no white man was found with heart large enough and purse long enough to entertain these noble women, there was a colored man possessing both the heart and the means to entertain them."

"There were colored men," she continued, "whose names are well known among the champions of freedom, who were always there to escort them."[35] Records and newspaper coverage of the 1870 D.C. hearing do not explicitly mention the presence of black women at this event, but this letter in the *New Era* suggests their interest in the proceedings, if not their presence.[36] The biographer of Mary Ann Shadd Cary, the first black woman to attend the newly founded Howard Law School, has speculated that Cary attended the 1870 woman suffrage convention held in D.C. the week after the D.C. committee hearing.[37] By 1872 Cary was a contributor to the *New Era*, she had known Douglass since the 1850s, and it is quite possible that she wrote this anonymous letter.

This brief letter in the *New Era* underscored the complicated realities faced by the proponents of woman suffrage, black and white, who in 1870 were trying to insert themselves into a congressional debate over D.C. government. For some, the debate over the best type of government for the District represented a crucial referendum on black male voting rights and a test of congressional commitment to black men's enfranchisement. For others, the debate was an opportunity to press for woman's rights, white and black. And for still others, it was a chance to pit the claims of white women against those of black men. For all participants, the question of reorganizing D.C.'s government was a concrete lesson that national debates over voting rights for any one group touched on the voting rights of everyone, that black male suffrage, black woman suffrage, and white woman suffrage were related and overlapping concerns.

Taking place so soon after the passage of the Fourteenth Amendment, and just before the ratification of the Fifteenth, the D.C. committee hearings provide an extraordinary glimpse of individual efforts to work out the meaning of these radical and sweeping changes in the nation's fundamental law. When Stanton stood to give her remarks before the House and Senate committees charged with overseeing District government, her arguments reflected this sense of flux. To make her case for women's votes in D.C., Stanton first reached outside the Constitution itself to the democratic theory of inalienable, natural rights as developed by the *Federalist* writers John Jay and Alexander Hamilton. As she told the committee, "The right [to self-government] itself is antecedent to all constitutions. It is inalienable, and can neither be bought, nor sold, nor given away."[38] While she conceded that "the mode and manner in which the people shall take part in the government of their creation may be prescribed by the constitution," she emphasized that "in framing a constitution the people are assembled in their sovereign capacity; and being possessed of all rights and powers, what is not surrendered is retained."[39] Stanton argued here that women, like men, were entitled to self-government through the vote, since the vote marked the fundamental way in which individuals consented to government.

Stanton spoke in a language of eternal principles, but her arguments were also framed within a specific political context. To Stanton, the Civil War, like the American Revolution, was a foundational moment in the nation's history, a time when the organic law of the land could be revisited, and eternal principles reaffirmed through specific political acts. Congress's decision to reconstitute the government of D.C., to establish it on new principles after it was "resolved into its original elements," represented another such foundational moment when eternal principles could be affirmed through new laws. By restructuring the government of D.C., Congress was doing "fundamental work," and Stanton believed that "all the people should have a voice" in this work.[40] In other words, the reorganization of D.C.'s government provided a specific political context in which Congress might recommit itself to the democratic sentiments of the American Revolution.

Stanton also took the opportunity provided by the D.C. hearing to offer a new argument for woman suffrage that interpreted the Fourteenth Amendment in a novel and more radical way, one that reflected a dramatic shift in her thinking about this amendment over the last two years and one that might actually eliminate rather than exacerbate tensions between blacks' and women's rights. This new reading of the Fourteenth Amendment was first circulated in St. Louis in 1869 by the Missouri suffragists Virginia Minor and her lawyer husband, Francis. Together the Minors had begun to think through the meaning of the Fourteenth Amendment for women, and they had come up with something extraordinary, something they believed would "stand the test of legal criticism."[41] To the Minors, women's right to vote, like black men's right to vote, could be based upon their new Fourteenth Amendment status as national citizens. If voting was understood to be a privilege of citizenship, and the Fifteenth Amendment on its way to being passed certainly suggested that it was, then the important work of the Fourteenth Amendment was that it made all persons born or naturalized in the United States citizens of the United States. Since women were citizens, perhaps they too had become potential voters by the Fourteenth Amendment. Perhaps state constitutions that limited the franchise to male citizens contradicted the new Fourteenth Amendment. What if women simply took what was already theirs and voted?

Francis Minor urged women to do just that. If they were stopped at the polls, so much the better, because "in no other way could our cause be more widely, and at the same time definitively brought before the public. Every newspaper in the land would tell the story, every fireside would hear the news." By the time the question would be favorably decided by the Supreme Court at some time in the future, Francis Minor predicted "the popular verdict would be in accord with the judgment that is sure to be rendered." Here was a way for women to move forward: "We no longer beat the air—no longer assume merely the attitude of petitioners. We claim a right, based upon citizenship."[42] In the days just prior to the 1870 hearing, suffragists had printed up 10,000 extra copies of an issue of Stanton and Anthony's *Revolution* that laid out these new ideas and placed a copy "on every member's desk" in the Congress.[43]

The Minors' belief, that voting inhered in the condition of national citizenship, was very much a product of its particular historical moment. Before the passage of the Fourteenth Amendment, the relationship between citizenship and voting was ambiguous. Property qualifications for the vote existed from the colonial period through the American Revolution and into the first decades of the nineteenth century. With the exception of the years 1776 to 1807 in the new state of New Jersey, women citizens had never consistently voted.[44] Yet the Minors' understanding of the meaning of the Fourteenth Amendment, that voting and citizenship went hand in hand, captured how in the postwar moment black men's citizenship and voting rights were linked.[45] Indeed, black men's citizenship, like black and white women's citizenship, had long been governed by a patchwork of laws that reflected ambiguity about their relationship to the polity, and the Fourteenth Amendment at once resolved black men's citizenship status and gave them equal protection under the law. Freed by the Thirteenth Amendment in 1865, made citizens and potential voters by the Fourteenth Amendment in 1868, black men in 1870 seemed to embody a new, crucial link between citizenship and suffrage in the postwar nation and thus point to something larger than their own enfranchisement.[46]

The Minors' equation of citizenship and suffrage appeared to be further supported by the Fifteenth Amendment, just months away from ratification. The Fifteenth Amendment's first clause declared that a "citizen's right to vote shall not be abridged." This phrase implied that citizens already enjoyed a right to vote. That the Fifteenth Amendment's full text read that a "citizen's right to vote shall not be abridged on the basis of race, color, or previous condition of servitude" could be understood as merely an emphatic, but not exhaustive, list of special conditions. And this is the way the Minors, and those like Stanton who agreed with them, were beginning to interpret it. In the Minors' reading, the Fourteenth Amendment established voting rights for all national citizens, including women. The Fifteenth Amendment, in their eyes, underscored this fact.

From a contemporary vantage point, the Minors' reading may seem idiosyncratic, an overly complex effort to torture a larger meaning out of laws that were designed to protect newly emancipated black men in the South.

But many arguments for the Fourteenth and Fifteenth Amendments had been made in the language of universal democracy: that all men are created equal and share equally in the right to life, liberty and the pursuit of happiness. The Minors' reasoning extended these ideas to women. And because this new way of reading the Fourteenth and Fifteenth Amendments took "citizenship" and "suffrage" to be synonymous terms, it did not render the claims of race and sex antagonistic. Rather, it supported black women's rights and white women's rights, black men's rights and white men's rights, in equal measure. As Francis Minor described them, "These resolutions place the cause of equal rights far in advance of any position heretofore taken."[47]

Suffragists hoped to find allies among the congressmen who attended the D.C. Committee hearing for the Minors' new thinking, and they were especially attuned to how Senator Sumner would receive their remarks. In the recent past Sumner had disappointed suffragists. In the 1866 Senate debate over black suffrage in the District, Sumner had agreed with Cowan's critics that the question of votes for women was a distracting side issue from the more important question of black male suffrage.[48] In 1870 Sumner disappointed suffragists again and refused to declare himself on the subject. Sumner commended the assembled suffragists and those congressmen who supported them, noting that after twenty years in the Senate "he had never seen a committee in which were present so many Senators and Representatives, so many spectators, and so much interest manifested in the subject under discussion."[49] Even so, the day's proceedings were not enough to garner his outright support.

Although the woman suffrage amendment to the D.C. government bill failed to pass, when suffragists left the capital their spirits were ebullient, and many were eager to test the Minors' new theory—soon labeled the New Departure—at the polls. It would take Congress until the winter of 1871 to decide D.C.'s new status; in February 1871 both houses would approve a measure to turn D.C. into a federal territory. But animated by plans to test the New Departure and by their decision to push a new Sixteenth Amendment, modeled on the Fifteenth, that would prohibit states from disfranchising citizens on the basis of sex, suffragists left the capital convinced that their work in D.C. had been a great success.

DEBATING ANNEXATION: SANTO DOMINGO, 1870

Focused on the politics of Reconstruction that in January 1870 provided the backdrop to the D.C. committee hearings, suffragists were largely unaware of the other events that were just then coming to occupy legislators' attention.

On January 10, 1870, little more than a week before suffragists' congressional hearing, President Grant sent two treaties to the Senate for consideration. The first committed the United States to the annexation of Santo Domingo and to bringing the island republic into the Union as a new federal territory. A second, less ambitious, treaty contracted for the ninety-nine-year lease of Samana Bay, the principal harbor on Santo Domingo's northern coast.[50] On January 18, a week after the D.C. hearings took place, Sumner chaired the first meeting of the Senate Foreign Relations Committee to examine Grant's Santo Domingo treaty. During the preceding week, local and national newspapers had begun picking up the story of U.S. plans to annex Santo Domingo. Throughout suffragists' stay in D.C., their activities shared space in the press with commentary, editorials, and predictions about when and how annexation would take place.

Grant's enthusiasm for annexation combined what he believed was a very obvious national self-interest with a somewhat less convincing humanitarianism. As Grant told Congress, Santo Domingo possessed "one of the richest territories under the sun" and the "most capacious harbors" at the entrance to the Caribbean Sea.[51] For American businessmen looking to increase the domestic production of sugar and coffee among other imports, as well as to ensure easy trade with Latin American markets, President Buenaventura Báez's offer to annex his country to the United States looked too good to refuse. Grant also believed that annexation held out the possibility of other, less material, rewards. After centuries of Spanish colonial rule, Dominican democracy was relatively new and seemingly fragile. Threatened by internal rebellions, border disputes with Haiti, and the designs of European powers, Grant was certain that the people of Dominica must "yearn for the protection of our free institutions and laws; our progress and civilization."[52] In Grant's eyes, the United States had a role to play defending Dominican democracy, one spelled out by the Monroe Doctrine's 1823 prescription that the American hemisphere was no longer open for European colonization.[53]

In addition to protecting Dominican democracy, Grant offered up yet another, even more humanitarian reason for annexation, one designed to resonate deeply with those Americans who held abolitionist sympathies and had supported the Republicans and the Union in the recent Civil War: abolishing slavery in the Caribbean. There had been several abolitions of slavery in Spanish Santo Domingo, the first in 1801 when the Haitian rebel Toussaint L'Ouverture invaded the Spanish colony during his uprising against the French. The Spanish reinstated the practice when they regained control of the colony between 1809 and 1821, and slavery continued until Haiti invaded Spanish Santo Domingo again in 1822. By 1870, slavery had been abolished for good in both Haiti and Santo Domingo, yet the institution still thrived in the nearby Spanish colonies of Cuba and Puerto Rico.[54] Grant promised Congress that under U.S. protection the economy of Santo Domingo would blossom, drawing laborers from the surrounding islands of Cuba and Puerto Rico. These islands would then, "as a measure of self-preservation," be forced to abolish slavery in order to retain their workforce.[55] It was hoped that Brazil, another site of slavery in the Americas, would soon follow suit. With Santo Domingo as a thriving example of free labor, black Americans might even choose to quit the U.S. South, easing American racial tensions. Given these outcomes, Grant asked Congress to consider how annexation could possibly fail "to redound greatly to the glory of the two countries interested, to civilization, and the extirpation of slavery?"[56] With a Republican majority in Congress and the Republican Charles Sumner chairing the Senate Foreign Relations Committee, Grant hoped that annexation might sail through Congress as a Republican measure.[57]

The initial public responses to Grant's treaties were, however, mixed. Some Americans approved of the plan and considered it an important first step toward a much greater U.S. presence in the Caribbean. The *New York Times* happily predicted that the annexation of Santo Domingo was "but a preliminary movement to the acquisition of the entire island," and that "Hayti [*sic*] will come in due time."[58] Other press included Cuba as well as Haiti on a list of new territory that would, it was hoped, eventually follow Santo Domingo into the Union as a new state.[59] In 1870, much of Cuba was engaged in an anticolonial insurgency against Spain that sought emancipation for Cuba's slave population in addition to national independence. Many former American abolitionists sympathized with the Cuban insurgents. Others hoped an independent Cuba would provide an important export market for American products.[60]

Sympathy for the Cuban insurgents did not necessarily translate into support for the annexation of either Santo Domingo or Cuba, however, and Grant's critics were as vocal as his supporters. Some skeptics wondered publicly if the president's enthusiasm for acquiring new territory in the Caribbean meant that Grant was dabbling in land speculation. In January 1870, it was easy to be suspicious of Grant's motives. In the previous months, the president's association with financiers Jay Gould and James Fisk's illegal attempts to manipulate the market in gold had become a public scandal that seriously tarnished his reputation.[61] Leaving Grant's speculative ventures aside, still other critics of Grant's expansionist foreign policy worried that despite Báez's protestations to the contrary, the Dominican people did not truly want annexation to the United States and might resist with force. For Americans still recovering from the destructive violence of the Civil War, the thought of a new military conflict in the Caribbean was an alarming one.[62]

Anti-annexationists' most widely shared and deeply held concern, however, had to do with the "character" of the Dominican people themselves, and with the ability of the United States to incorporate territory—willing or otherwise—that was not, in the vocabulary of Reconstruction era America, sufficiently "civilized." Equating civilization with whiteness and Protestant Christianity, and estimating Santo Domingo's largely Catholic population to be only one-tenth white—although "what their color really is we have no means of knowing"—a writer for the *Nation* summed up the Santo Domingo situation this way: "Were its population in any sense of the word a civilized population, or had we a civil service so officered and managed as to furnish a civilizing agency, we should have very little to say against the acquisition."[63] Without such an agency, this correspondent feared the problem of "civilizing" the Dominicans was beyond the capacity of the present government.[64] The notion that civilizing projects required the services of a trained staff of civil servants was, of course, a specious one. U.S. missionaries had been doing civilization work among Indians and overseas for decades without the formal support of government agencies. But this critique served the purpose of implicitly placing the U.S. annexation project on a par with the more formal colonial projects of European powers in the Caribbean, like Spain, to which the United States often contrasted its own enlightened democracy.

In 1870, many Southern Democrats agreed in spirit with the sentiments advanced by anti-annexationists in the *Nation*, that civilizing Santo Domingo was beyond the capacity of the present government, and argued that "instead of our elevating those degenerate races in the tropics, they will rather drag us down to their level."[65] In the antebellum period, there had been a significant amount of support among southern slaveholders for American expansion into the Caribbean, particularly into Cuba, as one possible means of protecting and strengthening the institution of slavery.[66] As a result, abolitionists in the 1850s objected to territorial expansion overseas as part of their opposition to the extension of slavery into new territory in the American West.[67] After the Civil War, however, when Grant linked expansion to abolition and the Constitution forbade slavery, these positions reversed. In 1870, the thought of incorporating Santo Domingo's multiracial population into the Union without the framework of slavery became anathema to many of those who had formerly pushed for a greater U.S. presence in the Caribbean, and racist arguments became the common currency of Grant's opponents.[68]

In this context support for annexation, the willingness to open up the polity to new, nonwhite citizens could be considered an explicitly antiracist stance, as a refusal, in the words of one *New Era* writer, to "defer to the sophisms of prejudice."[69] It was this position that informed Douglass and his colleagues' decision to line up behind Grant in favor of annexation. "There was a time not many years back, when colored men, both here and in Saint [*sic*] Domingo, repelled with abhorrence such measures as we now advocate," ran one *New Era* editorial, but "this feeling has passed away with the oppression and wrong-doing which gave it birth."[70] In February and March 1870, while Sumner's Foreign Relations Committee considered Grant's treaties, writers in the *New Era* began claiming that U.S. expansion into the Caribbean was part of the project of constructing a multiracial democracy at home and "heartily sympathizing with their brethren" in the Caribbean urged the U.S. Senate to vote for annexation on behalf of "colored men" in the United States and Santo Domingo.[71]

The notion that bringing Santo Domingo's multiracial population into the Union signaled an ongoing commitment to black civil and political rights within U.S. borders—that U.S. expansion abroad could be linked to the expansion of U.S. democracy at home—may have had the force of simple logic, but it was not the only way to read the situation. Convinced that "providence" intended the islands of the West Indies as "the seat of a great black republic, where the colored race, in a congenial climate…could work out their destiny as an independent Power to a glorious fulfillment," Sumner was increasingly emphatic that any friend of the "African race" should oppose annexation.[72] In contrast to Douglass, Sumner believed that annexation would threaten rather than enhance black democracy at home and abroad by undermining the independence and sovereignty of Haiti; and Haiti in 1870, as Sumner was continually reminding his colleagues, was the only free black republic in the hemisphere.[73] Sumner's concern for Haiti was long-standing. In 1862, he had worked with President Lincoln to secure American diplomatic relations with Haiti, and he was well informed about the territorial claims underlying Haiti's ongoing border disputes with its Dominican neighbor.[74] As Sumner wrote one friend, he considered the Haitians "almost my wards."[75]

Prominent members of the antebellum abolitionist reform cohort, including William Lloyd Garrison, Gerrit Smith, and the black abolitionist and woman suffragist Robert Purvis, shared Sumner's fears that U.S. annexation of Santo Domingo would eventually encompass the entire island. Garrison's newspaper columns railed against what he called "American Swagger and Manifest Destiny" and criticized Grant's pretensions that the American desire to annex Santo Domingo grew out of a concern "for her special elevation and advancement." "Heaven knows," he wrote, "that we are not yet so far delivered from our deep rooted prejudices against the negro race as to make us care a straw for the mental, moral, or material condition of the Dominicans."[76]

[handwritten margin note: true motives]

The former abolitionist and suffrage sympathizer Lydia Maria Child agreed with Garrison, writing both privately and publicly in support of Sumner and against what she termed this "insane rage for annexation" and our "national greed for territory."[77] Child was especially concerned, however, with how annexation might add weight to the influence of Catholic voters and by extension the Catholic Church, which she deemed "in its spirit and its form...utterly antagonistic to republican institutions."[78] Child's reputation as an author and activist in the cause of equal rights for blacks was almost unparalleled, and Sumner had long acknowledged her influence on the development of his own antislavery opinions.[79] But Child's anti-Catholicism mirrored racial arguments about Dominican incapacity for civilized government, which in part explains why annexation could appear to men like Douglass as an important antiracist stance. Sensitive to these complexities, Child sought to refute those who might "hastily infer" from her anti-annexation position any notion "that the colored race is incapable of self-government."[80] Turning her attention to Haiti, Child conceded that in Haiti "it is a lamentable truth that education, agriculture, and commerce have been dreadfully impeded," but Child urged readers to consider the historical legacy of slavery, as well as the policies of the Catholic Church, which she believed "dwarf[ed] the souls of people by keeping them from thinking for themselves." "It is not possible for any people to entirely outgrow, in a short space of time, the ignorance and poverty of spirit that derived from that soul-killing institution," Child wrote in the *National Standard*, an important antebellum abolitionist venue.[81] Child's suggestion that ignorance and political capacity were rooted in history, not nature, coincided with one of the central claims of the woman's rights movement: that women's dependence and ignorance were a social construction supported by laws and therefore could change over time. Child echoed these sentiments in her defense of the political capacity of Haitians and Dominicans to govern themselves.

In Child's public interventions into the annexation debate the link she had begun to make between women's right to self-government, and the Haitian and Dominican right to self-government remained implicit. But writing to Sumner privately, Child was more expansive. Child had been urged by many to write to Sumner on the topic of woman suffrage, she admitted, but in the past she had "forborne" because in her estimation Sumner's "shoulders [already] had sufficient weight to carry," and having "perfect confidence in the moral and intellectual insight of a man," Child was "not desirous to hurry his conclusions."[82] But in the midst of the Santo Domingo debate Child was finally moved to prod Sumner, reminding him that "sooner or later you will see that the republican ideas you advocate so earnestly cannot be consistently carried out while woman [*sic*] are excluded from a share in the government."[83] "Any class of human beings to whom a position of perpetual subordination is assigned, however much they may be petted, must inevitably be dwarfed morally and intellectually," Child wrote to Sumner in defense of woman suffrage.[84]

Sumner and his supporters' opposition to Grant's annexation plans may have been well grounded in a respect for the independence and sovereignty of Haiti, but by the fall of 1870 this opposition was creating what many considered to be an "unseemly" alliance between a senior member of the Republican Party and Senate, and House Democrats like James Bayard of Delaware who considered the Dominicans a "semi-barbarous race" that was "permanently," and "naturally disqualified" for constitutional government.[85] After all, in the fall of 1870, the Republican Party was still doing the work of Reconstruction, and that work required party unity. In March 1870 the Fifteenth Amendment had become law, but it was immediately apparent that enforcing this law and protecting black men's voting rights in the southern states would require additional legislation. In May 1870 Congress passed the first of a series of enforcement acts toward this end.[86] Likewise, Sumner had introduced his own civil rights bill into the Senate.[87] Like all Reconstruction era legislation that enabled the federal government to protect black political and civil rights in the U.S. South, the 1870 Enforcement Act was passed against the will of the Democratic minority.[88] Grant's supporters were eager to point out the irony of the situation in which Sumner, as an opponent of annexation, now found himself: a political ally of the very Democrats whose political power he had devoted his career to circumscribing.

During the spring and summer of 1870, as Grant's treaties wound their way from the Senate Foreign Relations Committee to the Senate floor, suffragists' attention was focused elsewhere. In March 1870, when Sumner's committee reported both treaties adversely, to the chagrin of the administration, Stanton, Anthony, Stone, and Blackwell were occupied by organizational challenges at home. Both the AWSA and the NWSA intended to hold meetings in New York on the same day in May, a situation that threatened to invite ridicule from the movement's critics and confuse movement sympathizers unfamiliar with the ins and outs of the personal and political disharmonies between members of both groups. As bystanders to this train wreck in the making, members of both organizations urged their respective leaders to reconcile their differences and merge the two associations. In addition to personal differences, NWSA members intended to pursue a Sixteenth Amendment, modeled on the Fifteenth Amendment, that would explicitly prohibit discrimination against a citizen's right to vote on the basis of sex. In contrast, members of the AWSA were turning their attention away from Congress toward individual state legislatures, although in early 1870 these differences in strategy were not hard-and-fast. In early May 1870, a conflicted NWSA renamed itself the Union Woman Suffrage Association and encouraged AWSA members to join the new organization.[89]

While suffragists debated union, Sumner led the opposition against annexation. By the end of June 1870, both treaties were defeated in the Senate when Grant failed to get the two-thirds majority required for their passage. Yet the issue was not entirely closed. Since April 1870, a House bill to annex Santo Domingo by congressional joint resolution, as opposed to by treaty, had been on the table, and by the end of the 1870, the bill was in the Senate.[90] On December 21, 1870, to the horror of many of his Republican colleagues and the delight of the Democrats, Sumner arrived in the Senate and delivered a vitriolic and caustic critique of Grant's continued push for annexation.[91] In addition to rehearsing the by now familiar criticisms that the Dominicans did not want annexation, that Báez was corrupt, that the plan had been cooked up by the very same American speculators who pushed for annexation before the Civil War, Sumner detailed the Haitian opposition to U.S. annexation by reading into the Senate record personal correspondence he had received from the Haitian government and Haitian contacts.[92] In a particularly hostile gesture toward Grant personally, Sumner likened the president to Germany's Bismarck, who in December 1870 was completing his victory over the French in the Franco-Prussian War.[93] The parallels between Grant's and Bismarck's militaristic unification of sectional confederations within their home countries into new, more fully national states may have been ripe for comparison, but the not-so-subtle suggestion that Grant intended to invade Haiti, as Bismarck invaded France, was considered an egregious insult to a sitting president by a member of his own party. In response to Sumner's critique of Grant, Douglass wrote Sumner privately and spelled out the difficulty faced by many Republicans in 1870. "Personally, he [Grant] is nothing to me," Douglass wrote Sumner, "but as the President, the Republican President of the country—I am anxious if it can be done to hold him in all honor."[94]

Sumner looked to Europe for analogies that might help him crystallize public opposition to Grant's plans, but he also found examples closer to home. Warning his colleagues that the annexation of Santo Domingo would be "kindred to the outrage upon Kansas, and, if possible, of more historical importance," Sumner linked his anti-annexation stance directly to his antebellum antislavery politics.[95] Sumner's Kansas comment referred back to the passage of the 1854 Kansas-Nebraska Act that allowed these two newly organized territories to decide the slavery question for themselves within their own constitutional conventions.[96] At the time, antislavery legislators and abolition-ists, including Douglass, had vehemently opposed the act because of its poten-tial to open territory north of the line of the 1820 Missouri compromise to slavery.[97] Clearly, Santo Domingo was not Kansas; the slavery question in the United States in 1870 was moot. But by analogizing Santo Domingo to Kansas, Sumner brought to the forefront of the annexation debate that aspect of Grant's foreign policy which sought to export America's racial problems to the Caribbean in much the same way as the Kansas-Nebraska Act exported the slavery question to the western territories before the Civil War. Grant had made the case to Congress that annexation would ease American racial tensions by creating a haven for black Americans in the Caribbean. Doug-lass saw this as an opportunity to embrace new black fellow citizens. But Sumner believed annexation signaled the abandonment of new black citizens at home.[98]

The Republican press was critical of Sumner because of his personal attacks on Grant, but Sumner's allusions to Kansas resonated with the public, if not the party, and he received numerous letters of appreciation from across the states. As one Michigan man told Sumner, "All intelligent Republicans in the West indorse [sic] you on the Santo Domingo question."[99] In January 1870, it may have seemed likely that annexation would sail through Congress as a Republican measure, but by January 1871, when many suffragists returned to the capital for a new round of meetings, the Santo Domingo question was one of the most visible examples of emerging fissures within the Republican Party.

OVERLAPPING DEBATES: ANNEXATION AND WOMAN SUFFRAGE, 1871

"Arrived in Washington this A.M.," Anthony wrote in her diary on January 10, 1871, and "found papers full of Victoria C. Woodhull's Memorial to Con-gress."[100] On January 10, 1871, the D.C. newspapers were actually filled with the Santo Domingo debate and Sumner's attack on the president, but Antho-ny's eyes were drawn to the small announcement that a hearing before the House Judiciary Committee had been granted to Victoria Claflin Woodhull for the following day.[101] Just three weeks earlier, on the same day that Sum-ner castigated Grant so vehemently in the Senate, John Spoffard Harris, the Republican senator from Louisiana, and his House colleague George Julian of Indiana had introduced into their respective chambers a woman suffrage memorial on behalf of the very controversial stockbroker, newspaper edi-tor, and, in April 1870, self-declared presidential candidate, Victoria Claflin

Woodhull.[102] Woodhull's memorial asked Congress to pass a law, a declaratory act, that would affirm immediately women's right to vote under both the Fourteenth Amendment and the Fifteenth Amendment in every state in the Union.[103] Premised on the same legal reasoning first circulated by the Minors in St. Louis in 1869 and presented by Stanton to the Committee on the District of Columbia in 1870, Woodhull's memorial asked Congress to declare that state constitutions which discriminated against women voters were in conflict with the federal Constitution because women were U.S. citizens and U.S. citizenship carried with it the right to vote. Francis and Virginia Minor had hoped that women would test this legal theory in the courts by attempting to register and to vote. By taking this argument directly to Congress, Woodhull sought to bypass the courts.

To Anthony and more especially to Isabella Beecher Hooker, who had been in D.C. since December organizing the upcoming woman's rights convention, the news of Woodhull's hearing before the House Judiciary Committee came as a surprise.[104] It was not that Woodhull was entirely unfamiliar to Anthony and Hooker, but by birth, background, and life experience, she stood firmly outside the circles of friendship and familiarity that by 1871 had bound together many of the women who were joining the newly founded NWSA and ASWA for more than two decades. Unlike many of the middle-class women who were beginning to swell the suffragists' ranks, Woodhull had spent her childhood in poverty. Indeed, she had spent many of her thirty-one years, including her married ones, supporting herself through spirit-reading, fortune-telling, and casual prostitution. In December 1870, when her memorial was presented to Congress, Woodhull had never attended a suffrage convention or joined a state suffrage society.[105]

The opening of Woodhull's stock brokerage in January 1870 earned Woodhull a great deal of publicity, and while suffrage activists may not have known Woodhull personally she had certainly come to their attention; at the time, Anthony had visited Wall Street and interviewed Woodhull's sister Tennessee Claflin for the *Revolution*.[106] If Woodhull's achievements as a woman on Wall Street had not brought her to Anthony and Hooker's attention, the first publication of *Woodhull and Claflin's Weekly* in May 1870 would certainly have done the trick. Published with financial backing from Woodhull's patron, the fabulously wealthy and influential railroad tycoon Cornelius Vanderbilt, *Woodhull and Claflin's Weekly* was devoted to presenting radical points of view on the issues of the day, which included woman suffrage, but also such controversial topics as Spiritualism and free love.[107] As Anne Braude has shown, the radicalism of the Spiritualist belief that individuals could be "vehicles of truth" supported and reinforced demands for woman's rights, and many reform-minded women had been drawn to Spiritualism ever since the movement began to take shape in upstate New York beginning the late 1840s.[108]

No matter how compatible Woodhull's Spiritualist beliefs and her commitment to woman's rights, however, the majority of women in the organized suffrage movement steered well clear of publicly claiming any affinity for free love. The reform of marriage laws that gave men control over property, wages, children, and even sexuality within marriage, what Stanton called the "compulsory adulteries of the marriage bed," were at the core of the antebellum woman's rights program.[109] Yet despite offering a sustained critique of marriage laws, most advocates of woman's rights did not reject the institution outright and felt that the free love tenets that a "true marriage" should be an entirely private contract based on mutual respect and affection, and that divorce should be easily obtainable for men and women, went too far.[110] Indeed, Stanton's outspoken support for divorce and her tendency to alternate lectures on woman suffrage with lectures on marriage reform were as controversial within suffragist circles as they were outside them.[111] Even Lucy Stone and Henry Blackwell, whose own marriage ceremony included a public protest against the laws of marriage that made women unequal partners, felt that Stanton's advocacy of divorce should be kept separate from woman suffrage.[112]

Hooker and Anthony were later to learn that Benjamin Butler, Sumner's Massachusetts's colleague, and chair of the House Judiciary Committee, helped Woodhull write her memorial and orchestrated its presentation to the committee. In 1871, Butler was a notorious figure in his own right. He had voted for Jefferson Davis at the 1860 Democratic convention and then gone on to become one of Lincoln's most important generals, infamous for his 1861 declaration that fugitive slaves should be treated as "contraband of war," which prevented runaways from being returned to their owners.[113] During his 1862 capture and occupation of New Orleans he had earned the nickname "Beast Butler," in part for his threat to insult any Southern woman who heckled Union soldiers by treating her "as a woman of the town plying her avocation."[114] In December 1870, many thought that Butler was Grant's "man" in the Senate.[115] After all, it was Butler's bill to annex Santo Domingo by congressional joint resolution that was occupying the Senate on the day Woodhull's memorial was first introduced into Congress. The combination of Butler and Woodhull promised to make Woodhull's January 1871 hearing a D.C. event.[116]

Butler's help aside, the Judiciary Committee's willingness to give Woodhull a hearing was also an admission of how widespread this new thinking about the meaning of the Fourteenth and Fifteenth Amendments for woman suffrage had become by 1871.[117] As early as 1868, Stanton and Anthony's *Revolution* had begun carrying stories of women's attempts to register and to vote across the states.[118] Marilla M. Ricker of Dover, New Hampshire, described as "a young widow of large property," is credited as the first to do so with the expressed intention of testing the Minors' legal theory in the courts. Ricker successfully registered to vote in a local election in March 1870, although her ballot for the straight Republican ticket was refused on election day.[119] In October 1870, after five black women successfully voted in South Carolina, the election managers were promptly arrested.[120] Some women went to the polls in groups, and sometimes these were black and white women together. Between the 1868 passage of the Fourteenth Amendment and December 1870, when Woodhull's memorial was presented to Congress, nearly 800 women from New Jersey, Kansas, Maine, Michigan, New York, Washington Territory, and South Carolina went to the polls and, importantly, in some cases succeeded in voting in local, state, and federal elections.[121]

Stone and Blackwell were much less sanguine about the persuasiveness of the legal reasoning that inspired these attempts. "In regard to the claim made by Mr. Francis Minor and others 2 years ago & lately revised by Mrs. Woodhull under the 14 & 15 Amendments, I *doubt* its validity, but shall be glad to be convinced," Blackwell wrote Isabella Beecher Hooker's husband, the Connecticut lawyer John Hooker. "The whole question," he asserted, "hinges on this—is suffrage a privilege and immunity of citizenship in the case of classes hitherto disfranchised? It has never been so considered."[122] Despite their doubts, the *Woman's Journal* joined with the *Revolution* and the *New Era* in carrying stories of women who attempted to register and to vote, and contributed to the popularization of the idea that the Fourteenth and Fifteenth Amendments enfranchised women. One *Woman's Journal* editorial under the heading "Are Women Not Already Legally Enfranchised?" declared that "startling as the proposition may appear to many, the Fourteenth Amendment is much more far-reaching than was at first imagined, and will yet be seen to have enfranchised woman as well as man."[123] "The highest courts in some of the States—and among them, we believe is Massachusetts—" the article continued, "have settled that the elective franchise is one of the 'privileges and immunities of citizens.' "[124]

Like suffragists' hearing before the House and Senate Committees on D.C. the year before, the Judiciary Committee hearing granted to Victoria Woodhull in January 1871 drew an audience from across the capital.[125] In January 1870, the reporters covering suffragists' appearance at the D.C. committee hearing were struck by the image of the reform veterans Stanton and Sumner facing each other across the long table of the committee room; in January 1871, reporters' attention was captured by the sight of Hooker, Anthony, Paulina Davis, and Josephine Griffing, among other well-known suffrage activists, arranging themselves in a row behind Woodhull, at once lending her their credibility and yet taking a backseat.[126] The importance of this gesture was not lost on members of the audience either inside or outside the committee room, and suffragists would debate the wisdom of this decision to associate themselves with "notorious Victoria" for years to come. At the time, however, the promise of a Judiciary Committee report on their argument seemed much more important than Woodhull's credentials or her character.

Accounts of Woodhull's performance as a public speaker vary; she was a self-declared novice, but she was also credited with a certain innate charisma and dashing sense of style that commanded attention. Like Stanton before her in D.C. in 1870, Woodhull based her argument to the Judiciary Committee on the premise that under the Fourteenth Amendment women had become national citizens, and that the Fourteenth and Fifteenth Amendments together recognized a U.S. citizen's right to vote. Woodhull differed from Stanton in the weight she put on the Fifteenth Amendment.[127] When Stanton made these arguments previously, much of her emphasis had been on the notion that the right to vote is inalienable, that it precedes all law. In Stanton's reading, the Fifteenth Amendment did not confer suffrage but, rather, recognized a preexisting, "vested" right. That the Fifteenth Amendment did not confer extra protections of this right on the basis of sex, Stanton held, did not mean that women had legislated their rights away. Woodhull also emphasized a woman citizen's "inalienable 'sovereign' right of self-government in *her own proper person*."[128] Instead of speaking to how the Fifteenth Amendment ignored women, however, Woodhull asked the committee to consider how the Fifteenth Amendment could be said to include women as members of races and as part of the special categories protected by the Fifteenth Amendment. Indeed, for Woodhull, one of the most crucial aspects of her argument was that white women, like black women, were members of races because "color comprises all people, of all races and both sexes."[129]

As part of her effort to convince the committee that women were included in the protections given to race, color, and previous condition of servitude, Woodhull briefly pointed to the notion that marriage itself might be understood as a "condition of servitude." Speaking in support of Woodhull at the hearing, the D.C. lawyer and suffragist Albert Gallatin Riddle made this point emphatically. On one hand, to liken marriage to servitude invited ridicule. Butler was rumored to have said that on these grounds the Fifteenth Amendment should apply only to widows.[130] On the other hand, as Riddle lectured the committee, the laws governing the relations between husbands and wives in postbellum America remained grounded in a system of "coverture" imported from England to the colonies that merged a married woman's legal identity into that of her husband. Under coverture, as Riddle explained it, "the law calls her husband 'baron,' and she is simply a woman—'fem[m]e.' "[131] The law gives her to the man, not the man to her, not the two mutually to each other."[132] Riddle argued that the Fourteenth and Fifteenth Amendments spoke to women's condition in marriage, not simply because marriage could be analogized to servitude, but because the Fourteenth Amendment recognized women as full citizens, not women, under the law.

In 1871, the notion that the Fourteenth Amendment recognized women as full citizens was an unsettling and potentially revolutionary proposition in its own right with unforeseen implications for far more than voting rights. As scholarship on the rights of married women has shown, the principle of marital unity informed legal thinking in many different areas of law.[133] In most states, married women could not sue or be sued, write wills without their husbands' consent, or sign contracts. Linda Kerber has drawn attention to how this principle of marital unity was extended to naturalization law in 1855, when Congress made it possible for foreign women to become naturalized citizens through marriage to American men, because "they absorbed citizenship through their husbands' identities."[134] If Riddle was correct, and the Fourteenth Amendment made women full citizens, perhaps women could now naturalize men through their own marriages? Or act as their own economic agents without the consent of their husbands? At the time of Woodhull's hearing, much of the way that the Fourteenth and Fifteenth Amendments might affect women's civil rights was left unexplored in favor of attention to the vote.[135]

Woodhull's final claim was, in many ways, her most radical. In asking for a declaratory act that would overturn state constitutions that disfranchised women citizens, Woodhull challenged the notion that states, and not the national government, were primarily responsible for protecting and delimiting citizens' rights. The Constitution had left the control over suffrage laws in state hands, and state control of the ballot was one of the foundational principles of U.S. federalism.[136] And yet the Fourteenth and Fifteenth Amendments were federal laws that shifted at least some of the burden for determining citizens' right to vote to the federal government. Woodhull saw this shift in absolute terms and told the committee that the effect of these amendments "must be to annul the power over this subject [voting] in the States ... [because] the restrictions in the Constitution as to color, race, or servitude, were designed to limit the State governments in reference to their own citizens."[137] To her mind, the entire suffrage question was now a federal matter. In contrast to those who regretted the way the Reconstruction amendments appeared to drastically alter relations in federal authority, Woodhull embraced this shift.[138]

At the close of Woodhull's Judiciary Committee hearing, Anthony, like many visitors to the nation's capital that day, went to the Senate galleries to listen to Carl Schurz, the Republican senator from Missouri, lecture his colleagues on the "Santo Domingo Muddle."[139] That afternoon Schurz was making a final effort to prevent the Senate from authorizing a formal commission of inquiry to travel to Santo Domingo and investigate the political, social, and economic conditions of the country. It was hoped that the commission's report would facilitate a final decision on the annexation question. The commission was intended as a fact-finding mission, but both Schurz and Sumner were convinced that to vote for the commission was to vote for annexation, and they both argued vehemently against its authorization.[140]

In his speech that afternoon Schurz invited his colleagues to imagine what would happen if Congress added "new tropical states to the southern States we already possess…[and] people of the Latin race mixed with Indian and African blood…[were] sitting in the Halls of Congress?"[141] "Does not your imagination recoil from the picture?"[142] In January 1871, men of "African blood" like Senator Hiram Revels of Mississippi, and Congressman Joseph Rainey of South Carolina, were already sitting in the halls of Congress, and Schurz belonged to the party that put them there. But just nine months after the passage of the Fifteenth Amendment, Schurz defied the proponents of annexation to suggest "a single instance of the successful establishment…of republican institutions, based upon popular self-government, under a tropical sun."[143] The Fourteenth and Fifteenth Amendments sought to do just that in the U.S. South, and Schurz's comments were a clear indication of his increasing doubts for their success.

Schurz was particularly concerned with the problem of "securing to the South a tolerable state of order without giving to this Government too dangerous a measure of arbitrary power."[144] Here Schurz was surely referring to the May 1870 Enforcement Act, but also to the Ku Klux Klan Act then under discussion and likely to pass. Whereas Reconstruction legislation to this point protected black political rights from state discrimination, the Klan Act would respond to the growing problem of white violence against black voters in Southern states by making private criminal acts punishable by federal law. Even more than the 1870 Enforcement Act, the Klan Act seemed a sweeping enhancement of federal authority and a blow to state sovereignty.[145]

To Schurz, the problem of annexation was twofold. First and foremost, it was the problem of "incorporating the tropics into our political system," and by that Schurz meant the problem of governing a "people who have nothing in common with us; neither language, nor habits, nor institutions, nor traditions, nor opinions, nor ways of thinking; nay, not even a code of morals—people who cannot even be reached by our teachings, for they will not understand or appreciate them."[146] If the Dominicans were not ready for the American system of self-government, and Schurz did not think they were, because in tropical climates there was a "natural...tendency to government by force instead of by argument," what would annexation look like?[147] This question brought Schurz to the second problem of annexation: the method of rule. If Dominicans could not be trusted to participate as equals in the American system, what then was the alternative? "Will you govern those countries as provinces, as colonies, dependencies?" Schurz asked.[148] "Do you want to rule the West India Islands as England rules India?"[149]

Schurz's suggestion that the United States might rule Santo Domingo as England ruled India was not as far-fetched as it might seem at first glance. In 1871, the United States did not have in place a legal apparatus for governing colonies, and the ruling presumption was that any new territory under U.S. control would eventually enter the Union as a new state. As the constitutional historian Owen Fiss reminds us, Taney's decision in the infamous Dred Scott case not only denied black men and women U.S. citizenship but also sought to curtail Congress's ability to eliminate slavery in federal territories. To this end, Taney saw congressional control over federal territories as limited to that of creating new states. As Taney wrote, "There is certainly no power given by the Constitution to the Federal Government to establish or maintain colonies bordering on the United States or at a distance, to be ruled and governed at its own pleasure; nor to enlarge its territorial limits in any way, except by the admission of new States."[150] But Grant's original annexation treaty did not seek Santo Domingo's immediate incorporation as a new state, despite Douglass's hopes on this count. Rather, he intended for the republic to keep its territorial status for at least ten years in order to school Dominicans in the qualities necessary for citizenship.[151]

It was precisely the quasi-dependent relationship inherent in territorial status that was at the heart of the opposition voiced by Douglass and other friends of black equality to the proposed governmental reforms in Washington, D.C. In the D.C. case, African American leaders believed that territorial status undermined the sovereignty of D.C.'s black and white inhabitants alike even though their primary concern was the political fate of D.C.'s black voters. Conversely, in the case of Santo Domingo, annexationists chose to see territorial status and eventual statehood, however long deferred, as progressive and inclusive.

Despite Sumner and Douglass's disagreements over annexation, both men framed the debate in Reconstruction terms, that is to say, in terms of creating new black fellow citizens and a new Republican state in Santo Domingo.

This framing had the effect of deflecting attention from the colonial aspects of Grant's expansionist foreign policy. Schurz's anticolonial critique reframed this debate by focusing attention on how the government of territorial possessions in Caribbean could, over time, look a lot less like the U.S. relationship to Kansas than the British relationship to India. "You might leave those possessions for a time in a territorial condition," Schurz warned, but to "reduce this to a permanent system, or merely continue it ten years," would "impart to our Government a military character most destructive of its republican institutions."[152] Schurz believed that the long-term control of territorial possessions was, in fact, a form of colonial rule, one that would only increase the need for a dangerous buildup of federal power and exacerbate the revolution in federal relations already set in motion in the United States by Reconstruction. In Schurz's very Reconstruction era critique of U.S. expansion, colonialism, like Reconstruction, was a problem of centralization.

To Anthony, fresh from Woodhull's hearing, listening to Schurz's comments that afternoon must have been especially striking, a complex juxtaposition of two separate yet overlapping discussions about political capacity and federal relations. That morning Woodhull had claimed suffrage as an inalienable right in broadly democratic and universal terms, while Schurz argued that constitutional self-government was a privilege of certain races in particular climates. Woodhull built her claims on an expansive reading of the Reconstruction amendments; Schurz spoke to their failure. And while Schurz opposed annexation because he decried the possibility of new African blood in the halls of Congress, Woodhull's case for woman suffrage depended on the very same laws that protected the rights of men like Revels and Rainey to sit there. Finally, while Woodhull linked woman suffrage to expansive federal authority over voting rights, Schurz outlined the dangers of centralizing political rights at the federal level. It was not that Anthony had not heard such arguments before, but more often, these sentiments about the dangers of enhanced federal power and the incapacity of certain races for self-government had come from the Democratic side of the aisle.

This complicated political moment presented Anthony, like Child before her, with an opportunity to weigh in on the annexation question. Directly engaging the problems of centralization and colonialism raised by Schurz, however, would have meant taking sides in a debate that was dividing the cohort of former abolitionists and Radical Republicans most sympathetic to woman suffrage. Instead, Anthony took the somewhat pragmatic position that if the annexation question continued to split the Republican Party, woman suffrage might become the rallying cry of a new reform party. In "After the Republican Party, What?" Anthony explained how the New Departure specifically, and

[margin handwritten note: anti-annexation = args against WS]

woman suffrage generally, might reunify the party by recalling it to its "republican principles," by which she meant the Reconstruction program of linking voting rights to national citizenship.[153] This argument served as the outline for a strategy that many NWSA members would pursue over the coming months: adding their voices to those of Grant's other critics with the hope that political vulnerability might turn the party to woman suffrage as its salvation. Anthony's refusal to address the annexation question specifically was indicative of what would later become an entrenched policy of steering the suffrage movement clear of what she perceived to be controversial side issues. In the winter of 1871, it kept the Santo Domingo question off the NWSA platform and out of the pages of the *Revolution*.

Woodhull, not surprisingly, was far less circumspect, and *Woodhull and Claflin's Weekly* jumped into the debate on the side of annexation.[154] In response to Schurz's claim that annexation would start the United States on a road toward a European style of colonialism, the *Weekly* argued that "the policy of the United States at this time should be that followed by older nations—viz, that of acquiring footholds in all parts of the world as bases of operations."[155] In response to Sumner's charge that the annexation project "is pushed in utter indifference to the African race," *Woodhull and Claflin's Weekly* claimed that, "Mr. Sumner's 'negrophily' carries him a little too far."[156] Given the close relationship between Butler and Woodhull, it is more than likely that *Woodhull and Claflin's Weekly*'s pro-annexation position—rooted in an economic analysis of trade and markets and very unsympathetic to Sumner—reflected the administration's position more than Woodhull's own. Writers in *Woodhull and Claflin's Weekly* never linked woman suffrage specifically to annexation or explored the topic of women's citizenship and woman suffrage together as Douglass's *New Era* had begun to think through the question of black citizenship and black suffrage.

AWSA suffragists had not been in D.C. to hear the Santo Domingo debates in Congress, but as it turned out, the *Woman's Journal* provided the venue for a woman suffrage perspective on annexation to emerge. "Our readers have undoubtedly missed the familiar initials 'H.B.B.' from our columns for the last few weeks," ran a notice in the *Woman's Journal* on February 25, 1871. "Mr. Blackwell, we expect [by now], has joined the government commission in San Domingo."[157] In mid-January Congress had approved Grant's commission of inquiry over Sumner's and Schurz's objections, and two weeks after the commission set sail aboard the *Tybee* from New York for Santo Domingo, Blackwell went on behalf of the farming magazine *Hearth and Home*. Blackwell had been commissioned by the paper to assess the Dominican situation as a representative of the "great agricultural interest of our country." His specific task was to answer the question of why, "with a vast amount of fertile soil still undeveloped upon our own continent...should we cross the sea to take possession of a region so distant?"[158] In one respect, this was Blackwell's own question. Blackwell had speculated in Wisconsin land in the 1850s with a mild degree of success, and he was always on the lookout for new business opportunities.[159] "Papa has really gone to San Domingo," his daughter Alice wrote to her cousin Kitty at the time of Blackwell's departure, "he has engaged to write enough letters to various newspapers to pay his passage, and has also, I believe, an eye to some private speculations there."[160] Blackwell's brother George thought that he had a "fancy to preempt half St. Domingo, round about the Bay of Samana."[161]

Once Blackwell landed in Santo Domingo, he, like other reporters from U.S. papers, spent his days shadowing Grant's three commissioners as they toured the island. All three of the men Grant had appointed to his Santo Domingo commission were respected and well-known Republican partisans: Andrew White, the president of Cornell University and much admired by Stanton; Benjamin Franklin Wade, the former senator and Radical Republican from Ohio; and Samuel Gridley Howe, the husband of Blackwell's compatriot Julia Ward Howe at the *Woman's Journal*.[162] In addition to his philanthropic work in Boston, which included establishing the Perkins School for the Blind, Howe's credentials included his service on the Freedman's Inquiry Commission.[163] Charged in 1863 with the task of laying out the precise nature of federal responsibility for the newly emancipated slaves, the commission created the Freedman's Bureau in 1865. Presumably, Howe's experience with the creation of the bureau, an institution designed to serve as the guardian for a people acclimating to self-government, provided him with rare insight into the likely success of annexation. It would fall to Douglass to investigate the condition of the approximately 13,000 black Americans who immigrated to Santo Domingo in 1824 when it was under Haitian rule.[164]

From the press reports that began trickling back to the United States during February and March 1871, it was apparent that the commission's impression of the Dominicans and of annexation was favorable. Blackwell's impressions were favorable as well. In the venue provided by *Hearth and Home*, Blackwell liberally employed the colonial rhetoric of the "white man's burden" to boost for annexation. In several articles, Blackwell characterized the Dominicans as a "simple and uneducated people [that] have never been roused to activity by the investment of capital," and painted lush pictures of land just waiting to be cultivated by enterprising "white" men.[165] As Blackwell wrote Sumner in an ill-judged bid to gain his support for annexation, "the experiment of isolating black and colored men from contact with whites has hitherto resulted in stagnation and retrogression towards barbarism." "The only islands which are improving," Blackwell continued, "are those where white men are in the ascendant."[166]

In Blackwell's rendering, Santo Domingo was a tropical paradise. The Dominicans might be Roman Catholics, as Child had pointed out, but as Blackwell remarked, they had established "freedom of religious opinion."[167] "The population might be only one-tenth white," the concern raised by anti-annexationists in the *Nation*, but Blackwell found "perfect social equality" among this "mixed race, descended from the Spaniards and Indians, with a considerable African admixture." Fears that Santo Domingo was a site of racial strife and religious bigotry, Blackwell assured his readers, were unfounded. Rather, travelers to Santo Domingo would find the people "honest and peaceful, and tired of the frequent political revolutions in which they are involved." Most important, for farmers reading *Hearth and Home* and thinking about the project of cultivating Santo Domingo's fertile lands, "white men, who are acclimated," Blackwell told *Hearth and Home* subscribers, "can live and labor here and raise healthy families."[168]

If Blackwell found Dominican men somewhat lazy, "less vigorous and active than our selves," what struck him most immediately about Dominican women was the contrast between the complete withdrawal of upper-class women from public life, and the very public presence and personal freedom of women from the poorer classes.[169] In Blackwell's letters to the *Woman's Journal*, he attributed what he termed the "almost Oriental seclusion" of Dominican "ladies" to their Spanish ancestry. Blackwell found that the end result of strictly limiting upper-class women to the domestic sphere was a lack of intellectual intercourse between the sexes, because "women know nothing of national questions," that made life "dreadfully monotonous."[170] But keeping women from public life also meant that Blackwell found no "public women," "no such evidence of gross and disgusting vice as appears even in moral and religious Boston."[171] Blackwell was willing to concede that in some respects the relations between the sexes in Dominica were "in advance of our people," but as a self-described student of political philosophy, he ultimately came to the conclusion that "the total abstraction of woman's influence from the domain of politics and ideas seems one cause of the want of political stability which is the curse of Spanish American nations."[172] In light of this link between overly domesticated women and unstable government, Blackwell told his readers that "the most beneficial result of annexation...would be the moral and intellectual emancipation of woman in Santo Domingo."[173]

The notion that annexation might emancipate Dominican women morally and intellectually drew on beliefs about the debased character of women in non-Christian societies that had circulated among missionaries in the evangelical Protestant churches since the antebellum period.[174] But Blackwell was no missionary, and his failure to include political emancipation on his list was a curious omission for a suffrage activist. It is tempting to think that Blackwell failed to mention political emancipation because U.S. women did not have the vote, and therefore annexation would not emancipate Dominican women politically. Just one year earlier, however, in one of his first *Woman's Journal* articles on the U.S. "Indian problem" in the context of U.S. encroachment into Indian Territory, Blackwell had come to a very different conclusion. Then, Blackwell had made a case for Indian woman suffrage and argued that, "the interests of Indian women cannot be ignored without guilt and folly" because the "condition of the squaw is that of slavery."[175] Blackwell echoed Justice Taney's words in his infamous Dred Scott decision, and claimed that the Indian woman had "literally no rights that the red man is bound to respect."[176] Blackwell believed that the Indian woman, unlike the black or white woman, "was not represented in theory" in political matters by Indian husbands.[177] In this context, an "Indian State, on the basis of manhood suffrage," would be an "organized brutality," "a political aristocracy of drunken idleness, resting upon crushed and degraded womanhood."[178] With respect to Indian women within U.S. borders, Blackwell urged readers of the *Woman's Journal* to consider the benefits of constructing this "incipient civilization on the basis of *universal* suffrage."[179] In Blackwell's view, the question of woman suffrage for Indian women was that of making her the "political equal of her tyrant," a project made especially urgent if Congress intended to enfranchise Indian men, and thereby create a "semi-barbarous aristocracy of sex."[180] This was Stanton's earlier language regarding the Fourteenth Amendment.

In Blackwell's analysis, the argument for enfranchising Indian women was grounded less in abstract ideas about women's equality, or even democratic principles about individual sovereignty and consent, than on what he perceived to be the barbaric character of Indian men and, by extension, the degraded character of Indian women. In 1870, with respect to Indian women within U.S. borders, Blackwell was beginning to advance arguments that would link woman suffrage to the process of civilizing the Indians, even though white and black U.S. women did not have the vote, and his efforts to render woman suffrage compatible with the project of lifting Indians up from savagery represents one of the earliest efforts to bring these sets of ideas together around woman suffrage.

Traveling across Santo Domingo in 1871, Blackwell was thus well positioned to make connections between the political emancipation of Dominican women and the project of civilizing the Caribbean.[181] Significantly, however, he did not. Blackwell may have been a suffragist, but he was also a failed sugar-beet farmer looking for investments. And, in 1871, many Americans were unwilling to take on another civilizing mission, as anti-annexationists had made clear. In this context, emphasizing the barbarism of Dominican men could only work against annexation. Blackwell was wearing two hats, that of a suffragist and that of an annexationist, and with respect to Santo Domingo, he seemed far more at home in the pages of *Hearth and Home* than he did in the *Woman's Journal*. In the context of Santo Domingo, arguments for Dominican woman suffrage that were grounded in Dominican barbarism cut across arguments for annexation that depended on the Dominican's readiness for U.S. civilization. In the particular context of the Caribbean, Blackwell did not, or could not, bring expansionist arguments and woman suffrage together, although he advocated both.

Returning to New York from Santo Domingo in March 1871, Grant's commissioners continued on to D.C. to attend a dinner at the White House and report the success of their mission to the president.[182] Looking ahead to the 1872 presidential election, however, and considering the deep fissures already extant within the Republican Party, Grant was ready to give up on annexation, and in his message to Congress on April 5, 1871, he suggested that no further action be taken on the Santo Domingo question.[183] Douglass, however, remained committed to the project. Douglass's homecoming had been quite different from that of Grant's other commissioners. He had not been included in the White House dinner, and the press carried rumors of the ship captain's attempts to keep him out of the dinning room during his return trip to New York.[184]

On April 20, 1871, just after returning to D.C., Douglass led approximately seventy black and white women to the D.C. polls in one of the largest New Departure efforts to claim the vote for women under the Fourteenth Amendment.[185] The group of women voters included the D.C. suffragists and NWSA members Josephine Griffing, Sara Andrews Spencer, and Mary Ann Shadd Cary.[186] At the end of January, while Douglass was in Santo Domingo, the House Judiciary Committee had reported against the claims of Woodhull's memorial.[187] Writing for the majority and against the suffragists, Ohio Republican John Bingham dismissed their claims that national citizenship guaranteed the right to vote, and agreed with the former U.S. attorney general Edward Bates that "the phrase, 'a citizen of the United States,' without addition or qualification, means neither more nor less than a member of the nation"—that is, not a voter.[188] In the face of this first negative, official response to the claims of the New Departure, women's efforts to register and to vote in D.C. in April 1871 were a self-consciously radical act of civil disobedience designed to bring their claims into court in the face of congressional disfavor.

The April 1871 D.C. election was the first election under D.C.'s new territorial government. D.C.'s voters, black and white alike, went to the polls to elect the members of the territory's lower chamber. Douglass's participation in the April 20, 1871, New Departure gathering at the polls was an example not only of his commitment to votes for women but also of his commitment to reaffirming the promises of the Fourteenth and Fifteenth Amendments to protect black men's presence at the polls. Douglass never explicitly linked the democratic vision of citizenship and suffrage underlying the New Departure to his support for annexation. It has thus been possible to read his position on annexation as one of partisan loyalty rather than a consistent belief in the interrelationship between expanding U.S. borders to include new black citizens in the Caribbean and ensuring black political participation in U.S. politics at home. Douglass's support for Grant's Santo Domingo plans had been unwavering, and many speculated that this loyalty to the president reflected his desire for a government appointment (Grant made Douglass a member of the new territory's upper council).[189] But Douglass's participation in this New Departure exercise was hardly an example of blind allegiance to the party or to Grant. Speaking at a church in Baltimore in support of annexation four days after joining suffragists at the polls in D.C., Douglass told the assembled audience that he firmly believed that the United States would annex Santo Domingo if its people were white or slaves; "they are always ready to welcome the colored man as a servant, but when it is as my fellow citizen, then it becomes a very different thing."[190] Three days later, Douglass expanded on this point when he asked his readers in the *New Era* to consider why "a people who have annexed Louisiana, Texas, California, and Alaska, and who are for annexing Mexico and Canada in good time, raise this question of destiny against Santo Domingo?"[191] The answer, of course, was that all conversation about the rights of nations to work out their destinies for themselves was "pretended," a code to keep colored men from U.S. citizenship. In April 1871, there was no better way to stand up for black voting rights in D.C. and, more broadly, to a racially inclusive United States—one that might even include new black fellow citizens in the Caribbean—than to advocate the principles of the New Departure by accompanying black and white women to the polls.

These particular links between woman suffrage, U.S. expansion, and citizenship remained implicit, especially as the discussion of annexation attenuated over the next several months. Had annexation remained a viable political project, it is entirely possible that these connections between woman suffrage and expansive politics might have become more explicitly linked, although perhaps not quite in the way Douglass might have hoped, that is, as different parts of a democratic and racially inclusive political nation that recognized both black men and black and white women as full citizens.

Any opportunity for suffragists to think through the woman question in the context of U.S. expansion into the Caribbean, however, came to an abrupt end on January 2, 1874, when Dominican rebels forced Báez to resign, and he fled to the United States.[192] The possibilities of the suffragists' New Departure were also seemingly brought to a close on March 29, 1875, when the Supreme Court handed down its decision in *Minor v. Happersett*.[193] Ruling against suffragists' claims that voting was a right of national citizenship, Chief Justice Morrison Waite declared, "The United States has no voters in the States of its own creation."[194] The Court's unanimous opinion that "the Constitution of the United States does not confer the right of suffrage upon any one" shut the door on the suffragists' hope to claim the vote under the Fourteenth and Fifteenth Amendments.[195] Waite's decision did concede that women were national citizens under the Fourteenth Amendment, a point that even in 1875 remained to be decided. The larger irony, however, was that even as the politics of Radical Reconstruction helped close down the first United States' efforts to expand its national borders after the Civil War in Santo Domingo, the United States had created a newly national second-class citizenship. It was not Dominicans in the Caribbean who would inhabit this second-class status, however, but U.S. women and black men at home.

3

WESTERN EXPANSION AND THE POLITICS OF FEDERALISM

Indians, Mormons, and Territorial Statehood, 1878–1887

In May 1878, Matilda Joslyn Gage, chair of the NWSA's executive committee, published an article in her woman suffrage paper, *National Citizen and Ballot Box*, on the topic of Indian citizenship. At the time, Gage was a resident of Fayetteville, a small town just outside of Syracuse, New York, one of the bustling cities on the Erie Canal. Fayetteville sat in the heart of Onondaga County, which was named for the Onondaga Indians, one of the Six Nations that together with the Mohawk, Oneida, Seneca, Cayuga, and Tuscarora made up the Iroquois Confederacy. Many members of the Iroquois Confederacy had been pushed west of the Mississippi during the 1830s and 1840s, and those who remained in New York after the Civil War lived on vastly reduced reservation lands held in trust by the state.[1] In the fall of 1877, the Republican senator John Ingalls, whose home state of Kansas had become a site of Iroquois reservation lands in the West, introduced a Senate bill that sought to turn Indians across the continental United States into U.S. citizens.[2] Ingalls's bill was intended to put an end to tribal sovereignty and to break up tribal lands, and in March 1878, a council of the Iroquois tribes met in Onondaga, New York, to "decline the gift of citizenship."[3] For Gage, the passage of any law that would either "*allow* or *compel* them to become citizens" stood in sharp contrast to suffragists' own hopes to gain full citizenship for women, by which Gage meant the vote. That January, Gage had once again joined with other NWSA members in D.C. for their annual convention and a new round of congressional hearings on the question of woman suffrage, or, in Gage's words, to "demand citizenship denied." Now she found herself witnessing an attempt to "force [suffrage] on the red man in direct opposition to his wishes, while women citizens, already members of the nation, to whom it rightfully belongs, are denied its exercise." The perceived injustice was provoking, and Gage asked her readers to ponder the question: "Can women's political degradation reach much lower depth?" For Gage the answer was a resounding no. As Gage wrote bitterly, "She, educated, enlightened, Christian, in vain begs for the crumbs cast contemptuously aside by savages."[4]

Looking west, and contemplating a future in which Indian men might vote before U.S. women, may have highlighted for Gage the depth of her own "political degradation," but like the creation of a new government for Washington, D.C., western territorial expansion also offered unanticipated political possibilities for woman suffragists. In 1869, the territorial legislature of Wyoming enfranchised women, and in 1870, the Mormon majority in Utah Territory had followed suit. In the decade before the Civil War, the Mormon Church made public its belief in the practice of plural marriage, or polygamy, and one result of Utah Territory's 1870 decision to enfranchise women was that some of the nation's first women voters lived in families whose domestic arrangements challenged the moral sensibilities of suffragists and antisuffragists alike.[5] When Gage turned her attention to the question of Indian citizenship in 1878, the fact of women's enfranchisement in Wyoming and Utah territories was forcing Congress to confront the possibility that turning these territories into new states might inadvertently set federal precedents authorizing women's ballots. Indeed, woman suffrage in the territories added a gendered dimension to the partisan battling that accompanied the admission of new states into the Union. When examined through the lens of gender, postbellum territorial expansion was far more controversial than we often suppose. While not nearly as divisive as the question of expanding slavery into the territories three decades earlier, women's enfranchisement in the territories turned statehood debates into unexpected national referenda on the question of woman suffrage and on the nature of national authority over the vote. Expanding U.S. borders thus aided suffragists' efforts to keep the woman question on the national agenda in unforeseen ways. The Supreme Court's 1875 decision in *Minor v. Happersett* may have sent suffragists back to the states to gain the vote from state legislatures, but western territorial expansion put the question of votes for women back into Congress and, by January 1887, helped set the stage for the only congressional debate over a woman suffrage constitutional amendment to occur in the nineteenth century.

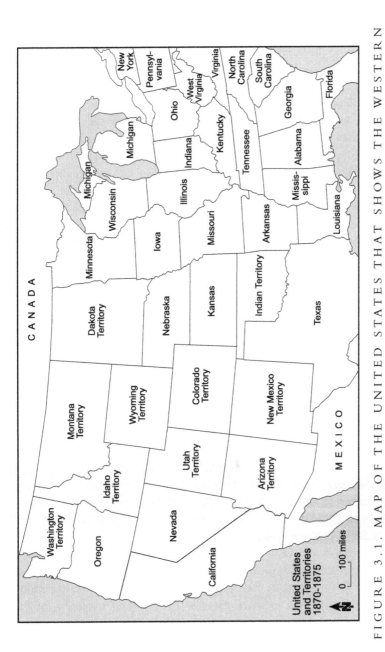

FIGURE 3.1. MAP OF THE UNITED STATES THAT SHOWS THE WESTERN
TERRITORIES INCLUDING INDIAN TERRITORY, CIRCA 1880

In the 1880s the question of votes for women at the national level was framed and reframed in the context of congressional efforts to bring woman suffrage territories in as new states and to resolve the political status of Indians and Mormons in the territories. Yet historical accounts of the suffrage movement have paid relatively little attention to how western territorial expansion drew national attention to local suffrage questions and reopened the woman question in Congress.[6] Meeting in 1887, the Forty-ninth U.S. Congress is remembered far less for its January defeat of the woman suffrage constitutional amendment, and far more for its other efforts to define the boundaries and the borders of American political community. The passage of the Dawes Severalty, or General Allotment Act, in February 1887 spelled out the conditions for establishing Indian citizenship and guaranteed those Indians living on allotted lands, who willingly "adopted the habits of civilized life," the same rights, privileges, and immunities as other United States citizens, which would ultimately include the vote.[7] One month later, the Edmunds-Tucker Act disfranchised the women of Utah Territory as one of a series of punitive measures directed against the polygamous practices of the Mormon Church.[8]

Expansion thus focused suffragists' attention on the twin problems of Indians and Mormons, whose "uncivilized habits" in the case of the former and "licentious practices" in the case of the latter were perceived as equal threats to the health and vitality of American institutions. The federal efforts to resolve these problems and to bring the western territories in as new states aided suffragists' efforts to keep the woman question alive in Congress. Gage, like many suffragists, disapproved of congressional efforts to turn Indians into citizens and opposed the disfranchisement of the women of Utah Territory. Yet both of these congressional projects helped create a political space for the woman question by reopening debates over the link between citizenship and voting rights presumably closed by *Minor*. As suffragists were only too happy to point out during discussions of the Indian and Mormon problems, enfranchising Indians and disfranchising Mormons through federal law effectively violated the constitutional principle established by *Minor*, that the "United States has no voters of its own creation."[9]

Between 1878 and 1887, Gage and other members of both the NWSA and the AWSA attempted to exploit this perceived inconsistency on the part of Congress by intervening in the national discussions of Indians, Mormons, and territorial statehood to make the case for a federal resolution of the woman question. In so doing, they challenged the postwar political settlement that treated the character of the electorate as a national concern, increasingly policed through immigration and naturalization law, but left control over voting rights in the hands of the states.[10] It was a testament to the success of this challenge that by 1887, debating and defeating the woman suffrage constitutional amendment had become as much a part of the politics of U.S. territorial expansion westward as was resolving the political status of Indians and preventing the spread of Mormon polygamy. The woman suffrage amendment was defeated, yet its emergence as a vibrant political question in 1887 was evidence not only of the growing strength of the suffrage movement but also of how the politics of territorial expansion reopened national discussions of voting rights. Looking back to the debate over the annexation of Santo Domingo and expanding U.S. borders into the Caribbean in the early 1870s, the problem of defining the gendered boundaries of political space and the physical boundaries of national territory remained largely separate questions. By 1887, however, in the context of the U.S. territorial system, they became inextricably intertwined because discussions of Indian citizenship, and voting women in Utah, Wyoming, and by 1883 Washington Territory, demonstrated that in certain instances Congress could and would exercise national authority over the vote.

INDIAN CITIZENSHIP AND THE QUESTION OF FEDERAL AUTHORITY OVER THE VOTE

In the spring of 1878, Gage's attention was drawn to the question of Indian citizenship in part because of her proximity to the New York meeting of the Iroquois council, but even without this local connection, the topic of Indian citizenship would have commanded her attention. When Federal troops were withdrawn from the South the year before, signaling the end of government-sponsored Reconstruction, Americans turned their attention westward. Between 1860 and 1880, more than 10,000 U.S. citizens, including a number of former slaves, migrated west, nearly doubling the population of the western states and territories.[11] As increasing numbers of U.S. settlers clashed with Indians on the western frontiers, expansion replaced Reconstruction on the national political agenda. By 1878, completing the project of national unification meant bringing the western territories into the Union as new states, and the necessity of creating a coherent Indian policy moved to the top of the list of national priorities.[12] It was the increasing frequency and violence of clashes between Indian tribes and U.S. settlers that provided the immediate impetus behind Ingalls's 1877 bill regarding Indian citizenship. These violent conflicts had been a problem in Ingalls's home state of Kansas since the 1850s, and by the 1870s the eastern press was filled with stories of the "Indian Problem." In the summer of 1876, Gage, along with other New Yorkers, would have read about the defeat of General George Custer by the Sioux at the Battle of Little Big Horn. "The victory of the savages will inflame the border," the *New York Times* warned its readers.[13] This prediction proved well-founded. Between Custer's defeat in the summer of 1876 and Gage's publication in May 1878, the "Indian Wars" raged across the West as settlers and Indians took up arms in Kansas, Nebraska, Texas, Oregon, California, Utah, Colorado, Montana, and Idaho.[14]

The notion that granting Indians citizenship could resolve hostilities between Indian tribes and U.S. settlers might seem, at first glance, a curious proposition. Despite the seeming incongruity of rewarding violence with citizenship, however, Ingalls's bill reflected an emerging consensus that creating citizen Indians was the most likely way to resolve these escalating conflicts.[15] From the Revolution through the 1830s, Indian tribes were viewed largely as separate sovereignties, and U.S. Indian policy had been conducted by treaty, although these treaties were frequently broken and often ignored. Unlike other independent nations with whom the United States might sign federal treaties, however, beginning in 1828, Indian sovereignty was qualified by a legal tradition that defined Indian tribes as "domestic dependent nations" of the United States.[16] As sovereign nations, Indian tribes were largely beyond the control of state governments, but as domestic dependents, they were wards of Congress. The "independent-dependency" of the Indian was a legal fiction that reflected a crucial ambiguity underlying U.S.-Indian relations across the nineteenth century. Federal treaties that acknowledged tribal sovereignty and title to lands were at odds with U.S. intentions to assert sovereignty over all lands and peoples within the geographic borders of the continental United States.[17] In 1871, when Federal troops leaving the South were redeployed to the West, Congress passed legislation declaring that "hereafter no Indian nation or tribe within the territory of the United States shall be acknowledged or recognized as an independent nation, tribe, or power with whom the United States may contract by treaty."[18] This 1871 law ended a century of Indian-U.S. relations based on a presumption of some Indian independence from U.S. rule. It did not, however, entirely resolve earlier ambiguities about the political status of Indians. The 1871 law no longer recognized Indian tribes as independent nations with whom the United States might sign treaties, yet it formally kept intact all previous treaties and continued to acknowledge tribes as distinct political bodies.

Turning Indians into citizens was one way of addressing the lingering ambiguities over Indians' residual independence within the United States that frontier violence made so visible. By dissolving tribal sovereignty, the extension of citizenship would bring individual Indians under the control of state governments, give Indians the vote, and convert collectively owned tribal lands into private property that new citizen Indians could sell off to settlers. In some cases, U.S. citizenship was already available to individual Indians willing to separate from their tribes and pay taxes to the states under whose jurisdiction they chose to reside. When the Seminole and Creek Nations sent delegates to D.C. to lodge a formal protest against Ingalls's bill, their particular concern was that this bill would allow Indians still living on reservations to apply for citizenship and, additionally, to claim an allotment, or share, of collectively owned tribal land as private property. As these delegates protested to Congress, "The presence among us on our own soil of those of our blood who have disowned our government would be an element of discord no one can doubt." Individual Indians who were U.S. citizens but remained on tribal property were guaranteed to "sow the seeds of discord and strife inside the tribe itself," an intolerable situation in its own right. Even more alarmingly, as the Seminole and Creek delegates pointed out, if Ingalls's bill passed, and all Indians became citizens, "the Creek Nation and the Seminole Nation would cease to exist."[19] Members of the Seminole and Creek Nations realized that granting Indian citizenship could wipe out the Indian far more effectively than wars along the border.

National legislators may have increasingly favored Indian citizenship as a solution to the Indian problem, but there was a current of opinion among suffragists that extending citizenship and voting rights to Indian men might make suffrage harder to achieve for U.S. women. A December 1877 announcement in the *Woman's Journal* for the January NWSA convention in D.C. indicated that the question of Indian citizenship and Indian suffrage was becoming a topic of movement concern. Signed by the new NWSA president, Clemence Lozier, as well as by Anthony and Hooker, the convention announcement warned suffragists that because Indian men "have always made of their women beasts of burden," Indian men as voters could create "an additional peril to the women citizens of the United States."[20] Suffragists feared that if Indian men joined with the "dram-seller, the drunkard, and the profligate" in the government of U.S. women, they were likely to "vote solid against woman suffrage" like "Mexicans, Half-breeds, [other] ignorant, vicious men."[21] In October 1877, voters in Colorado had rejected a woman suffrage amendment to the state constitution, and many members of the AWSA and the NWSA blamed "Mexicans" and "Half-breeds" for the defeat of the amendment in language that was not often in use during the heyday of the New Departure.[22] It was not that these sentiments had been absent from suffragists thinking in the early 1870s, but the universal claims that grounded the New Departure constitutional strategy de-emphasized race-based arguments for the vote.

Suffragists' claim that Indian men turned Indian women into "beasts of burden" recycled older ideas about the role of Indian women in native societies that dated from the seventeenth century. When British settlers first arrived in the colonies, they discovered that, in contrast to their own farming practices, many Indian tribes considered agriculture women's work. Kathy Brown has suggested that Indians and colonists in the seventeenth century viewed each other across a frontier of gender in which conflicting notions of masculinity and femininity contributed to colonial constructions of Indians as "savages."[23] In 1877, when suffragists worried about Indian men as voters because they used Indian women as "beasts of burden," they were employing a gendered construction of Indian savagery that had existed in American political discourse for more than two centuries. It was this concern over Indian men's treatment of Indian women that informed Henry Blackwell's 1869 suggestion that one solution to the Indian problem would be to enfranchise Indian women along with Indian men.

As Gage's reference to Indian "savagery" attests, she believed that Indian men were far less "civilized" than Christian women and far less deserving of the political privileges of citizenship. Americans had a long history of "Indian hating," and suffragists were not exempt from these sentiments.[24] Even so, suffragists' ideas about Indians were far more complex than they might seem at first glance. Notions of Indian savagery were pervasive among suffragists, but so to was attention to other long-standing tropes regarding Indians more "noble" qualities. Suffragists including Stanton, Child, Mott, and even Gage had, at different points in their careers, each looked to the Indians in their search for alternative models of social organization and family life that were more conducive to female freedom. Gail Landsman has investigated how contemporary writings on the Iroquois in particular drew suffragists' attention to matrilineal patterns of descent and the autonomy Indian women were said to retain within marriage.[25] In 1877, Lewis Henry Morgan's *Ancient Society, or Researches in the Lines of Human Progress from Savagery through Barbarism to Civilization* argued that Iroquois women had substantial political rights and freedoms within tribes that were unavailable to their U.S. sisters. Morgan's work was crucial to nineteenth-century woman's rights activists', particularly Gage's and Stanton's, search for examples of a matriarchal tradition to which they could appeal.[26] Suffragists were especially interested in the extent to which Indian women in different tribes had rights to their own children, to control property, and to initiate divorce. According to Morgan, Iroquois marriage was largely under maternal control, and women had the power to separate from husbands if they chose, moreover, without losing their tribal affiliation or their control of property within marriage.[27]

In addition to this burgeoning anthropological literature, suffragists also drew on their own firsthand experiences in forming more sympathetic and positive images of Indians and of the status of women in native societies. As a girl, Child lived for a time in northern Maine, where she came into frequent contact with members of the Abenaki and Penobscot tribes.[28] Her experiences during these years were at the core of what would later become a well-developed critique of the mistreatment of Indians by European settlers. By the beginning of the Civil War, Child had produced a substantial body of material criticizing U.S. Indian policy, and by the end of the war she was at the forefront of the emerging movement for Indian rights. In 1878, Child was an advocate of Indian citizenship, although she recognized quite clearly that assimilation could be as much of a tragedy for Indian nations and a violation of Indian rights as extermination. Carolyn Karcher has documented those moments in Child's fiction where her meditations on Indian life and Indian women created a perspective from which to think critically about how the expectations of "civilized" society circumscribed women lives.[29] Karcher notes that as early as 1824, when Child published *Hobomok, A Tale of Early Times*, she had already begun to explore the relationship between patriarchy and white supremacy that she would develop throughout her career by using the literary device of love and marriage between an Indian man and a New England woman. By 1878, attention to the Indian question, like attention to the slavery question in the antebellum era, was becoming an important way for suffragists to explore the meaning of female independence and dependence, and ideas about self-sovereignty that accompanied the extension of republican citizenship to women.

Thus, to suffragists, as to many Americans, Indians were noble savages whose plight at once elicited sympathy and disdain. Gage's essay on Indian citizenship reflected these competing attitudes. On one hand, Gage spoke repeatedly about Indian barbarism and her outrage that Indian men might be enfranchised before U.S. women. On the other hand, Gage also acknowledged that the Indians had been oppressed by U.S. policies and that "duty toward them demands…a faithful living up to its obligations on the part of the Government."[30] Acknowledging that Indian citizenship "would open wide the door to the grasping avarice of the white man" for Indian lands, Gage argued in a prescient analogy that to force citizenship on unwilling tribes without their consent would be much the same as proposing the "forcible annexation of Cuba, Mexico, or Canada to our government, and as unjust."[31] For Gage, racial prejudice as well as sensitivity to the long history of Indian mistreatment at the hands of the United States combined to form the basis of her opposition to Ingalls's bill for Indian citizenship. Her critique of U.S. expansion echoed those offered by anti-annexationists like Garrison during the Santo Domingo debate who mistrusted Grant's professed concerns for the welfare of the Dominicans. As a suffragist, Gage may not have fully empathized with the Iroquois' decision to decline the gift of citizenship and with it the vote, but she could certainly understand their resistance.

Empathy aside, Gage's discussion of Indian citizenship is most notable because of her effort to move beyond the framework of savagery and civilization and to use the Indian problem as a way to reopen the legal and constitutional questions supposedly settled by the Supreme Court's decision in *Minor* (1875). In *Minor*, the court had ruled against suffragists' claim that voting was an inherent right of national citizenship. Gage was interested in how federal legislation that turned Indians into citizens would create new voters and impose them on the states, thereby contradicting *Minor*. The belief that voting was a right of national citizenship was dear to Gage's heart and the underlying principle of her editorial endeavors. In addition to being a "general criticism of men and things," Gage's *National Citizen and Ballot Box* was dedicated to popularizing the position that "Suffrage is the Citizen's right, and should be protected by National Law."[32] In 1873, as an advocate for the New Departure, Gage had published an essay titled "Centralized Power vs. State Rights," in which she presented a stark reversal of the classic liberal fear of the inherent tyranny of centralized power. Arguing that "*state* centralization is tyranny; *national* centralization is freedom," Gage far outstripped even the most radical Republican anticipation of what became the modern liberal faith in the power of the federal government to protect individual rights and ensure individual freedoms.[33]

By addressing the question of Indian citizenship, Gage hoped to revive the issues of *Minor* and make the case that "although, theoretically, the power over the suffrage is held to be in the hands of the states alone…the United States has endowed whatever class it pleased with the suffrage."[34] In "United States Rights vs. State Rights," a companion piece to her essay on Indian citizenship, Gage opined that Chief Justice Morrison Waite's declaration in *Minor* that the United States has no voters was "false upon the face of it."[35] First Gage noted that "every enfranchised male slave had the ballot secured him under United States law, a law which overrode all State provisions against color."[36] Along with ex-slaves, Gage included on her list "every Southern man disfranchised because of having taken part in the war, and who was afterwards granted amnesty [and] the naturalized foreigner [who] secures his right to vote under United States law, and cannot vote unless he first becomes an United States citizen."[37] Finally, Gage noted the case of "foreigners who had served in, and been honorably discharged from the army."[38] For Gage, what made the Indian question most relevant to suffragists was that despite legal opinions that declared voting to be a state right, the Indian question demonstrated concrete links between national citizenship and the vote and served as a potential example of how Congress could create voters and impose them on the states through national law.

Intent on demonstrating that for Indians, if not for U.S. women, national citizenship and voting rights went hand in hand, Gage's article on Indian citizenship recalled her readers' attention to the 1877 case of *United States v. Elm*, which was heard in federal court in the Northern District of New York.[39] In this case, the conviction of an Oneida Indian man for illegal voting in the 1876 election was overturned because, in the words of Judge Wallace, "if the defendant was a citizen of the United States, he was entitled to exercise the right of suffrage" in the state of New York.[40] For Wallace, the primary issue at stake in Elm's case was not whether citizenship made Elm a voter—the answer to that was yes—but whether or not Elm was a citizen in the first place. Wallace noted that if Elm's tribe had continued to "maintain its tribal integrity," and if Elm personally maintained his relationship with his tribe, he would not have been a citizen under the terms of the Fourteenth Amendment, which specified that citizens must be subject to U.S. jurisdiction. Elm's tribe was defunct, and he paid taxes in the state of the New York, however; as a result, Wallace determined that he was entitled to the vote.[41]

In 1873, when Susan B. Anthony was tried in the U.S. Circuit Court of New York for illegal voting at the 1872 presidential election, she too had based her defense on her status as a citizen under the terms of the Fourteenth Amendment and its promise of equal protection under the law, which Anthony claimed included voting rights.[42] When Judge Ward Hunt found Anthony guilty of illegal voting, however, he sidestepped altogether the question of voting as a right of national citizenship. Hunt ruled against Anthony because she was a woman, and the New York State constitution limited the vote to men.[43] Anthony's 1873 trial had been widely publicized. When Gage drew suffragists' attention to the case of *United States v. Elm*, she implicitly juxtaposed the similarity of conditions but difference in outcomes between U.S. women and Indian men in the courts.

Gage's comparison of the treatment of Elm and Anthony in the courts was a reflection of how by 1878 the understanding of Indians' relationship to the federal government was coming to serve as a loose analogy for that of women. The language used to describe the status of both groups included references to the notion of "domestic dependency" and the problem of primary allegiances, in one case to husbands and families, in the other to tribes. Just as Indian men's voting rights depended in part on their separation from tribes and tribal government, so too did women's voting rights require a separation from family government. In his 1879 essay "Is the Family the Basis of the State?" the Connecticut suffragist John Hooker, Isabella Beecher Hooker's lawyer husband, argued that the "the first duty of the citizen is to forget that he belongs to any family in particular but is an individual citizen."[44] Instead of families forming the primary unit of society, Hooker conceived of the nation as an aggregate of individuals whose links to each other were primarily legal, and the nation as fundamentally constituted through law. To Hooker, family government and tribal government were equally weak foundations for the growth of strong nations. As Hooker wrote, "Civil government is supposed to have had its origin in family government, the patriarch becoming chief of the tribe which was substantially the outgrowth and expansion of a single family; but if a nation was to be formed of such tribes it would be essential to its peace and prosperity that they should as soon as possible mingle into one homogenous mass, and that no citizen should consider himself as of one tribe rather than another."[45] Analogizing the family to the tribe was an important and politically salient metaphor. After all, advocates of Indian citizenship hoped that that legal change could civilize "savages" within a generation. This belief echoed thinking among members of the woman's suffrage movement who had come to see the historically dependent status of women as a social construction embedded in law and similarly amenable to change. What is most striking about both Gage and Hooker's implied analogy between Indian and U.S. women's shared status as legal dependents or wards is that it grounded women's political emancipation on the transformative power of national citizenship and continued to privilege the ideas that had animated the New Departure. Rather than using the discussion of the Indian question as an opportunity to develop ideas that linked the vote to Christian women's "civilization," in contrast to Indian men's "savagery," Gage and Hooker focused on their shared dependency within tribal and familial relationships, and the power of national citizenship to change their dependent status.

NATIONAL SOLUTIONS FOR NATIONAL PROBLEMS

Gage was not alone in her hope that suffragists might find a way to overturn what NWSA suffragists called the "vacillating interpretations of constitutional law" that were reflected in the Court's decision in *Minor*.[46] Between 1870 and 1875, NWSA energies had been largely concentrated on the New Departure strategy of claiming the vote under the Fourteenth Amendment and later the Fifteenth Amendment, a moment Anthony described as "full of life and hope."[47] But agitating for a sixteenth, woman suffrage constitutional amendment had always also been an important option. In 1869, when George Julian introduced the first proposal for a woman suffrage amendment to the national constitution (had it been ratified it would have been the sixteenth amendment), his language was consistent with the logic of the New Departure, that voting was a right of national citizenship: "The Right of Suffrage in the United States shall be based on citizenship, and shall be regulated by Congress; and all citizens of the United States, whether native or naturalized, shall enjoy this right equally without any distinction or discrimination whatever founded on sex."[48] Three years later, in 1878, California senator Aaron A. Sargent's woman suffrage constitutional amendment echoed the simpler language of the Fifteenth Amendment: "The right of citizens of the United States to vote shall not be denied or abridged by the United States or by any state on account of sex."[49] Sargent's simpler language reflected a step back from the New Departure, however, because it did not assert the premise that suffrage was a national right; rather, it merely asserted that this state right should not be limited on account of sex.

Stanton, like Gage, however, was not entirely ready to give up on the New Departure, or to begin again the tedious process of "forming country societies, rolling up petitions against unjust laws, or in favor of further amendments to state and national constitutions." She preferred instead to "demand our rights at the ballot-box."[50] When the NWSA recommitted itself to pursuing a woman suffrage sixteenth amendment at its January 1878 meeting in D.C., Stanton inaugurated the new campaign. Yet her "National Protection for National Citizens" speech rehearsed many of the arguments made on behalf of the New Departure and continued to frame the question of women's ballots not as a problem of sex but as a problem of national power over the franchise.[51] To this end Stanton turned her attention to other examples of national problems, like the Indian problem, requiring national solutions. Urging her audience to remember the "losses sustained by citizens in traveling from one State to another under the old system of State banks," and to imagine "the confusion if each State regulated its post-offices, and the transit of the mails across its borders," Stanton pointed to "a growing feeling among the people in favor of more homogenous legislation," that is, laws that were uniform across the states.[52] Political rights, she believed, should necessarily follow the same path toward national regulation as mail and money.

In the late 1870s, when NWSA suffragists linked their cause to expansive national power, they swam against a powerful tide of postwar reaction to federal infringement on states' rights.[53] Demanding "national protection for national citizens" in 1878 was an argument that looked backward to the political exigencies of postwar Reconstruction but failed to resonate in the contemporary climate of a growing backlash against black male voters across the South, and toward immigrant voters across the states. When Republicans withdrew Federal troops from the South, as part of the political compromise that earned them the presidency in 1877, they signaled the abandonment of any significant national commitment to protect black voters. The reestablishment of white supremacist governments across the South was "hard work," requiring countless acts of murder and violence.[54] By 1878, this work was well under way as southern "redeemers," seeking to reclaim state governments for white Democrats only, successfully established redemption governments in every southern state capital.[55] Even D.C., after a fashion, was redeemed in 1878, when Congress reorganized the government there yet again and abolished all elected offices. When the NWSA met in D.C. that year, Democrats held majorities in both the House and the Senate. These Democratic majorities regularly used the phrase "states' rights" as convenient shorthand for describing a commitment to the progressive disfranchisement of southern blacks and the dissolution of southern Republicanism. Stanton's call for "national protection for national citizens" could not have fallen on deafer ears.

Other women speaking from the NWSA platform in January 1878 alongside Stanton advanced arguments in favor of a sixteenth woman suffrage constitutional amendment that attempted to deflect attention from the immediate issues of the postwar South. The thirty-five-year-old Elizabeth Boynton Harbert, an Illinois suffragist whose energy and enthusiasm placed her in the forefront of an emerging cohort of younger leaders, avoided the language of states' rights, citizenship, and black democracy and instead advanced suffragists' aims using the language of domesticity. In what might be regarded as a late nineteenth-century incarnation of "Republican motherhood," a set of ideas that justified women's political participation on the basis of their "womanly" talents for raising citizen-sons, Harbert told NWSA activists that the "new truth, electrifying, glorifying American womanhood to-day, is the discovery that the state is but the larger family, the nation the old homestead," and most important of all, "that in this national home there is a room and a corner and a *duty* for 'mother.'"[56] Harbert's argument for women's ballots emphasized the essential differences between women and men and represented an important shift away from the efforts of New Departure suffragists "to bury the black man and the woman in the citizen," in Stanton's famous phrase.[57]

Harbert's conception of the nation as a larger family was well suited to encouraging the participation of new women in the suffrage movement. When Frances Willard, the recently elected president of the Woman's Christian Temperance Union, endorsed woman suffrage in 1876, the majority of

WCTU activists were far more comfortable thinking about women's ballots as a means to expand the sphere of woman's duty and woman's work than to transform themselves from women into citizens. In this respect Harbert's vision was an inclusive one that accommodated the principles of womanly virtue animating the reform efforts of women working outside the suffrage movement. But the conception of the nation as a larger family advanced by Harbert and Willard also obscured a very divisive and exclusive set of racial politics behind a discussion of gender. To think of the nation as a larger family, as Harbert did, was to make organic what for New Departure suffragists was primarily a legal construction: to make qualities such as ethnicity and heredity important tenets of national identity. In contrast, to be a citizen of a nation that was conceived as a larger family emphasized the essential qualities and abstract capacity of individuals, rather than their universal rights as citizens. Although Harbert herself did not argue for the vote for white women only, her conception of women voters performing the work of motherhood on a national scale implicitly reinforced the idea of the nation as a family writ large, whose citizenry was linked by a shared racial and ethnic heritage.

It is tempting, for the sake of clarity, to imagine Stanton, on the one hand, and Harbert and Willard, on the other, constituting a spectrum of belief marked by a variety of types of argument that could be marshaled in support of a sixteenth amendment. At one end of this spectrum were claims for the ballot grounded in womanly virtue and racial essentialism; at the other, demands based on citizenship. This kind of imagining, however, simplifies the complex nature of suffragists' thinking about race, nation, sex, and rights during a moment of expanding democracy and violent backlash.[58] In most cases, suffragists' support for the proposed sixteenth amendment drew on both types of arguments in varied combinations. Stanton, too, employed the language of domesticity to make her case for women's votes. Despite her call for "national protection for national citizens," she asserted a familial conception of national belonging in her defense of the proposed sixteenth amendment. In her 1878 NWSA speech, Stanton reminded legislators that they had not trusted southern freedmen "to the arbitrary will of courts and States." Why, then, she asked, "send your mothers, wives, and daughters to the unwashed, unlettered, unthinking masses that carry our State elections?"[59] Here, Stanton's imagining of the national family was quite striking, precisely because it included freedpeople within the American family and drew the line of exclusion at newer immigrants. Stanton's reference to "unwashed, unlettered, unthinking masses" was more a thinly veiled dismissal of the waves of Catholic immigrants arriving in U.S. cities than of blacks or even Indians, both groups that in the 1870s NWSA suffragists tended to view as wholly American although located well below whites in the context of a complex racial hierarchy. In 1878, when Stanton asked legislators to consider "how can we ever have a homogenous government so long as universal principles are bounded by State lines," the meaning of the phrase "homogenous government" resonated differently with different audiences. To some it recalled the Reconstruction era hope that woman suffrage, like black male suffrage, would result from the expansion of national authority and the prohibition of state laws that denied women the vote on the basis of sex; to others it signaled the privileging of the rights of the "native born."

Black suffragists like Mary Ann Shadd Cary and Frederick Douglass who attended the 1878 NWSA convention supported the sixteenth amendment strategy of gaining the vote for women. Yet it was impossible to miss the ways that platform speeches and resolutions were contributing to a climate in which black suffragists could only feel less welcome within the organization, much as they were increasingly less welcome within the Republican Party. In violation of the Fifteenth Amendment, southern states were already using literacy tests to keep black voters from the polls. Douglass spoke of "anti-Black prejudice among white suffragists," and it is likely that he meant the NWSA debate over endorsing literacy tests as a means to ensure that "intelligence shall be made the basis of suffrage."[60] In this context, Stanton's assertion that "this measure in no way conflicts with the popular theory that suffrage is a natural right [because] women and black men can stand the educational test quite as well as the favored 'white male citizen'" was in many respects disingenuous.[61] Within two years Cary's frustrations with the NWSA led her to form D.C.'s Colored Women's Progressive Franchise Association and to continue the struggle for votes for women in this new venue.[62] This did not reflect her own abandonment of universality but, rather, a sense that despite the NWSA's commitment to pursing a woman suffrage constitutional amendment that would necessarily include black women in its protections, the NWSA had abandoned the racially inclusive principles underlying its New Departure strategy.

The demands for a sixteenth amendment represented a narrowing of the NWSA's radically egalitarian commitment to universal democracy under the New Departure, but this did not make the demand for a sixteenth amendment less controversial outside the organization. Lucy Stone was far from convinced that the proposed amendment had any hope of passage. The *Woman's Journal* encouraged its readers to sign petitions supporting the sixteenth amendment, but in 1878, members of the AWSA were devoting their main energies to state and local organizing.

Despite the difficulties standing in the way of the woman suffrage amendment, Stanton was not entirely off the mark when she pointed to the fact that in 1878 the United States faced national dilemmas requiring federal solutions. Indians, as Gage had pointed out in the *Ballot Box*, were one obvious example of a case where national sentiment was turning away from a piecemeal approach—that is, one that involved numerous separate treaties with individual tribes—toward national laws that could address the Indian problem wholesale. An expanding national economy provided numerous other examples of political problems that crossed state lines and required national solutions. Since the early 1870s, midwestern farmers had begun organizing themselves into cooperative associations, or Granges, and pressuring legislators for federal regulation of the railroads. In 1878, the Greenback Party, a national organization of paper money advocates, indebted farmers, and labor activists, entered the congressional elections and won several seats in the House.[63] Greenback Party demands included railroad regulation, an eight-hour day for government employees, and an increase in the supply of paper money to alleviate debt. In 1878, the national reform efforts of farmers and organized labor stood largely outside the mainstream of national politics, but they represented a growing current of opinion in favor of federal solutions to the problems of an industrializing economy. In her "National Protection for National Citizens" speech, Stanton had her finger on this weak pulse.

MORMON POLYGAMY AND THE QUESTION OF NATIONAL AUTHORITY OVER THE VOTE

When Stanton cast about for examples of a "growing feeling among the people for more homogenous legislation," she failed, significantly, to touch on the one local issue that in 1878 national legislators were willing to address as a national problem requiring a national solution: polygamy in Utah. In their 1856 national party platform, Republicans had labeled southern slavery and Mormon polygamy (the plural marriage of one husband and multiple wives) the "twin relics of barbarism."[64] By 1862, Lincoln had signed the Morrill Anti-Bigamy Act, which made plural marriage a federal offense and nullified territorial laws authorizing polygamous marriage.[65] Because Mormons controlled the Utah judicial system, the act was largely unenforceable. In 1874, Brigham Young's secretary George Reynolds, himself a bigamist, volunteered to test the law, claiming that federal intervention in Utah marriage law was a violation of his First Amendment rights.[66] Reynolds was found guilty in 1878. When Stanton made her "National Protection for National Citizens" speech, Reynolds's case had reached the Supreme Court. Examining this case, Sarah Barringer Gordon has argued that upholding states' rights to regulate marriage, which in this instance meant supporting the Mormon right to plural marriage in Utah Territory, was perceived by many as a "weakness" in the federal system, one that might allow the scandalous and licentious behavior of a few to corrupt the moral integrity of the many. Conversely, a Supreme Court ruling that upheld Reynolds's conviction would constitutionalize federal intervention in the law of marriage in Utah Territory, an area of law traditionally considered as falling within the domain of state self-government.[67]

Stanton's failure to mention the regulation of marital practices in Utah Territory as an example of a national problem requiring a national solution, like banking or the Indian problem, was out of character; she had never feared raising delicate issues for public scrutiny or taking unpopular stands. The problem of Mormon polygamy for the suffrage movement was, however, particularly complicated. Initially at least, suffragists had believed that women voters in Utah Territory would use the ballot to make polygamy illegal. It was this assumption that encouraged the Indiana Republican and suffrage ally George Julian to introduce a bill into Congress in 1869, asking for woman suffrage in Utah, that was entitled, "A Bill to Discourage Polygamy in Utah."[68] Congress had failed to act on Julian's bill, but in 1870, Utah Territory enfranchised women on its own. When Stanton and Anthony visited Utah Territory in 1871, as part of a western tour, they were optimistic about the success of woman suffrage to end legalized plural marriage in the territory. Stanton gave a closed lecture to Mormon women at the Mormon Tabernacle in Salt Lake City, during which she discussed different forms of marriage. Stanton remembered the event as one of "full and free discussion," and while she found that "Mormon women, like all others, stoutly defend their own religion," she was convinced that they were "no more satisfied than any other sect."[69] Seven years later, it was clear, however, that many Mormon women voters in Utah Territory supported plural marriage. The Mormon suffragist Emmeline B. Wells, for example, viewed polygamy as crucial to the expansion of woman's rights because it allowed women to combine motherhood with more control of "her individual self," by which she meant control over sex within marriage.[70] As the editor of the Utah *Woman's Exponent*, Wells popularized the pro-polygamy sentiments of Mormon suffragists. By 1878, woman suffrage in Utah Territory had become an embarrassment for the suffrage movement because of the way polygamy linked votes for women and sexual scandal in the public mind.

Stanton was well aware that the enforcement of the Morrill Act was not the only way that antipolygamists hoped to put a stop to plural marriage in Utah Territory. Almost immediately after the territory enfranchised women, antipolygamists introduced legislation into Congress calling for women's disfranchisement.[71] In 1876, when Anthony disrupted the official celebration of the U.S. centennial in Philadelphia, she included this anti–woman suffrage legislation in a list of grievances that she read as part of the *Declaration of Rights of the Women of the United States*.[72] In this context, Stanton's decision to stay clear of the Mormon question was well founded. Drawing attention to Mormon women's failure to illegalize polygamy could only hurt suffragists' efforts to make a case for women's votes. Stanton's decision to avoid the topic, however, did not prevent suffragists in either the AWSA or the NWSA from being drawn into the debate. As the NWSA began its sixteenth amendment campaign in 1878, a growing women's antipolygamy crusade led by Protestant women in Utah reached outward from the territory, hoping to engage the energies of eastern women. Many suffragists responded sympathetically: Julia Ward Howe and Frances Willard became two of the most prominent suffragists to speak out against the practice of polygamy specifically and Mormonism generally.[73] In contrast, NWSA members aided Emmeline B. Wells, as a fellow suffragist, when she came to D.C. in 1879 to protest the enforcement of the Morrill Act.[74]

In 1882, Congress appointed standing committees in both houses devoted to the question of woman suffrage. Stanton and Anthony would later claim that this meant Congress was "at last raising [women's] political status to the dignity of the Indian," but it was already clear that the Mormon question would have far more salience for the political fate of woman suffrage than would the Indian question.[75] Antipolygamy legislation was a dominant topic of the 1882 legislative session, and in March, Congress added prohibitions against voting, jury service, and running for public office to the list of penalties for polygamous marriage and cohabitation.[76] The 1882 law took the name of its primary advocate, the Vermont Republican senator George Edmunds. Edmunds was a former Radical Republican, opponent of woman suffrage, and, in 1882, a member of a loose cohort of independent, "half-breed" Republicans who had successfully defeated Grant's renomination for a third presidency. This coalition of Grant opponents within the Republican Party included Henry Laurens Dawes, a primary architect of the Indian Allotment Bill that five years later would bear his name, and his Massachusetts colleague, George Frisbee Hoar.[77] Whereas in 1869, Julian's proposal that Congress should enfranchise women in Utah Territory was indicative of a belief that votes for women would end the practice of polygamy, the 1882 Edmunds Act reflected no such faith in the power of women's votes.

Although many suffragists believed Mormon women were the victims of the "crime" of polygamy, and not criminals in their own right, defending polygamous Mormon women's right to vote without publicly associating themselves with their challenge to traditional marriage was a conundrum.

Many shared the pervasive hostility toward plural marriage expressed by the Nebraska suffragist Clara Colby when she editorialized in the *Woman's Tribune* that "as long as the Mormons retain polygamy, so long will their religion be abhorrent to civilization and a synonym for the unhappiness and degradation of women."[78] Colby never explicitly compared the Mormon "degradation" of women to the "degradation" of Indian women, but her language reflected the popular sentiments that the marital practices of polygamous Mormons were evidence of their equally "un-civilized" character. In later years, Stanton would antagonize members of the suffrage movement by indicting all religions in the degradation of women, including Protestant Christianity. To Stanton, if Mormons perpetuated "their abominable system of polygamy" through religion, religion also made "the Hindoo woman burn herself on the funeral pyre of her husband" and held "Turkish women in the Harem." Similarly, Stanton felt that "so long as ministers stand up and tell us as Christ is the head of the Church, so is man the head of the woman," Christian women were also held in bondage.[79]

In 1879, the NWSA resolved to protest the disfranchisement of any woman in Utah Territory, but by 1884 Colby tried to have it both ways. She wrote in the pages of the *Woman's Tribune* that if the Edmunds Act succeeded in disfranchising only Mormons who believe in polygamy, "then the vote in the hands of the Gentile women and non-polygamous Mormon women will be the safety of the territory."[80] Gage was not nearly as sanguine as Colby about how the disfranchisement of polygamous women might affect the suffrage movement. If Colby looked forward to the future success of woman suffrage in Utah Territory after the disfranchisement of polygamists, Gage focused on the act of disfranchisement itself. As early as 1879, Gage urged her *Ballot Box* readers to consider how "the Utah question, which now comes up again, is not simply a religious question," but rather touches on women's political rights. In much the same way she had tried to lift the Indian question out of the framework of savagery and civilization, Gage similarly attempted to lift the discussion of the Mormon question out of its religious framework. To this end, Gage pointed attention to the constitutional questions at stake in congressional efforts to use disfranchisement as punishment for the crime of polygamy. As Gage explained carefully in the *Ballot Box* "the general government did not confer this right...[therefore] the United States according to its own theory, has no authority to interfere with this right, because according to that theory, it has nothing at all to do with the suffrage question."[81] Writing on Indian citizenship in May 1878, Gage hoped to point attention toward the absurdity of the principles in *Minor*: that the United States had no voters of its own creation, and that voting rights were not the proper objects of federal legislation. But one year later, without any hint of sarcasm, Gage upheld *Minor* in defense of women's voting rights in Utah Territory. In 1879, when the NWSA formalized its opposition to the Edmunds bill, its resolution of protest closely followed Gage's reasoning, stating that "WHEREAS, The general government has refused to exercise federal power to protect women in their right to vote in the various States and territories; therefore, *Resolved*, That it should forbear to exercise federal power to disfranchise the women of Utah."[82] Even as the organization took this stand, polygamist suffragists were not allowed to speak at the 1882 NWSA convention because the NWSA commitment lay with protesting this exercise of national disfranchisement and not in supporting polygamy.

If antipolygamists had been satisfied with the Edmunds bill, the topic might have dropped off suffragists' radar. In 1886, however, Congress turned its attention to a second antipolygamy bill that included a clause disfranchising all women voters in Utah Territory, Mormon and non-Mormon alike. Suffragists across the board were united in their opposition. Even Colby was outraged. Pointing her readers' attention to the non-Mormon women who would be disenfranchised by Edmunds's second bill, Colby wrote heatedly in the *Woman's Tribune* that, "the injustice and tyranny of that section [of the Edmunds bill] ...has no parallel in history." "Certainly no condition exists," she protested, "which would warrant the de-citizening [of] the innocent thousands."[83] In 1884, Colby's *Woman's Tribune* had replaced Gage's *Ballot Box* as the NWSA's official organ. Colby's awkward use of the word "de-citizening" recalled the NWSA's New Departure era efforts to link citizenship to the vote.

Writing in the *Woman's Journal*, Lucy Stone advanced similar sentiments, protesting "if Senator Edmunds had undertaken to do the same thing to Irishmen or to colored men, the whole country would ring with it."[84] Stone's analysis of the likely reaction to the "decitizening" of Irishmen and colored men was only partially correct. The Irish vote in New York had been crucially important to the successful election of the New York Democrat Grover Cleveland to the presidency in 1884; both the Republican candidate James Blaine and the Democratic candidate Cleveland had actively competed for the votes of these citizens.[85] If Republicans fought Democrats for the votes of Irish citizens in 1884, they largely ignored black voters in the South. Or, rather, they ignored the ongoing disfranchisement of black voters in the South, despite the importance of the black vote to a successful Republican campaign. Douglass publicly protested this Republican failure to stand up for black political rights in 1884 and chastised the party for forgetting "its high mission as the party of great moral ideas." The country did not "ring" with Douglass's protests, however.[86] Indeed, Douglass's marriage to a white woman that year was a lightning rod for racist sentiments in the national press. Stanton supported the Douglass marriage, but Anthony urged her not to do so publicly because she did not want the suffrage movement "to be any party to this indiscretion." "Neither Douglass, nor you, nor I, have the _right_ to complicate nor compromise *our question,*" Anthony wrote Stanton heatedly. Anthony claimed that she had "but one question—that of equality between the sexes." "That of the _races,_" she insisted to Stanton, "had no place on our platform."[87]

Congressional attention to the second Edmunds bill rightly alarmed suffragists, yet it simultaneously offered them an opportunity to bring the woman suffrage question to the floor of the Senate in much the same way as the debate over a woman suffrage amendment to the D.C. government bill in 1870. In January 1886, one of Edmunds's Republican colleagues, George Hoar of Massachusetts, introduced an amendment to Edmunds's second bill that sought to remove the clause disfranchising women voters. Nearly ten years had passed since Aaron Sargent had first introduced a woman suffrage constitutional amendment into the Senate, and despite a series of positive committee reports, the bill had yet to make it out of committee. Hoar deliberately proposed the amendment to the second Edmunds bill as a means of putting the question of woman suffrage back into the Senate in a way that the anti-woman suffrage Edmunds had never intended. Arguing in much the same vein as had Gage when she protested the 1882 Edmunds law, Hoar defended Utah women's right to vote by drawing on the principle of *Minor.* Woman suffrage, he asserted, was "a thing to be left to the people of the Territories and the people of the States as a matter which comes within the domain of local self-government." "It seems to me, " Hoar told his Senate colleagues, "that we ought not to undertake to violate that principle in dealing with the Mormons of Utah."[88]

In defense of his bill, and Congress's right to disfranchise women voters, Edmunds fell back on Congress's special powers to manage the territories. Edmunds assured his colleagues that if Congress disfranchised women voters in Utah, "we are not invading any vested right." In Edmunds's view, disfranchising the women of Utah Territory did not violate the principles of *Minor* because when it came to the territories, *Minor* simply did not apply. "We do not violate that principle at all," Edmunds argued, "because we could take away the whole government of the Territory." As Edmunds reminded the Senate, "every Territorial law ...[holds only] until disapproved by Congress."[89] Suffragists avidly followed the Senate debate over Hoar's amendment to the Edmunds bill. The *Woman's Journal* reprinted the *Congressional Record* transcript so that suffragists might track the course of the debate in minute detail. For Gage and other opponents of *Minor,* it must have been hugely satisfying to watch anti–woman suffragists like Edmunds work to get around *Minor's* provisions. After all, *Minor* was an anti–woman suffrage decision, but through his efforts to protect the voting rights of women in Utah Territory, Hoar was turning the logic of *Minor* on its head by arguing that its principles forbade national intervention in Utah Territory's decision to enfranchise women.

The Senate debate over Hoar's woman suffrage amendment to the second Edmunds bill offered suffragists a second, possibly even more satisfying, twist in what was already a very complicated plot. By framing the defense of woman suffrage as a defense of the local right to self-government, and states' right to legislate the ballot, Hoar put southern Democrats in the unenviable position of having to choose between their opposition to woman suffrage and their defense of states' rights. Watching Democrats negotiate this delicate trap turned the *Congressional Record*, often a dry read, into a page-turner. Suffragists would have read the remarks of the anti–woman suffragist Joseph E. Brown, the former Confederate governor of Georgia, and now its Democratic senator, with particular glee.[90] Despite his long record as an advocate of states' rights and an opponent of woman suffrage, Brown supported Hoar's amendment to the Edmunds bill, telling his colleagues that "if the question [of woman suffrage] was up in his own State, he would vote against it; but, as the question before the Senate was one affecting the right already given to the women of Utah by the Laws of that Territory, he would vote for Mr. Hoar's motion."[91] Brown had no sympathy for suffragists, but he opposed federal intervention in this case because he feared its implications closer to home.

The problem for Democrats like Brown was that using disfranchisement as a means to punish the crime of rebellion, in this case the Mormon rebellion against the moral sensibilities of the American Protestant majority, was so closely modeled on Republican willingness to use disfranchisement as a means to punish the crime of confederate rebellion in the South after the Civil War.[92] Brown opposed Republican antipolygamy legislation because it recalled the Republican disfranchisement of Southern secessionists in the 1870s. He also opposed the Edmunds bill because this willingness to interfere with local franchise decisions suggested that congressional Republicans might now recommit themselves to enforcing national prohibitions against state disfranchisement on the basis of race. Republicans lost the presidency in 1884 to a solid Democratic South that kept black male Republicans from the polls through a combination of fraud and violence. Any future Republican victories in the southern states would presumably depend on either protecting black voters and recommitting the Republican Party to enforcing the Reconstruction amendments, or abandoning black voters entirely and turning the southern Republican Party into a whites-only organization. Georgia had actively resisted Reconstruction in the 1870s, refusing to ratify the Fifteenth Amendment, to allow elected black representatives to take their seats in the Georgia legislature, and to outlaw the Klan.[93] For a brief time after the war, Brown had become a Georgia Republican, representing that wing of the party willing to work with Democrats to redeem the South. But in 1886 Brown had returned to the Democratic fold and was protecting Georgia's redemption government by standing up to Republican efforts to interfere with the voting laws of Utah Territory—even if that meant that women would continue to vote in that territory. Despite his anti–woman suffrage sentiments, Brown opposed the idea of black Republicans at the Georgia polls far more than women voters in Utah Territory.

Despite the unlikely support of men like Brown, Hoar's woman suffrage amendment to the Edmunds bill was defeated. This defeat ensured the passage of the Edmunds-Tucker Act in 1887 and the disfranchisement of women in Utah Territory. For a brief moment during the debate over Hoar's amendment, concern for the broader implications of Edmunds's proposed interventions into the suffrage policies within Utah Territory placed anti–woman suffrage Democrats like Brown in a strange and uneasy alliance with suffragists. A decade earlier, the debate over the annexation of Santo Domingo had created an equally strange alliance between Sumner and the Democrats. In this earlier case, race-based opposition to the creation of new black citizens in the Caribbean combined with Sumner's commitment to preserving the independence of black democracy in Haiti to create a significant opposition to Grant's policy of expansion. Territorial Utah, however, was already a part of the United States in a way that Santo Domingo had never been. By 1886, when Congress turned its attention to the Edmunds bill, legislators were not in a position to disown the Mormon question, as they had the Dominican question. In 1886, the process of expanding national borders westward forced legislators to engage in a debate on woman suffrage that they would have preferred to avoid.

In April 1886, just three months after the defeat of Hoar's amendment seemingly signaled the end of any serious congressional debate over woman suffrage for the near future, senators were forced to take up the issue once again when they considered a bill to admit Washington Territory into the Union as a new state. In the Senate's discussion of Washington statehood, the two questions of woman suffrage and national authority to regulate the ballot returned full-blown and in a seemingly inseparable fashion. Because the Mormon question did not color this debate, the issue of states' rights, woman suffrage, and national authority over the vote emerged more clearly as divisive and contentious issues.

In November 1883, Washington's territorial legislature had granted women the vote, and women began to participate in territorial elections on equal terms with men. Therefore, admitting Washington as a new state meant admitting women voters into the Union. The Kentucky Democrat Senator James Beck was vehemently opposed to admitting Washington Territory's women voters into the Union. The logic underlying his opposition, like Brown's opposition to the Edmunds bill, indicates how the discussion of new women voters in the West was inflected by the politics of black disfranchisement in the South. But Beck's opposition also demonstrates that what many legislators feared most was neither the black vote nor a growing national government, but the challenge to male authority that enfranchised women, white or black, would pose. Beck was particularly concerned with the prospect that admitting Washington into the Union with woman suffrage would create federal precedents that might encourage woman suffragists in Kentucky. Beck complained to the Senate that he was "unable to see how Congress can deny the application of the principle of female suffrage everywhere if it establishes it in this case, over which it has absolute and unquestioned power to do as it pleases." "If women vote," Beck warned, "it will be only because Congress authorizes them by this act." Admittedly, it was not just the idea of women voters that bothered Beck, but black women voters in particular, or, in his words, the "ignorant Negro woman." Beck was adamant that "Congress can not allow the most intelligent woman in any State of the Union to vote without allowing the most ignorant negro woman in any State in the South to vote." But Beck's opposition to the Washington statehood bill was not limited to his abhorrence of black women voters, but of all women voters. To Beck, Washington statehood was the "entering wedge to universal female suffrage for white and black, refined and ignorant." "There is no disguising that fact," he declared, "and gentlemen can not shut their eyes to it."[94]

Beck was joined in his opposition to the Washington statehood bill by his Democratic colleague from Louisiana, Senator James Eustis, who offered an amendment to the Washington statehood bill, modeled on the Republican Edmunds bill, which would disfranchise the women of Washington Territory.[95] While it was not surprising that Kentucky white supremacists would oppose any bill they viewed as an "entering wedge" that might open the polls to black women, it was surprising that in this case they were willing to compromise the principle of states' rights to achieve this end. After all, much of the Democratic opposition to the Edmunds bill was rooted in the fear that this "second reconstruction in the West" might revive a Republican commitment to Reconstruction more generally and encourage new federal efforts to prohibit the Southern rush toward black disfranchisement.[96] The South Carolina Democrat Matthew

Butler shared Beck's and Eustis's hostility toward votes for women, but unlike Beck, Butler would rather see women voters admitted to the Union than to compromise his states' rights position. Butler thus opposed the efforts of fellow Democrats to disfranchise the women of Washington Territory because he believed that "the people of that Territory have the power to regulate those matters for themselves."[97] Insisting, "it is their affair and not mine," Butler voted against the amendment disfranchising Washington women.[98]

In 1870, during the Santo Domingo debate, Democrats took great delight in watching how different approaches to the issue of black suffrage divided Republicans on the annexation question. In 1886, Republicans similarly enjoyed watching woman suffrage in Washington Territory divide the Democrats. Beck was a longtime states' rights ideologue who believed that "Nation" was a "contemptible" word and one that "no good Democrat uses, when he can find any other, and when forced to use it, utters in disgust."[99] Henry Teller, a Republican from Colorado, was thus only too happy to point out the hypocrisy of Beck's willingness to use national law to challenge women's voting rights in Washington Territory after decades of standing firm for state control of the ballot. As Teller reminded Beck, "The power of the voter does not come from Congress; it comes from the State; and on the other side of the Chamber, I will venture to say, it never was disputed until yesterday."[100] If Beck felt that "the colored women of Kentucky are not fit to vote," Teller suggested, that "is a question for Kentucky," just as "colored" women's voting rights in Mississippi "is a question for the people of Mississippi."[101] Teller's position was, of course, somewhat disingenuous in its own right. Beck had only to point to the recent debate over the Edmunds–Tucker Act, which disfranchised Utah women, to dispute Teller's claim that the Senate "have everywhere treated the question of electors, as question for the Territory, as we have treated it and as we are compelled by law to treat it, as a question for the State."[102] Edmunds had defended his bill by making distinctions between territories and states, but most legislators conflated the two in such a way that made both the Edmunds–Tucker Act's disfranchisement of women in Utah Territory and Eustis's efforts to disfranchise the women of Washington Territory seem like dangerous threats to the principle of state control over the vote.

Neither Eustis nor Beck ever offered a convincing explanation for why they feared women voters in faraway Washington enough to compromise their states' rights positions. Washington woman suffrage may have been an "entering wedge" to universal female suffrage, but so too had the Fourteenth and Fifteenth Amendments been entering wedges for black male suffrage, and in 1886, Kentucky and Louisiana whites were well on their way to resurrecting white control of the political process in their states despite these amendments.

It is possible to speculate that the specter of black women voters in Kentucky and Louisiana was in some way more threatening to white supremacy in the South than were existing black male voters. It was not that their femininity would protect black women from the kind of violence black men suffered; it had never done so. Yet the increasing salience of the rhetoric of "protection" in U.S. political discourse offers some clues as to what may have animated Eustis and Beck. Rebecca Edwards has made the case that the emerging language of "protection" represented a new way of gendering American politics, one that justified expanding federal power as a defense of the American family.[103] Just as Frances Willard justified women's growing political presence and the creation of formal links between the WCTU and the Prohibition Party on women's need to "protect the home," the language of "protection" infused the Republican approach to tariff reform and the demands of western farmers and eastern labor for railroad regulation and a minimum wage. In the 1880s, Republicans were increasingly adept at rendering innovative policies familiar through the power of this domestic ideology. In contrast, the Democrats tended to see expansive federal power in terms of "encroachments on the patriarchal home," a framework that linked states' rights to the defense of white womanhood, and envisioned white men as defenders of a private domestic sphere that was conceived of as separate from the nation.[104] In this framework Beck's and Eustis's willingness to compromise dearly held principles of states' rights, in order to head off the possibility of creating women voters in Kentucky and Louisiana, suggests that what was at issue was not simply keeping black women from the polls but keeping all women from the polls and the defense of patriarchal family more generally. In the past, the Southern defense of states' rights and patriarchal family had reinforced each other. In the context of admitting Washington Territory's women voters into the Union, these two concepts stood in opposition, and Beck and Eustis were willing to compromise their states' rights position in order to preserve an all-male electorate.

By June, Eustis's anti–woman suffrage amendment had been defeated, but Washington's fate remained undecided as the House had yet to take up the debate. By contrast, the NWSA push for the sixteenth woman suffrage amendment had been making steady progress. In 1884 and again in 1886, the Senate Select Committee on Woman Suffrage reported the measure favorably, and the NWSA hoped that its allies in the Senate might get the measure to the floor for a full debate in the upcoming months.[105] The defeat of Eustis's amendment to the Washington statehood bill had been a small victory, but it also revealed the strength of the anti–woman suffrage opposition, as did several unfavorable House reports on the question.[106] Anthony thought "there may be force in the plan" of delaying the sixteenth amendment question until after Washington had been admitted.[107] As Anthony wrote Elizabeth Boynton Harbert in June 1886, "Our friends in the U.S. Senate think it best to let our 16th Am't [*sic*] resolution wait until after the House has acted on the *Washington* Territory Bill for Admission—lest the full discussion and vote might wake up the enemy to combine against the admission of Washington into the Union!!! because of its *women* holding the ballot!!"[108] In general congressional Republicans supported the admission of Washington Territory into the Union because it was expected to come in as a Republican state, adding much-needed electoral votes and congressional colleagues on the Republican side of the aisle. But not all Republicans were woman suffragists, and if Democrats succeeded in making Washington's admission a national referendum on the woman suffrage question, many Republicans would be forced to vote against Washington's admission.

With the Washington question still undecided at the end of the year, the New Hampshire Republican and suffrage ally Senator Henry Blair called for a debate on the woman suffrage constitutional amendment. Suffragists antici-pated the Senate discussion of the woman suffrage amendment with a great deal of unease and a growing sense that senators might be willing to take up the question of votes for women if only to resolve it in the negative so as to ensure that future discussions of territorial statehood would no longer become national referenda on the woman question. Senators seemed eager to take up the question of woman suffrage if only to get it off the table. When Blair called for a full Senate debate in December 1886, he offered an odd endorsement, urging the Senate to vote on the sixteenth amendment, "so that we may be relieved of the question, for at least this session, and perhaps for some Con-gresses to come."[109] Stanton had gone to England that fall to visit her daughter Harriot, but even from this vantage point, she found time to criticize "our champion." In an open letter to the NWSA Stanton complained that Blair's desire to be "relieved" of the question "rather grates on my heart strings": "If he had said I desire a vote, that women may be relieved from their crushing disabilities, that would have had a touch of magnanimity."[110]

In the context of lukewarm support from their allies, the Senate's defeat of the woman suffrage amendment in January 1887 came as no surprise. The defeat of the Hoar amendment to the Edmunds antipolygamy bill and the disfranchisement of Utah women was fair warning that a woman suffrage con-stitutional amendment would not pass at this time. The January 1887 debate on the woman suffrage constitutional amendment is often viewed as evidence of woman suffrage's growing popularity, and as one early, if incomplete, victory in the movement's long history. It was also a demonstration of how congres-sional control over the territories could turn local franchise decisions into national issues. In the early 1870s, NWSA suffragists argued that the right to vote should be considered a question of national, and not state, politics. Legislators and jurists rejected this argument, but the politics of western territorial expansion and the federal efforts to resolve the problems of Indians and Mormons, in the 1880s created a political opening for suffragists to push their question at the federal level. By 1887, territorial statehood debates and congressional efforts to stamp out polygamy in Utah combined to put the question of woman suffrage into the Senate, and the woman suffrage amendment acquired a headlong momentum of its own, giving the woman suffrage question both life and death at the national level.

The defeat of the sixteenth amendment was only the first of many defeats that spring. In February 1887, women voters in Washington Territory were disfranchised there by a controversial decision of the territorial supreme court. In March 1887, women in Utah Territory were disfranchised when the Edmunds-Tucker Act became law.[111] The passage of the Dawes-Severalty Act in February 1887 granting citizenship and voting rights to Indians who separated from their tribes went largely unremarked by suffragists still reeling from the defeat of their own amendment, although for a brief moment Colby tried to use the passage of the Dawes Act as a way to revisit the constitutional questions Gage had raised ten years earlier. "In view of the fact that Nebraska, by no act of its own, has voters in the Omahas, the Winnebagoes and the Santees," Colby asked her readers to ponder "what becomes of Senator Ingalls' claim in his *Forum* article on the Sixteenth Amendment that the 'question of Suffrage belongs exclusively to the States?' "[112] Colby's query, like Gage's before her, however, went largely unanswered. In 1878, when Gage first attempted to draw suffragists' attention to the analogous situation of Indians and women under the law, she hoped that Indians might serve as a model for how federal law could be used to transform domestic dependents into full citizens. The passage of the Dawes Act turned some Indians into voters within the states, as Colby complained, but for others it merely held out the possibility of citizenship, and well into the twentieth century Indians remained an example of how citizenship and wardship could be legally compatible, and not oppositional, categories, a fact that made their situation increasingly less useful to suffragists as a model of change for women.[113]

On July 10, 1890, Wyoming Territory became the forty-fourth state, and the only full woman suffrage state in the Union.[114] During the congressional debate over Wyoming's admission, members of Congress rehearsed the arguments for and against woman suffrage that had been presented during debate over the Hoar Amendment to the Edmunds-Tucker Act, the Eustis Amendment to the Washington statehood bill, and the proposed woman suffrage amendment to the federal Constitution. While certainly a victory for woman suffrage, Wyoming's admission was also a kind of defeat. Admitted on the heels of

Congress's failure to pass the woman suffrage constitutional amendment, Wyoming statehood did not represent the ringing endorsement for woman suffrage that suffragists had hoped for and did not create a national precedent. "The Republic will not go to pieces, the Union will not be dissolved," Senator Orville Platt of Connecticut assured some of his more anxious colleagues, because women voters in Wyoming "does not determine the question of whether they shall vote anywhere else."[115] Had the proposed sixteenth amendment remained on the table, this would not have been so clear. In public, suffragists spoke of victory, yet privately they admitted that Wyoming's admission had less to do with support for woman suffrage than the exigencies of partisan politics. "It is a piece of politics on the part of the Republicans," Francis Jackson Garrison wrote Anthony that spring, "but it will be a satisfaction to have one _State_ in which women will be able to vote."[116]

Sitting in the gallery, listening to the Senate debate Wyoming's admission, may have recalled for Anthony the moment fifteen years earlier when she had listened to the Senate debate the annexation of Santo Domingo. She had returned to the Senate galleries many times in the intervening years, but this was the first time that admitting new states into the Union included the admission of women voters. None of the arguments on either side were entirely new, of course; the opponents of woman suffrage remained firm in their belief that woman suffrage was not only "contrary to the experience and history of the country" but "fraught with great danger to the free institutions under which we live, and to the harmony, welfare, and good order of society."[117] But even if the arguments for and against woman suffrage were familiar, the national discussion of Indian citizenship, Mormon polygamy, and Washington statehood also established that in the context of expanding national borders suffrage questions in the territories were always national issues. Fifteen years earlier, during the Santo Domingo debate, Anthony would have been hard-pressed to describe exactly how territorial expansion might affect the woman question other than to weaken the Republican Party. But in 1887, it was clear to all parties, suffragists and antisuffragists alike, that expanding borders had the potential to nationalize the suffrage question. The politics of territorial expansion made clear that under certain circumstances the physical expansion of national borders could reconfigure the gendered boundaries of political space, as indeed Wyoming's admission brought women voters into the Union. This was a lesson that Anthony would not forget, and in 1898, when the United States debated the acquisition of new territorial possessions in the Pacific and the Caribbean, she would look back to lessons learned through western expansion as a guide to how suffragists might approach the question of U.S. expansion overseas.

4

IMPERIAL EXPANSION AND THE
PROBLEM OF HAWAII, 1898–1902

"The war prospects look portentous today," Susan B. Anthony wrote her friend and colleague the Pennsylvania suffragist Rachel Foster Avery on April 17, 1898, "but my hope is that Spain will yet see that the better part of valor for her is to let Cuba go free!!"[1] The day before Anthony dashed off her note to Avery, the Senate voted to approve President McKinley's request for a war resolution, and one week later, on April 25, 1898, the United States officially declared itself at war with Spain.[2] Anthony's Quaker background made her a pacifist by inclination, and she believed that "there is, there can be no justifiable cause for war."[3] Like many Americans, however, she was also sensitive to the Cuban desire for independence and personally "ashamed" that over the years she had taken so little notice of "those liberty-loving Cubans."[4] Spain's conflicts with its Cuban colony had been ongoing for decades, but the insurrection that began in 1895, and was already three years old, had been paid an unprecedented amount of publicity within the United States. In 1897, it appeared as if Spain and Cuba might reach a political solution that granted Cuba domestic autonomy but kept it formally under Spanish sovereignty. Despite this potential for compromise, McKinley's neutrality policy was under constant challenge from pro-war Americans eager to intervene on Cuba's behalf. When the U.S. battleship *Maine* sank in Cuba's Havana harbor in mid-February, pro-war, anti-Spanish sentiment within the United States intensified.[5]

Anthony certainly understood the rush to war. If she could not personally support the U.S. intervention in the Spanish-Cuban conflict, she comforted herself with what she felt was the "only excuse": that through this war "another people may be able to secure their liberty."[6] The suffragist and senator George Hoar, one of the few Republicans who failed to vote for McKinley's war resolution, consoled himself with similar thoughts. Despite his reluctance to see the United States engaged in a military conflict with Spain, there was some comfort in the belief that this war would be "the most honorable single war in all history."[7] Anthony and Hoar may have had a shared sympathy for the Cuban desire for independence from Spain, as well as an antipathy to the increasing belligerence that characterized U.S. anti-Spanish sentiment, but Anthony's antiwar position was not merely a reflection of her pacifist principles. Her opposition to the war also grew out of a strategic fear, born of her experience of the Civil War, that any war could only distract attention away from the suffrage question. As Anthony wrote Avery, "It looks now as if there were no escape from the clash of arms, and of course, when so many families have the men of their households at the front, and are constantly fearing news of their death, it will be exceedingly hard to rouse them to work for women's enfranchisement."[8] The war with Spain would likely be bloody and all-consuming, and if this "campaign against the slaughters of Cuba" could not be avoided, the best that Anthony thought suffragists might hope for was to wait it out, "to lay on our oars and study and prepare ourselves to enter more vigorously into the work after peace had been proclaimed."[9]

In April 1898, Anthony thought that the war with Spain would last only several months, and in this she was correct. By mid-August, the United States had defeated the Spanish fleet in the Philippines' Manila Bay, occupied the Cuban city of Santiago, and taken the island of Puerto Rico.[10] At the end of the summer, the United States signed an armistice with Spain, and the terms of a more lasting peace treaty were already under discussion. The U.S. victory over Spain raised more problems than it solved, however. Winning the war brought with it the real possibility of keeping control over Spain's colonial empire in the Caribbean and the Pacific, a possibility that forced the United States to confront more fully the nature of its own imperial aspirations.

Hoar had hoped that the war with Spain would be fought without "the slightest thought or desire of foreign conquest."[11] His opposition to the war, like that of many other antiwar advocates, reflected his mistrust of the imperial ambitions that underlay a good deal of the pro-war sentiment, however much this sentiment was disguised as a defense of Cuban liberty. Hoar had good reason to be suspicious. Six months earlier, in January 1897, Congress had considered signing a treaty of annexation with Hawaii. Hawaii had been the site of "civilizing" work by U.S. missionaries for more than seventy years.[12] In 1893, the growing population of white settlers in the Hawaiian Islands had deposed Queen Liliuokalani and imposed a government with the U.S. planter Sanford B. Dole as president. The Dole government sought annexation to the

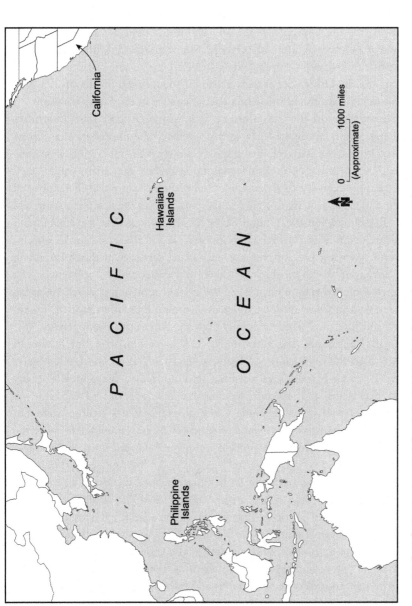

FIGURE 4.1. MAP OF THE PACIFIC THAT SHOWS HAWAII, THE PHILIPPINES, AND THE U.S. WEST COAST, CIRCA 1898

United States by a treaty that recalled an older style of expansionism in which new territory would come into the Union as a new state, thus turning territorial inhabitants into U.S. citizens. Nevertheless, the discussion of the Hawaiian question, like the Dominican question before it, could not be kept entirely outside of an imperial frame of reference. Annexation might formally preserve the distinction between empire and expansion, but anti-annexationists in both Hawaii and the United States viewed the U.S. acquisition of Hawaii as a dangerous step toward the creation of a Pacific empire in the European mold.[13]

Thus well before the U.S. armistice with Spain in August 1898, Americans were engaged in an imperial debate that conflated the future status of Spain's colonial possessions with the final status of Hawaii. Anti-imperialists were concerned with how the political incorporation of native Hawaiians would "corrupt the homogeneity of the nation."[14] The rhetoric of racial hierarchy and Anglo-Saxon superiority flowered in the press during the war with Spain and again in 1899, when the United States turned its attention toward Filipino pacification, informing both the opposition to, and justifications for, U.S. imperialism.[15] Asserting U.S. sovereignty over island territory without extending U.S. citizenship to the inhabitants of these territories raised a different sort of problem. Colonial rule might violate the Constitution and corrupt American democratic principles equally as much as the political incorporation of "uncivilized" and "barbaric" alien races might corrupt American "homogeneity."[16]

In the short term, the advocates of U.S. expansion won this debate. In July 1898, in the midst of the military conflict with Spain, the United States annexed Hawaii by congressional joint resolution, over the protest of many native Hawaiians, and without deciding the precise terms of U.S. rule on the island. Hawaii was to become a federal territory and a future state, but unlike past practice in other federal territories Congress intended to write the Hawaiian territorial constitution itself, a project it delayed until after the end of the war.

On December 10, 1898, the United States signed the Treaty of Paris and took formal control over Spain's former colonies with the exception of Cuba, although it retained an occupying army on the island.[17] It would take the United States several decades to work out the legal and constitutional terms of its relationships to these island territories, but by January 1899, it was clear that the United States intended to set the terms of these relationships unilaterally and to retain control over Spain's colonial possessions. Filipino rebels under the direction of Emilio Aguilnaldo had declared the birth of an independent Philippine Republic on January 23, 1899, and wanted the United States out of the Philippines. The war with Spain was over, but by February, the Philippine-American War had just begun.

Many anti-imperialists assumed that members of the U.S. woman suffrage movement would be staunch critics of antidemocratic U.S. efforts to establish sovereignty over foreign peoples against their will because of suffragists' own aspirations for self-government. But suffragists proved to be complex critics of U.S. imperial ambitions.[18] Suffragists approached the question of U.S. imperialism in 1898 in much the same way they addressed territorial expansion in the 1880s, concerning themselves largely with the strategic question of how U.S. control over new island territories might provide opportunities to set national precedents for women's voting rights, rather than with the abstract question of the Filipino or Puerto Rican right to self-government. In the spring of 1898, some suffragists protested the war with Spain, and others supported it, but by the end of the year Anthony began urging suffragists to focus their energies less on opposition to the war and more on keeping the word "male" out of the territorial constitutions and "organic acts" that Congress would create to govern its new possessions. This policy echoed suffragists' efforts in the 1870s to keep the word "male" out of the Fourteenth Amendment. Primarily concerned with preventing U.S. imperialism from extending the boundaries of what she called "male oligarchy" overseas, rather than the antidemocratic nature of empire itself, Anthony, now president of the NAWSA, substituted a critique of patriarchy for a critique of empire and in the process lent the NAWSA's tacit approval to the U.S. imperial project.[19]

Overseas empire raised new questions about the meaning of national belonging and the capacity of "alien races" for citizenship. Still, viewing island territories as future states, suffrage leaders who came of age during Reconstruction tended to see the complexities of U.S. imperialism as a problem of federal relations. In this context, the substance of the suffrage movement's official approach to the complexities of U.S. imperialism was to focus on the specific content of the new territorial constitutions that would be drafted by Congress over time. The first result to emerge from this strategy was the "Hawaiian Appeal," a petition that suffragists presented to Congress in January 1899, which demanded that Congress enfranchise all women in Hawaii Territory, both native and those of U.S. descent, on the same terms as men in the territory.[20] The Hawaiian Appeal was not aimed only at white women in the territory. Couched in the rhetoric of protection for native Hawaiian women, the petition merged views about native men's savagery and notions of essential womanly virtues across races to make a case for native and white women's voting rights. In some cases, suffragists would argue that native Hawaiian women needed the vote more than U.S. women, because of the "uncivilized" character of native men. Premised on U.S. women's concern for their less "civilized" sisters, the Hawaiian Appeal thus grafted the Reconstruction era focus on federal constitution writing to the new realities of U.S. imperialism. During the debates over Indian citizenship and Mormon polygamy, suffragists had moved back and forth between justifications for the vote that were grounded in the vocabulary of citizenship and rights, and those grounded in the vocabulary of race and civilization. The Hawaiian Appeal merged these two vocabularies.

SUFFRAGISTS DEBATE THE WAR

The weeks leading up to and following McKinley's declaration of war in April 1898 saw a lively debate in the pages of the *Woman's Journal* over the role of women in foreign affairs. Henry Blackwell launched the debate the week before the United States declared war on Spain when he insisted that the cause of woman suffrage and that of peace were the same and that "if women were voters there would have been no war."[21] "Women would endeavor to intervene by conciliation and moral appeal," Blackwell editorialized, "but so long as political society is composed of male citizens only, so long will the belligerent instincts of masculine humanity override higher considerations."[22] William Lloyd Garrison, son of the famous abolitionist, seconded Blackwell's idealized vision of American womanhood and chastised pro-war suffragists for their bellicosity in the next issue of the *Woman's Journal*. "It is a common claim made for women that, when they shall obtain their political rights, their influence at the ballot-box will make for a higher civilization." "Where stand women at this hour?" Garrison asked.[23]

The women who responded to Garrison's query were interested equally in interrogating Garrison's assumptions about womanly virtue as they were in arguing for, or against, the war. Some respondents were willing to accept the mantle of the "peace-loving sex" and the notion "that womanly tenderness would be an enormous factor in national affairs," but others criticized Blackwell and Garrison's suggestion that "women as a class should be more opposed to war than men."[24] Writing into the *Woman's Journal*, a suffragist named Florence Burleigh, for example, warned that "woman suffragists make a great mistake in advocating the granting of the franchise to women on any other ground than justice." Burleigh was willing to concede that "women as a class may be more moral than men," but she wondered if they were truly "any wiser."[25] Stanton used every opportunity to speak on the war as a means to undermine the essentialized vision of U.S. womanhood that informed both the pro- and antiwar positions inside the NAWSA. "The war goes bravely on and I am glad of it," Stanton wrote her son Theodore. "I am sick of all this sentimental nonsense about 'our boys in blue,' and 'wringing mother's hearts.' "[26]

At the end of July 1898, just weeks after the annexation of Hawaii and the U.S. military victory in Manila Harbor, a *New York Tribune* reporter asked several prominent women reformers for their opinions on the war with Spain. In response to the query, "Do women still favor the war?" Stanton applied a lesson learned from the Civil War and replied "war under many circumstances [is] a great blessing....Justice, liberty, equality for all first, and then that peace 'that passeth all understanding.'" Indeed, Stanton's "one regret" was that "we did not thrash that cruel, brutal nation, with her bullfights and inquisitions, long ago."[27] Ellen M. Henrotin, the recently retired president of the General Federation of Women's Clubs, joined Stanton in her support of the war. The General Federation was a national association of women's voluntary organizations devoted to community improvement, education, and self-culture.[28] A few months earlier, Henrotin had felt some doubt over the rightness of the war and announced, "Members of the General Federation would condemn a war which was undertaken for aggrandizement or territorial acquisition."[29] By July, however, she was firmly convinced that the war with Spain reflected the disinterested benevolence of a right-minded people, and that the United States was "destined to carry the flag of liberty to the oppressed."[30] Julia Ward Howe was also pro-war. As Howe told the *Tribune*'s reporter, she considered the war with Spain "to have been inevitable." "Suffering Cuba has long agonized under Spanish misrule," and as a result, Howe could only "thank God that we are doing something to retrieve this disgrace by rising up to help our neighbor in her sore need."[31] Taken together, Stanton's, Howe's, and Henrotin's responses challenged any assumptions that women, by nature, necessarily opposed war. This may have been the *Tribune* reporter's intention from the outset; their statements lent a certain irony to the article's promise that members of the "peace-loving sex" would answer the "war question."[32]

In 1898, when the *New York Tribune* polled members of the "peace-loving sex" on their opinions on the war, the paper did not ask the heads of black women's associations to weigh in on this question. Had the *Tribune*'s reporter thought to poll black suffrage activists, he would not have found much antiwar sentiment. On one hand, the black press was divided on the question of the war with Spain. The irony of the U.S. rush to war to defend Cuban liberty, while greeting the violence and disfranchisement of its own citizens with relative equanimity, was obvious; as one headline in the *Washington Bee* made clear, "The Negro Needs Freedom as Much as the Cuban."[33] Yet despite a widespread sense that civil rights at home should come before Cuban independence, the war offered an opportunity for black men as soldiers to claim U.S. masculinity for themselves. As they had done during the Civil War, many rushed to volunteer as soldiers despite the fact that black men in uniform provoked violent responses from white racists.[34] Over the course of the Philippine-American war, individual black suffragists would develop a critique of U.S. imperialism grounded in the racial politics of southern disfranchisement and white violence, but in April 1898, perhaps because of the opportunities provided by the war for black men to "prove their manhood," black suffrage leaders were silent on the war question.[35]

Despite their shared pro-war sentiments, Stanton, on the one hand, and Howe and Henrotin, on the other, did not often find themselves in agreement on other matters. If anything, the time that had elapsed between the formation of the AWSA and the NWSA in the early 1870s had only shown more clearly the differences among these well-known women reformers. In addition to her suffrage work, Howe spent much of the 1890s engaged in the cause of universal peace, and in 1894, Howe had become president of the Friends of Armenia. Since the 1880s, Christian Armenians living within the borders of the Muslim Ottoman Empire had been agitating for political independence, and Howe's organization was dedicated to providing aid and relief to the Armenian survivors of Ottoman violence. Characterizing her peace work as service in behalf of "Christian civilization against barbarism," Howe reached out to members of other national women's organizations, including the American Red Cross, founded by Clara Barton in 1881, and Henrotin's General Federation of Women's Clubs, where she sat on the board of directors before becoming an honorary vice president.[36]

In contrast to Howe's central position within a growing national network of mainstream women reformers, Stanton was increasingly isolated both politically and philosophically inside and outside the suffrage movement. In 1895, Stanton and a small cohort of fellow radical thinkers published the first volume of the *Woman's Bible*, a set of critical commentaries on biblical passages that illustrated the precise ways that the Bible, the Christian tradition, and the clergy acted in concert to perpetuate women's subordination. Stanton's Bible project challenged the Christian female moral authority that was foundational to the majority of U.S. women's reform efforts, including those of Howe and Henrotin. As Kathi Kern has shown, the publication of the *Woman's Bible* inspired one of most heated debates among women reformers in the last decade of the nineteenth century. Stanton's feminist critique of the Bible was perceived as an attack on the principle of women's natural piety that was crucial to the public activism of women in a growing number of clubs and organizations, especially those in Frances Willard's Woman's Christian Temperance Union, and in the thousands of women's missionary societies, church organizations, and voluntary associations that had spread across the nation. Many of these women grounded their increasingly visible public work in religiously based gender ideologies that privileged notions of women's natural moral capacity as women. By challenging the "progressive orthodoxy" of Christian women reformers, Stanton's Bible project placed her outside the circle of acceptable belief inhabited by organized womanhood in the United States at the end of the nineteenth century.[37]

Ten years earlier, Stanton and the NWSA leadership had made a concerted effort to bring women like Henrotin and Willard and the constituencies they represented into the suffrage tent. To this end, in January 1888 the NWSA invited delegates from hundreds of women's organizations within the United States and in Europe to join them in D.C. to celebrate the fortieth anniversary of the 1848 woman's rights convention at Seneca Falls. The NWSA hoped to mark this anniversary by founding the International Council of Women (ICW). Stanton had originally hoped that the ICW would become the first international woman suffrage association, but this plan was abandoned in one of the first skirmishes marking the emergence of a new and younger cohort of leaders within the U.S. suffrage movement. Many years later, the Indiana suffragist and former AWSA leader May Wright Sewall recalled that "all the older women, or pioneer suffragettes, at first desired the proposed international meeting to be limited to the advocacy of equal political rights."[38] In contrast, Sewall remembered that "the younger women of that period," those women who belonged to "various other progressive movements in which conservative women and even anti-suffragists were associated," hoped that the ICW would be expansive enough to include "workers along all lines of human progress."[39] Younger suffragists like Sewall saw the ballot less as the key to individual emancipation and a crucial right of national citizenship, than as a necessary precondition for the fulfillment of public "womanly" obligations to home and society. Like WCTU president Frances Willard, who became the American National Council of Women's first president, Sewall embraced traditional conceptions of women's duties as wives and mothers.[40] In sharp contrast to the sense of entitlement and confrontational style that had informed the illegal voting tactics of New Departure era activists, Sewall advanced women's entry into political life in the spirit of harmony and cooperation.

Those wishing to host the most inclusive gathering possible, including Sewall, prevailed. NWSA invitations to the first meeting of the ICW in 1888 explicitly stated that it was "neither intended nor desired that discussions in the International Council shall be limited to questions touching the political rights of women."[41] Anthony was excited to see that "very many conservative associations have appointed delegates—and accept the National's invitation—apparently gladly!!"[42] The remarkable sight of pro-suffrage women sharing a platform with women from the Christian Women's Board of Foreign

Missions and from the Ladies of the Grand Army of the Republic, among others, vividly demonstrated the possibilities the ICW held for suffragists seeking to broaden their constituency at home.[43] To suffragists, the presence of clubwomen at the ICW indicated a latent constituency for women's votes. M. Louise Thomas, president of Sorosis, a women's literary club founded by the journalist Jane Cunningham Croly in 1868, confirmed this line of thought when she confessed that "there are three subjects that are never talked about in the club—religion, politics, and woman's suffrage." Yet "Sorosis is alive to the influence of the advanced thought of the age," she insisted, as was evidenced by the fact that "three of its original incorporators are now present with us" at the ICW.[44] Thomas's sentiments made it possible for NWSA activists to hope that through the ICW women would come to learn, in Stanton's words at the meeting, that "sympathy as a civil agent is vague and powerless until caught and chained in logical propositions and coined into law."[45]

The *Tribune's* decision to poll the "peace-loving sex" on their war positions reflected, in part, the success of women's own efforts to frame their public activism as an extension of their womanly duties to home and family, and their special capacities as women, rather than on the incidental relationship of sex to citizenship. The war debate in the *Woman's Journal* indicated the impact of this changing constituency on the suffrage movement. Sewall, for example was a dedicated suffrage activist, but she also believed that the reform most needed by women today was not the ballot, but "dignity, refinement, broad culture, 'sweetness and light.'"[46]

NWSA suffragists' desire to reach out to organized women who had not yet taken up the suffrage cause and the presence of new younger women in the suffrage movement created the conditions for a merger between the AWSA and the NWSA. Stanton became the first president of the new National-American Woman Suffrage Association formed in 1890 and was succeeded by Anthony in 1892. Despite the presence of former NWSA leaders at the helm of the new organization, and Lucy Stone's death in 1893, the new NAWSA's strategy followed more closely the AWSA's plan of state organizing than it did the NWSA's strategy of gaining the vote by federal constitutional amendment.[47] One result of this state-by-state approach was that after 1895, NAWSA meetings were held in D.C. only every third year.

The NAWSA's turn to state organizing also made the organization more hospitable to white southern suffragists who joined the NAWSA in increasing numbers throughout the decade. Black suffragists had lent their active support to the campaign for a woman suffrage amendment to the federal Constitution.[48] In contrast to black women's support for the proposed sixteenth amendment, white southern suffragists rarely worked toward a constitutional amendment and instead committed their energies toward getting the vote through the emendation of state constitutions. The racist sentiments that underlay this "states' rights" approach were never difficult to discern as over and over again white southern suffragists made the case that white women's votes should be viewed as a "means to the end of securing white supremacy."[49] Historian Marjorie Wheeler points to the fact that the racial arguments employed by late nineteenth-century white southern suffragists ranged across a "narrow" spectrum. At one end the Louisiana suffragist Kate Gordon advocated explicit "negrophobia" and supported women's votes for white women only. At the other end, women like Laura Clay of Kentucky shared Gordon's belief in the inequality of blacks and whites, but nonetheless believed that literacy tests and educational requirements for the vote would ensure that black women would become enfranchised only gradually and under white stewardship.[50] Privately Anthony was critical of the racist sentiments of white southern suffragists, but publicly she acquiesced with the NAWSA's decision to gain a foothold in the South by accommodating the views of white women. She went so far as to ask Frederick Douglass not to attend the 1895 NAWSA convention in Atlanta and refused to help black women in that state set up their own suffrage organization.[51] Henry Blackwell and Stanton both endorsed educational qualifications for the vote in the 1890s, in spite of the very obvious ways that literacy tests were being employed to disenfranchise black male voters. In "A Solution to the Southern Question," Blackwell explicitly made the white supremacist case for woman suffrage. Arguing that the "'race' question in the South is really to a great extent a question of illiteracy," Blackwell provided statistics that "proved" how the enfranchisement of literate white women would reinstitute good government by the "civilized, responsible members of the community."[52] In 1893, when the ICW met for a second international congress in Chicago in conjunction with the World's Fair, the effect of the suffrage movement's efforts to reach out to white southern suffragists was vividly illustrated in the exclusion of black women and black women's organizations from the public spaces and public platforms reserved for white women claiming to speak for all U.S. women.[53]

In the spring and summer of 1898, suffragists debated women's natural affinity for war, and the rightness of the war with Spain itself, but any consensus on these subjects was well beyond the NAWSA's reach. Rebecca Edwards has noted that there was no "women's position" on the war.[54] This lack of consensus was particularly visible within the suffrage movement because the war issue divided long-standing allies and friends like Stanton and Anthony, and Howe and Blackwell, and did not provide an easy framework in which to forge future strategies. By the end of the summer, the war with Spain was over, and suffragists, like all Americans, turned their attention to its una-voidable consequences. When McKinley sent delegates to the U.S.-Spanish peace conference in Paris in October 1898, he had not publicly decided to keep the Philippines or the other island territory of Spain's colonial empire under U.S. control.[55] At the beginning of the war, Congress had attached the Teller Amendment to its war resolution, which prohibited the United States from annexing Cuba. With the Cuban question theoretically off the table, U.S. negotiators in Paris, and citizens at home, were primarily concerned with the fate of the Philippines and Puerto Rico. In fall of 1898, anti-imperialist sentiment in the U.S. was increasingly visible and in some ways quite familiar. More than twenty-five years after he first laid out his anti-imperial arguments against the U.S. annexation of Santo Domingo, the former Missouri senator Carl Schurz was still an active force in U.S. political life and an outspoken critic of U.S. expansion overseas. In 1898, Schurz revived his earlier, anti-annexation arguments in a series of articles and speeches that warned against the dangers to the nation of trying to incorporate "savage" and "alien" races, and the dangers to U.S. constitutional traditions of governing island territories without bringing them into the family of states. Schurz's racial and constitu-tional anti-imperialism was echoed in different forms in the writings of anti-imperialists across the country.[56]

William Lloyd Garrison was a founding member of the Anti-Imperial League that formed in Boston in November 1898, and one of the first to demand that suffragists adopt a principled anti-imperial position.[57] After returning from a meeting of the Universal Peace Union in Connecticut at the end of August, Garrison wrote to the *Woman's Journal* to criticize the recent annexation of Hawaii: "Behold a country that has had its century of dishonor with the Indians and its infamy with the negro, prating on of its new found duty to swarms of people of whose nature and needs it knows nothing! ... The Women who rebel against taxation without representation will have a difficult task to prove they are entitled to suffrage more than the disfran-chised masses of the Sandwich Islands [Hawaii]."[58] Garrison's reference to the "disfranchised masses" of Hawaii spoke to the political status of most native Hawaiians, and the resident immigrant populations from China, Japan, and the Philippines under the Dole government. The 1893 constitution for the Hawaiian Republic was the handiwork of white planters of U.S. descent who made up only about 4,000 of the more than 110,000 inhabitants on the island. Through property qualifications, literacy requirements, and racial exclusions, the total number of eligible voters in Hawaii in 1893 stood at about 2,700.[59]

"Imperial rule abroad necessitates imperial rule at home," Garrison warned, and for proof of this axiom, Americans needed only look to the "crime of Mississippi."[60] Earlier in the year, the Supreme Court's decision in *Williams v. Mississippi* declared that the literacy test in the 1890 Mississippi constitution did not violate the Fourteenth and Fifteenth Amendments, despite the fact that black voters had disappeared from the Mississippi polls almost entirely.[61] McKinley had sent a commission to Hawaii at the end of the summer to take stock of the political, social, and economic conditions on the island before Congress drew up a new territorial constitution, but Garrison was convinced that in the context of Mississippi, one could not expect that this constitution would reflect a commitment to democratic principles that crossed the lines of color. In Garrison's view, Mississippi was the constitutional precedent for a host of future disfranchisements on racial grounds. Since 1882, the Chinese Exclusion Act had prohibited Chinese in the United States from becoming citizens, and now the nation was rushing to "annex whole populations of Asiatics." Garrison believed that war and imperialism were both "fatal to self-government," and that suffragists needed to weigh in on the question.[62]

Given his antiwar position, Blackwell's general agreement with Garrison was not entirely surprising. As early as June 1898, Blackwell had drawn suffragists' attention to the fact that "the advocates of 'imperialism' are already discussing, in advance of possession, the proper method of governing the Eastern and the Western Indies, the Ladrones, the Carolines, and even the Canaries."[63] To Blackwell, it was important that suffragists insist that the United States "maintain for every community which it severs from Spain, the sacred right of independent self-government."[64] In the 1870s Blackwell had subscribed to Grant's expansive vision of the Monroe Doctrine, as a justification for the U.S. annexation of Santo Domingo, but in 1898 Blackwell argued that the principle of preventing European colonization on the American continent should be understood as a doctrine of "home rule."[65] Upholding this doctrine in the context of Spain's former colonial possessions meant a "firm and enlightened policy of non-intervention."[66] Such a policy, Blackwell argued, would be consistent with the democratic sentiment that governments derive "'their just powers from the consent of the governed.'"[67] If the United States were to guarantee Spain's former colonies protection from foreign aggression without instituting U.S. sovereignty over these populations, Blackwell believed that the United States would become "the beloved and respected mother of republics."[68] "Home rule is the American principle," Blackwell insisted, and "Aguilando is entitled to it equally with Commodore Dewey."[69] In making his case for "home rule for the Philippines," Blackwell "observed with profound disapproval and regret the too general assumption that free institutions are adapted only to certain favored races and localities."[70] If American women "are not willing to live forever in subjection," he argued, "let them demand the application of the Republican principle to these outlying territories."[71]

On the surface, Blackwell's and Garrison's anti-imperial sentiments appeared much the same, but when it came to Hawaii, Blackwell felt that the opponents of imperialism could go "too far."[72] Garrison's position was informed by the belief that the "Anglo-Saxon" civilizing project had been a failure. It had "sheltered negro slavery, robbed and murdered the Indian, and committed atrocities against the Chinamen."[73] Civilization, to Garrison's mind, had no "narrow prefix of Anglo-Saxon," and the long history of U.S. rule on the American continent, along with the ongoing politics of black disfranchisement in the South, suggested that the United States was equally incapable of carrying civilization across the oceans as it was incapable of living up to its civilizing pretensions at home.[74] For Garrison, home rule meant keeping the United States firmly within its own continental borders and embarking on a policy reform and a recommitment to democratic principles on U.S. soil.

In contrast, Blackwell believed firmly in the U.S. civilizing mission, and that expansion itself was not "necessarily injurious or fatal to the republic."[75] In the context of the long history of U.S. continental expansion west, and the importance of these "successive annexations" to U.S. prosperity, Blackwell argued that some annexations, specifically those of Florida, Texas, Louisiana, New Mexico, California, and Arizona, must be seen as forms of rescue, in which the United States had taken territory from the "despotic colonial governments of Spain, France and Russia" and re-dedicated it to "civilization and liberty."[76] "What we ought to oppose," Blackwell felt, "was not an enlargement of our territory, but a lowering of republican ideals," by which he meant any failure to guarantee political rights to the inhabitants of island territory in the possession of the United States, not relinquishing that territory.[77] In the Hawaiian case, this would mean extending equal suffrage to all the inhabitants "on reasonable educational qualifications, irrespective of race, color, or sex," and "when the population has become Americanized and homogenous," considering Hawaii's "eventual admission as a State."[78] To Blackwell, the difference between Hawaii and the Philippines was that the civilizing project in Hawaii was likely to succeed whereas in the Philippines it would not. "Home rule" in Hawaii meant literacy tests, and educational and property requirements for the vote, a "militant republicanism," which Blackwell believed was compatible with both the project of civilization and the principles of U.S. democracy.[79] By contrast, in the case of the Philippines, home rule meant establishing a temporary protectorate over the islands during their transition from "colonial vassalage to independent self-government."[80]

Many suffragists did not understand Blackwell's fine distinctions between Hawaii and the Philippines, or the distinctions being made between Cuba and Hawaii, or between Cuba and any of the other island territories in the former Spanish empire. Puerto Rico and Cuba were just one hundred miles from the eastern coast of the United States, but Hawaii and the Philippines were thousands of miles across the ocean, and all of these places, with their distinctive political and social histories, were difficult for suffragists to think about in specific and individual terms. As May Wright Sewall noted, "One can hardly pick up a newspaper of any party, or even a religious newspaper of any sect, without encountering such phrases as 'Our new territory,' 'The conquered provinces,'...'Our new colonial possessions,' etc." "What do these phrases mean?" she asked. "Do we own the Ladrones by conquest? Have we a right to replace in Cuba the domination of the Spaniard by the domination of the United States? What is the meaning of this discussion of whether we shall annex the Philippines as a group, or be satisfied with taking a few of the islands?" Sewall could only conclude that "we are maddened by the taste of blood." In this context, it was "the immediate first duty of every good American...to expunge the obnoxious, monarchical, anti-democratic, anti-Christian phrases that are polluting our speech."[81] Sewall wanted Americans to "stand by American principles," but as the debate between Garrison and Blackwell indicated, the concept of "American principles" was difficult to define. It could mean, variously, "civilizing savages" and stewarding foreign peoples toward the kind of democratic government that was imperfectly realized at home, or leaving the inhabitants of other places to work out their destinies for themselves. Suffragists had no easy answer to this question.

In "Our Duty to the Philippines," a Vermont suffragist questioned "whether expansion necessarily leads to imperialism," as Garrison implied, or whether republican government "might be secured even if ignorant races should have to go through a preparatory course of tutelage," as Blackwell suggested.[82] Anthony tended to view the question through Garrison's lens. She was far less sanguine than Blackwell about the successes of the American civilizing mission and convinced that having made war on Spain "because of her cruelties to her Colonies in the Isles of the Sea—we should stretch our national government's hand to crush out the worse than Spanish cruelties under our flag."[83] By "Spanish cruelties under our flag" Anthony meant the widespread violence directed against black Americans. "The old slavocrats are bound to push out every man and woman of color from the *enjoyment of civil rights*," she complained to Stanton.[84] In this context, American expansion would only export American racism because "on every hand *American Civilization* which we are introducing into isles of the Atlantic and the Pacific is putting its heel on the head of the negro race."[85]

The New York suffragist Carrie Chapman Catt, who in 1900 would succeed Anthony as president of the NAWSA, heartily disagreed. She had no doubt as to the U.S. ability to take its civilizing mission overseas and thought "the manifest duty of the United States is to so direct the affairs of these peoples as to lead them to establish a stable, wise, and tolerant government."[86] Catt was careful to point out that this would be no easy task, "since they range through all stages, from the primitive savage to civilized man."[87] Nonetheless, Catt was willing to embrace "our new responsibilities," to add a new phrase to Sewall's list of euphemisms for colonial rule. After all, Catt argued, "the Cubans at close range proved disappointing. The Porto Ricans are yet of untested quality, and the Hawaiians are a heterogeneous people, with a low grade of development."[88] To Catt, suffragists' duty was clear: "Women will welcome any method which can help these men to higher manhood and better civilization."[89] Catt's focus on men suggests that in some instances, at least, foreign and non-Christian women might be considered, like Christian women in the United States, "naturally" more moral than men and therefore in less need of civilizing. It would be a sacrifice, of course, "one full of humiliation for American women," to see "our mighty nation" enfranchise "these unknown and untested Americans," but Catt was confident that woman suffrage would one day be the "crowning glory of democratic government."[90] Stanton did not share Catt's assumptions about women's more moral nature, but she agreed with Catt that the U.S. civilizing mission should be embraced as necessary to progress. As she told her son Theodore, "The great public topic just now is 'expansion,' of which I am in favor....what would this continent have been if we had left it to the Indians?"[91]

Catt and Stanton agreed that U.S. expansion represented progress, but Catt was no favorite of Stanton. In 1896, Catt had led the charge within the NAWSA to censure the *Woman's Bible*, and perhaps for this reason, or out of deference to her friendship with Anthony, Stanton did not argue the pro-imperial position in public.[92] Rather, she sent a letter to the *Woman's Journal*, written by her daughter Harriot Stanton Blatch, which offered a somewhat novel critique of the situation.[93] In 1898, Stanton's daughter Harriot was married and living in London, and her perspective on the imperial question was informed by her location at the heart of the British Empire. Beginning in 1869, the British suffragist Josephine Butler had led a campaign to repeal the Contagious Disease Acts, a series of laws that mandated medical exams for British prostitutes both at home and in the British colonies. To Butler and her allies in the Ladies National Association, the regulation of vice promoted rather than prevented sexual immorality. Stanton had met Butler and heard her lecture in 1882 when she went to London for Harriot's wedding. By 1886, when Stanton returned to England as Congress took up the federal suffrage amendment, Butler's campaign had been partially successful. That year the British Parliament voted to repeal the Contagious Disease Act in England, and Butler was turning her attention to other parts of the British Empire, particularly India, where similar laws remained in force.[94]

In 1898, when the *Woman's Journal* published Blatch's article "Mrs. Stanton Blatch on Imperialism: The Manifest Destiny of Women," British reformers had discovered ample evidence that despite the formal repeal of the Indian Contagious Disease Act in 1888, the medical examinations of prostitutes in India were continuing.[95] In addition, there was a significant and growing movement to reinstitute laws regulating prostitution in order to protect British troops in India from venereal disease.[96] It was against this backdrop of British suffragists' engagement with the problems of prostitution, contagion, and morality in the British Empire that Blatch weighed in on the U.S. imperial question. To Blatch, U.S. women needed to concern themselves less with manifest destiny than with precisely what destiny, as she cleverly put it, "expansion will manifestly bring them."[97] To answer this question, Blatch urged U.S. women to look to England. She claimed that the creation of the standing armies necessary for the management of Britain's vast colonial interests abroad was creating an imbalance of the sexes at home with unforeseen and damaging results. "Do the women of America wish to out-number the men of their country; do they wish prostitution to increase; do they wish to be pushed out of their work of home-building into that of field and factory?" "If not," warned Blatch they needed to "tell their men-folk that it is not the nation's destiny to raise the Filipinos and lower their own women to the level of Continental Europe."[98] Blatch's critique of the British imperial project did not address the success or failure of England's civilizing mission but focused instead on the impact of empire within the borders of England itself. This approach had the potential to open up the discussion of U.S. empire in new ways by focusing less on the perceived success of U.S. expansion than on the novel domestic problems that might result from overseas colonialism. By steering her analysis away from women's special abilities as women, Blatch did not question U.S. women's ability to shoulder the "white woman's burden" if they chose. Rather, she asked them to consider the costs. American women and men might be able to "raise the Filipinos" up from savagery," but only if they were willing to accept the necessary sacrifices colonialism entailed.

Raising the prostitution issue as a way of demonstrating the costs of British imperialism to British women, Blatch avoided a discussion of the concrete ways that British suffragists, including Butler, were simultaneously using the cause of protecting Indian women to make a case for themselves as a necessary force in the political life of empire. As Antoinette Burton has shown, British suffragists justified British women's intervention in the world of politics, and their demands for the vote, on their special ability as women to protect their Indian sisters. Premised on the presumption of natural bonds of sisterhood between women, but also on British women's special ability as *British* women to protect, reform, and civilize, British suffragists linked women's moral authority to the health and vitality of the empire, and woman suffrage to imperial stability. British colonialism, as Burton demonstrates, thus provided British suffragists with a crucial field for demonstrating their capacity for political citizenship as they worked with English men as allies in the construction of "civilized empire."[99] In many ways, the principles underlying British imperial suffragism were echoed in the logic driving the reform and missionary efforts of U.S. women. In 1884, Willard had founded the World Woman's Christian Temperance Union, in order to ban alcohol and the use of other narcotics worldwide, and was urging the members of her organization to take up the suffrage question as a way to protect the home; for Willard, as with Butler, home protection needed to take place on a global stage.[100]

The imperial question, like the war question, divided suffragists, but neither Garrison's hope that suffragists would support the anti-imperial movement nor Catt's desire that suffragists take up the work of civilization in the Philippines or Hawaii translated into a concrete strategy for pushing the question of woman suffrage itself. Joining the anti-imperial movement might provide suffragists with new allies, but the anti-imperialists' commitment to woman suffrage was tenuous at best.[101] Conversely, linking woman suffrage to the construction of U.S. empire might provide a new arena for women to demonstrate their capacity for political rights by demonstrating the ways that women could be important and necessary allies in the work of civilization, but this was similarly a tenuous strategy for gaining women's votes. Catt never spelled out exactly how helping foreign men to "higher manhood" would translate into votes for women. In the fall of 1898, the way forward for the NAWSA remained unclear.

THE "HAWAIIAN APPEAL" AND "OUR DUTY TO THE WOMEN OF OUR NEW POSSESSIONS"

"The morning's depiction of the Hawaiian Commission's report for the provisional government of that new U.S. Territory [states that it] is to be based on sex regardless of intelligence—instead of intelligence regardless of sex," Anthony wrote Ida Husted Harper on December 7, 1898.[102] An active participant in the

Indiana and California state suffrage campaigns in the 1890s, Harper had moved to New York in 1897 to become Anthony's official biographer. The first two volumes of her three-volume history of Anthony's achievements had come out earlier in the year, and the two women were in constant communication. In his annual presidential message to Congress the day before, McKinley had reaffirmed the U.S. commitment to govern Hawaii as a territory that would eventually come into the Union as a new state, and he was urging Congress to begin deliberations on a Hawaiian bill that would lay out the governing structure for the new territory.[103] The Hawaiian Commission had included a draft constitution for the territory in its report to Congress that limited the franchise to men, and included both literacy tests and property qualifications for the vote.[104] Anthony was concerned that the congressional Hawaiian bill would create a dangerous precedent for future annexations. Conversely, if the United States intended to embark on an aggressive program of territorial acquisition, and if Congress could be persuaded to enfranchise the women of Hawaii, it would create a federal precedent with vastly different implications.

As president of the NAWSA, Anthony was compelled to find a way to translate the discussion of U.S. imperialism into a strategy for gaining woman suffrage. Initially she had felt that the discussion of the woman question was destined to remain in the background until the war was over. By December 1898, when the United States signed the Treaty of Paris with Spain, it was clear that McKinley was determined to keep U.S. control over the Philippines and Spain's other island territory with the exception of Cuba. In this context, the details surrounding congressional decisions regarding the new provisional government of Hawaii took on new weight. To Anthony, the prospect of setting up new precedents for woman suffrage seemed to offer hope in an imperial debate that for the most part had left the woman question on the sidelines. The prospect of a vast U.S. civilizing mission may have created new spaces for women in public life, but that was not the same as opening up space for the question of women's ballots, which territorial constitution writing had the potential to do. In contrast to her earlier pessimism about what the war with Spain would mean for women, Anthony assured Harper in December 1898 that "there never was a time that could be called the *crucial moment* in women's chances for freedom like the present with all these provisional government schemes to be brought before Congress."[105] As Anthony knew well from her experience with D.C. in 1870, and Utah in the 1880s, federal constitution writing provided opportunities to push the woman question if suffragists were willing to seize them.

Younger suffragists needed to be convinced, however, and to her frustration, Anthony spent most of December trying to turn the attention of her closest NAWSA allies to the congressional discussion of the Hawaiian bill. "I wonder if when I am under the sod—or cremated & floating in the air—I shall have to stir you & others up," Anthony wrote heatedly to Clara Colby. "How can you not be on fire—when the Senate Foreign and *Territorial Com.* are considering the Hawaiian Commissions' damnable proposition to restrict the right to vote & hold office to *male citizens?*"[106] Anthony informed Colby that since McKinley had spoken of the Hawaiian Commission's report in Congress she had been trying to "rouse Mrs. Harper to open fire through the papers—but I see nothing....I really believe I shall explode if some of you young women don't wake up—and raise your voices in protest against the impending crime of this Nation upon the Islands it has clutched from other folks."[107] In December 1898, the imperial/anti-imperial debate was raging across the country, but for Anthony the true crime of empire was not that of seizing island territory but of failing to include women (native as well as future U.S. settlers) in new island governments. "Do come into the living present," Anthony urged Colby, "and work to save us from more barbaric *male governments.*"[108] As Anthony wrote heatedly to Rachel Foster Avery, "It does seem as if the very stones ought to cry out against thus placing the ignorant native men of those islands in the position of sovereigns over the intelligent, tax-paying women, black or white, who shall reside there."[109] To Anthony male government was in and of itself "barbaric," but in the case of Hawaii doubly so because unlike the white and black Christian men who ruled U.S. women, native Hawaiian men were uncivilized.

By the end of December, Anthony was "ashamed" of herself for letting the Hawaiian bill "slip through the Senate Committee—without getting a hearing before it" but determined not to let the same thing happen in the House.[110] A month of "stirring-up" her colleagues proved to be sufficient, and in January 1899, Anthony and the officers of the NAWSA sent a copy of what they called the Hawaiian Appeal to Congress.[111] In the "Appeal" suffragists requested that "in the qualifications for voters in the proposed constitution for the new Territory of Hawaii, the word 'male' be omitted."[112] "The declared intention of the United States in annexing the Hawaiian islands is to give them the benefits of the most advanced civilization," the petition declared, "and it is a truism that the progress of civilization in every country is measured by the approach of women toward the ideal of equal rights with men." Given this state of affairs, suffragists argued that "it would be inopportune to impose upon our new possessions abroad the antiquated restrictions which we are fast discarding at home," and formally requested that Hawaiian women, both native women and those of U.S. descent, be granted the right to vote "upon whatever conditions and qualifications the right of suffrage is granted to Hawaiian men," including literacy tests and property qualifications.[113] The NAWSA petition on behalf of the women of Hawaii specifically addressed the potential precedents that might be set by the Hawaiian constitution for other island territories acquired through the war:"Heretofore Congress has ignored our plea for the rights of women as citizens, but it has never legislated against these rights." The case of Utah, of course, was "unjust and inconsistent," although the "crime" of polygamy gave that "a show of excuse"; but "if the Congress of the United States today enters upon a system of class legislation…who can tell where it will end?" "Hawaii may offer advantages to Americans to settle there," but Anthony feared that if women were disfranchised in Hawaii by national law, "the only women of this country who could consistently go there would be the anti-suffrage association."[114]

Despite arguing for women's enfranchisement on the same terms as men, the Hawaiian Appeal did not reflect the commitment to the principles of universal democracy that had characterized suffragists' demands during the 1870s. NAWSA members noted that "consistently with their principles suffragists can ask for nothing less than full justice, which would make no distinctions of sex," but the appeal also stated that suffragists would be amenable to "whatever other limitations might be thought necessary for the time being."[115] The NAWSA's reference to "other limitations" spoke to the property and educational qualifications for the vote that were already in operation in Hawaii, and that effectively disfranchised most native Hawaiians as well as Japanese, Chinese, and Filipino migrants to the island.[116]

Immediately after the Hawaiian Appeal became public, it was attacked in the *New York Evening Post*, a weekly journal under the editorial stewardship of E. L. Godkin. Godkin was a well-known critic of America's democratic experiment who believed that it was possible to have entirely too much democracy.[117] In the 1870s, as editor of the *Nation*, Godkin vociferously opposed Grant's plans to annex Santo Domingo and shared Schurz's horror over turning "ignorant Catholic Spanish negroes" into U.S. citizens.[118] In the 1890s Schurz had joined Godkin as an editor at the *Post*, and the *Post* became an important venue for airing antiwar and anti-imperial sentiment. Neither editor supported woman suffrage.

The attack on the Hawaiian Appeal appeared in the form of an anonymous letter to the editor of the *Post* signed by a writer named "D."[119] In the 1870s "D" could have stood for Democrat, since the Democratic Party had been unanimously opposed to the annexation of Santo Domingo. In 1898, "D's" identity was less easy to guess, although the writer espoused a very similar kind of racial anti-imperialism. Indeed, what made the "Hawaiian Appeal" such a patently "absurd" document to "D" was that it indicated suffragists' willingness to compromise democratic principles by colluding in the government of island territories against the will of native inhabitants, and then sought to give this imperial project a democratic gloss by enfranchising women who "D" believed were incapable of citizenship. "Do they fancy that, among what they term our new possessions, we have acquired a Utopia, where every black, every brown, and every white woman can at least write her name…or read a word of the Constitution?" "D" asked, "or do not any of these things matter when the 'consent of the governed' seems to have lost its virtue as theory?"[120] In addition to challenging the underlying logic of the Hawaiian Appeal's particular brand of imperial suffragism, "D" sought to undermine suffragists' efforts to base their claims for the women of "our new possessions" on U.S. women's special and "sisterly" knowledge of womanly nature. To this end, "D" asked suffragists to consider "why the American officer finds the finest Cuban and the finest Porto Rican woman so agreeable to his taste, and so admirable to his sense of what constitutes womanhood?" "D's" answer was that unlike the "forward American woman," the "white" Spanish women in Spain's former colonies would "resent the imposition" of the vote.[121]

Finally, "D" turned his attention to the problem of sexual licentiousness more generally. "D" urged suffragists to read the recent spate of pro-imperial articles coming out in U.S. periodicals that suggested how the sexual habits of native Filipino men might create a different type of threat. As one writer in *Collier's* pointed out, many Filipinos were Muslim, and "by the Koran, polygamy is not only permitted, but, when a believer is rich enough to support more wives than one, enjoined." To extend constitutional government in the Philippines, then, would be to admit at least "a million Mohammedans" into the body politic, all of whom were "polygamists in theory." The *Collier's* solution was to keep Spain's island territories as "subject dependencies," although "whether a plurality of wives can be tolerated in an American dependency" would ultimately be a question for "American husbands."[122] The Protestant consensus that underlay the recent history of national antipolygamy legislation with respect to Utah Territory suggested that polygamy in U.S. dependencies would not be tolerated.

Stanton and Anthony's decision to respond to "D's" charges was a curious one. After all, "D's" attack on suffragists' essential femininity was hardly a new anti–woman suffrage argument and required no special effort to ignore. The fact that the two chose to respond, however, reflected in part the novelty of the position in which they found themselves: that of explicitly linking women's enfranchisement to the political realities of governing new U.S. colonial possessions overseas. In response to "D's" suggestion that American officers might prefer Spanish women, Stanton and Anthony conceded that "the preference of our sires and sons for Spanish women, if true, would be as great a calamity for Anglo-Saxon civilization as if our women should all prefer Spanish men." Fortunately, they assured "D," "even those women demanding political rights...know that the best type of race yet attained is Anglo-Saxon."[123] Stanton and Anthony's suggestion that even suffragists preferred Anglo-Saxon men may have been a tongue-in-cheek response to "D's" claim that men preferred women who did not want the vote. In "Statement on Territorial Constitutions," however, Anthony went even further in her defense of the virtues of Anglo-Saxon marriage and domestic life, and argued that to deprive the native women of "our possessions" of the franchise was an even more serious matter than to deprive U.S. women of the ballot because of the "half-savage character of the men of these countries."[124] Echoing British suffragist Millicent Garret Fawcett's concerns over how the introduction of British law in India had given "the Hindoo the slavery of the Anglo-Saxon wife," without providing "the Hindoo that spirit of Anglo-Saxon marriage and home life which has made that slavery often scarcely felt," Anthony built on the imperialist rhetoric of the British suffrage movement to make the case for woman suffrage in new U.S. territory overseas and claimed that "if to-day, in the Hawaiian Islands or in Cuba we fail to recognize the native women...we shall not only do them an injustice, but we shall forcibly give the Hawaiian and Cuban men lessons in the wrong side not the right side of our domestic relations."[125]

Stanton and Anthony's defense of the Hawaiian Appeal restated suffragists' willingness to accept educational and property qualifications for the vote in Hawaii as long as these restrictions weighed equally on women and men. As to "D's" suggestion that women in Hawaii, Cuba, Puerto Rico, and the Philippines were illiterate, the two stated that this was of little consequence when faced with the possibility of a national precedent denying woman suffrage in overseas territory. "In making our demands for educated women in the United States," Stanton and Anthony wrote, "we do not deem it necessary to consider the status of those in Indian Reserves or on Southern Plantations...neither was it ever a question with us whether American gentlemen preferred African and Indian women to those of their own nationality, as their social proclivities had nothing whatever to do with our civil and political rights."[126] These statements asserted a certain consistency in the suffrage position over time, but suffragists who participated in the antebellum woman's rights movement and created the national suffrage associations during Reconstruction had been very concerned with the status of those on "Southern Plantations" and, for a time, with the political rights of black women. Initially, at least, Anthony had been careful to distinguish "ignorant foreign men" from both black and white Americans. In defense of the Hawaiian Appeal, however, Anthony elaborated on the racial distinctions between Anglo-Saxon U.S. women, on the one hand, and Hawaiians and Filipinos, on the other, in ways that pushed black woman suffragists and immigrant women to the side.

Therefore, one of the most immediate consequences of suffragists' efforts to accommodate NAWSA policy to the political project of empire was to deepen the racial divisions within the movement. It is crucial to recognize how important this context was for the widely noted upsurge in racist arguments for white women's ballots on the NAWSA platform. The call to the 1899 NAWSA convention to be held in Grand Rapids, Michigan, in late April announced that the question of U.S. empire would be a primary topic of consideration because it was of "vital interest to millions of women—both the women of our new possessions...and the women of the United States, whose sons will be brought into intimate connection with Hawaii, Cuba, Porto [*sic*] Rico, and the Philippines."[127] Framing the imperial question as one of preventing "intimate connection" between different races created a climate in which it was impossible to address the specific concerns of black suffragists. When Mrs. Lottie Wilson Jackson, the black delegate from Michigan, asked the convention to pass a resolution condemning segregation on Southern railroads, her resolution was tabled as being "outside the province of the convention."[128]

While Jim Crow practices in the South were deemed beyond the proper sphere of suffragists' legitimate concerns, the convention's major speech, delivered by the Rhode Island suffragist Anna Garlin Spencer, was a "strong, philosophical presentation of 'Our Duty to the Women of Our New Possessions.'"[129] In her welcoming address to the audience that gathered in the auditorium of St. Cecilia Club House that April, Anthony had explained how "since our last convention the area of disfranchisement in the possessions of the United States has been greatly enlarged."[130] The problem, as Anthony saw it, was that in the past the settlers of new territories would have framed their own governments, but with the ratification of the Treaty of Paris in February 1899, "to-day Congress itself assumes the prerogative of making the laws for the newly-acquired Territories."[131] Previously, there had been no examples of universal suffrage to guide Congress, but now, "after fifty years' continuous agitation of the right of women to vote," which included the full enfranchisement of women in four states, and numerous instances of partial suffrage in more than one-half the other states, where women voted in school board and municipal elections, "it would seem that no member [of Congress] could be so blind as not to see it the duty of that body to have the provisional governments of our new possessions founded on the principle of equal rights, privileges and immunities for all the people, women included." Anthony hoped that the convention would "devise some plan" for getting Congress to adopt this position.[132]

Despite Anthony's hopes, Spencer's talk did not address the specific opportunities for woman suffrage at the national level presented by territorial constitution writing, or the idea of forming woman suffrage associations within
the new possessions themselves. Rather, Spencer's speech urged suffragists in
the United States to lend their energies to the Anglo-Saxon civilizing mission and made a case that the moral uplift of "backward races" must come
before any efforts to bestow political rights on the men and women of native
populations. Adopting the evolutionary model laid out by Morgan's anthropological studies of the Iroquois, which had so captivated Gage in the 1870s,
Spencer explained to her NAWSA audience the process by which uncivilized
tribes progressed from a state of barbarism, through savagery, to civilization.
Women in savage and uncivilized societies existed in some degree of transition from primitive "matriarchates," which privileged motherhood, tribal
relations, and the transmission of property and children through female lines
of descent, to societies ordered on the principle of "father-rule" and "mono-
gamic" marriage, which more closely matched the system of Christian marriage within the United States. The uninformed might believe that the native
system gave women more freedoms, but to Spencer's way of thinking, "the
subjection of woman to man in the family bond was a vast step upward from
the preceding condition."[133]

To Spencer, U.S. civilization in 1899 reflected the penultimate point in
a long process of women's moral and mental development within Christian
marriage. If U.S. women had not yet succeeded in writing into law and political life that respect for woman which she believed characterized American
civilization, that was because the United States itself was still "inconsistent,"
and not yet out of the transition stage from the "father-rule to the equal
reign of both sexes," which would be marked by woman suffrage.[134] Anthony
wanted equal political rights for men and women in the new U.S. possessions, and Spencer agreed that enfranchising native men would only introduce
"every injustice of women's subjection to men, without giving these people
one iota of the sense of family responsibility, of protection of, and respect
for woman, and of deep and self-sacrificing devotion to childhood's needs,
which mark the Anglo-Saxon man." But whereas Anthony was focused on the
project of federal constitution writing for the new island territories, Spencer
wanted to send a woman's commission to "all the lands in which our flag now
claims a new power of oversight and control." The object of this commission
would be the study of "domestic rather than political conditions."[135]

Spencer's vision of a woman's commission that might devise a plan for
social and moral uplift before agitating for women's ballots did not go unchal-
lenged. Some suffragists felt that since Congress was bound to establish some

form of male voting rights, surely the NAWSA should hesitate to acquiesce in the establishment of "sex supremacy."[136] Others thought that the commission idea was the more valuable plan. Blackwell agreed with Anthony's position that enfranchising the women of Hawaii, including native women, was the proper way forward, despite, or rather because, of the "barbarism" of native men. Despite Spencer's good speech, he warned NAWSA members not to "imagine that the so-called 'matriarchate' of early ages was an ideal condition of society."[137] Blackwell would have preferred that the United States relinquish control of the Philippines entirely. But given the U.S. decision not to do so, and in the context of the ongoing Philippine-American War, he warned suffragists that the real trouble is when "Western civilization interferes with Oriental abuses [but] does not go far enough."[138] In the case of the new U.S. possessions, where there are "peoples ranging from absolute savagery to mediaeval civilization," Blackwell again agreed with Anthony and argued that "such women, even more than those of our own States, will need the ballot as a means of self-protection."[139]

The 1899 NAWSA convention resolved both to protest the introduction of the word "male" into the suffrage clause of the proposed constitution for Hawaii and to recommend that McKinley appoint a women's commission to investigate the condition of women in "our new island territories."[140] While pro-imperial suffragists of varying degrees compromised between an active national strategy centered around the immediate problem of the Hawaiian constitution, and a more long-term approach focused on investigation and moral uplift, anti-imperial suffragists protested the ongoing Philippine-American War. In May, Blackwell attended the eightieth birthday celebration of Julia Ward Howe in Boston and used the opportunity to reminisce about his Santo Domingo days, while maintaining a steady stream of criticism about the U.S. war in the Philippines; his sympathies were with the "so called 'insurgents.'"[141] Other suffragists sent a special women's anti-imperial petition to McKinley.[142] In contrast, Anthony was increasingly public about her support for the Philippine-American War. Acknowledging that many of her "friends might think it strange that I do not join them in the protest," Anthony told one interviewer that "it is nonsense to talk about giving those guerillas in the Philippines their liberty." Anthony was convinced that if the United States relinquished control over the islands, "the first thing they [the Filipinos] would do would be to murder and pillage every white person on the islands, Spanish and American alike."[143] The contingent nature of Anthony's pacifist commitments is suggestive of how differently she had come to view the U.S.-Spanish and the U.S.-Philippine wars. Wars between nations like that with Spain were to be avoided, but the only way to avoid war with uncivilized races was to "go through it." In May 1899, with the suffrage requirements for the provisional governments of Hawaii and Puerto Rico yet undecided, it was still possible to imagine that victory would bring a new round of territorial constitutional writing that might provide a lightning rod for a national discussion of the woman question.

SYMPATHY AS A CIVIL AGENT

In May 1899, Anthony may have held out hope that the expansion of U.S. borders overseas would provide new contexts for suffragists to push the woman question in Congress, but the costs of her efforts to ignore the imperial question and to focus on constitution writing in the new U.S. possessions were already becoming clear. In April, Spencer's speech had indicated how quickly the rhetoric of protection for native women might shift attention away from immediate and specific plans regarding votes for women in favor of evolutionary schemes that held the ideal of woman suffrage up as part of an enlightened and progressive future but had little to say about immediate strategy. This point was brought home to Anthony when she traveled to London in July 1899, for a meeting of the International Council of Women. At a meeting to discuss amendments to the ICW constitution, council members from Great Britain and Ireland moved that a list of goals be inserted which included the language "to provide opportunities for women to meet together and confer upon questions relating to the welfare of the commonwealth and the family."[144] Anthony immediately took issue with this wording, telling fellow ICW council members that "she thought it rather vague to talk of the family and the commonwealth, because half of the commonwealth were not included in many of the Governments." Giving vent to her frustration that ten years after its founding the ICW had still not endorsed woman suffrage, Anthony complained that the members of the ICW "might as well beat the air as go on talking about the commonwealth when they had no voice in it."[145] The U.S. suffragist May Wright Sewall chastised Anthony for the stridency of her position. Sewall "did not undervalue the vote," she informed Anthony and the assembled members of the ICW, but "she would be reluctant to join an organization which should put it on record that the vote was the only instrument by which [women] allied themselves to the commonwealth."[146]

Anthony and Sewall had had a similar debate six months earlier during a discussion of resolutions that U.S. delegates might present to the ICW at this July meeting. That January, in the midst of her efforts to popularize the Hawaiian Appeal, Anthony had expressed her hope that "the time has now come when the Council should be ready to discuss what true citizenship really means."[147] In response to Anthony's claim that without the vote women were not "sovereign citizens," but "political slaves," Sewall had taken the opportunity to disagree publicly with Anthony and, to much applause, had declared that U.S. women "were born sovereign citizens, and no man could take sovereignty from them. The women of the United States were sovereign citizens even if they did not have the vote."[148] Anthony and Sewall's disagreement over the meaning of citizenship vividly illustrates generational and ideological divisions within the U.S. suffrage movement at the end of the century. For older leaders like Anthony, citizenship was inextricably linked to the vote and to women's ability to participate in the political life of the nation. For younger women like Sewall, who claimed for themselves the title of "representative women," women's citizenship was linked less to the vote and political rights than to their ability to speak for, and as, American women in both national and international arenas. In the context of U.S. empire, Sewall's position had increasing validity. Most U.S. women did not have the vote, but they were indeed increasingly "sovereign" to the extent that they claimed for themselves a share in the Anglo-Saxon civilizing mission over dependent territories under formal U.S. rule. Although initially a suffrage project, within ten years of its founding, the ICW had become an organization in which suffragism was marginalized by the vision of "representative womanhood" espoused by the very missionary and reform-minded women Anthony had originally hoped to convert.

DOMESTIC IMPERIALISM

By the fall of 1902, the Philippine-American War had ended in U.S. victory, and the United States had established different forms of territorial governments for its new island possessions, none of which enfranchised women. By inserting the word "male" into the Hawaiian territorial constitution, the Hawaiian Organic Act of 1900 left the question of woman suffrage in the hands of the U.S. Congress, although in other respects Hawaii's Organic Act created a territory in the same mold as other U.S. territories destined for eventual statehood. In contrast to Hawaii's new territorial status, the Foraker Act of 1900 set up only a temporary civil government for Puerto Rico (that would remain in place until 1917), left its territorial status undecided, and withheld U.S. citizenship from the local inhabitants. Unlike other territories in which inhabitants elected both houses of the territorial legislature, local government in Puerto Rico was to be conducted by a commission appointed by the U.S. president. The Foraker Act did allow for the creation of an elected lower house and left Puerto Ricans free to define the suffrage requirements for this body, which in 1900 did not extend the vote to women. The Philippine Organic Act of 1902, which created a locally elected lower house with property and tax qualifications for the vote, similarly did not include women. As with Puerto Rico, the Philippine upper house consisted of a set of commissioners appointed by Congress, with the head commissioner assuming the title of Governor General of the Islands. No elections were held in the Philippines until 1907, and it was assumed that at some future date, the Philippines would be granted independence. In the meantime, the United States would attempt to train the Filipinos in the capacities necessary for self-government.[149]

That November, Henry Brown Blackwell published an article in the *Woman's Journal* entitled "Domestic Imperialism," in which he tried to make the case that disfranchised women within the United States, much like Puerto Ricans and Filipinos, were internal colonial subjects.[150] In his earlier antiimperial writings, Blackwell had been primarily interested in urging fellow suffragists to join him in protesting against U.S. designs on the Philippines, but with that goal now historically foreclosed, his present tack was to persuade the "the men who call themselves 'anti-imperialists,' and denounce most vigorously the control of alien races abroad, [but] have no word of censure for similar control of one-half of our own citizens at home," to consider the problem of women's disfranchisement. In his efforts to define a concept of internal or "domestic" imperialism, Blackwell worked at the level of analogy and anticipated the links that women liberationists in the 1960s would begin to make between their own position in U.S. society and that of other colonized subjects engaged in liberation movements across the globe. Women's status as disfranchised citizens and the status of colonial subjects in U.S. colonies could be connected by law as well as by semantics. In *Downes v. Bidwell* (1901), one of the earliest Supreme Court cases to spell out the legal relationship between the United States and its colonies, the court cited *Minor* as precedent for the principle that political rights were incidental to national belonging.[151]

There is no evidence that suffragists in 1901 followed any of the legal cases emerging from the complicated new relationships between the United States and its new possessions. The number of suffragists still living who had participated in the movement during its New Departure days had dwindled, and in 1900, Anthony relinquished the presidency of the NAWSA to Catt. Nor was it likely that any knowledge of the similarities between the political status of U.S. women citizens and colonial subjects would have inspired or encouraged the younger generation of suffrage leaders, white or black, to describe their own condition as one of colonized subjects in the way that antebellum woman's rights activists had described themselves as political "slaves." White suffragists like Catt and Sewall preferred to think of themselves as "civiliz-ers," not as subjects of domestic imperialism. Despite being well positioned to see the analogies between their own status and that of U.S. colonial sub-jects overseas, black suffragists were similarly intent on claiming the mantle of "civilization" for black Americans and were themselves engaged in multiple projects of moral uplift both within U.S. borders and abroad.[152] Over the next decade, U.S. colonialism would provide a backdrop to the domestic politics of the U.S. suffrage movement, and while white and black suffragists would begin to participate in a new international movement for woman suffrage, they did not do so as colonized women or as victims of "domestic" imperialism but as representatives of American civilization on a global stage.

5

GETTING SUFFRAGE IN AN AGE OF EMPIRE

The Philippines and Puerto Rico, 1914–1929

On December 4, 1916, the Democratic president Woodrow Wilson was interrupted during a congressional speech when suffragists sitting in the gallery unfurled a banner of yellow sateen that read, "MR. PRESIDENT, WHAT WILL YOU DO FOR WOMAN SUFFRAGE?"[1] That December, Wilson was trying to keep the United States out of the war in Europe, but he was also concerned about resolving the issues of Philippine independence and the future status of Puerto Rico. Earlier in the year, Wilson had signed the Philippine Autonomy Act, better known as the 1916 Jones Act, a compromise between Republicans and Democrats that committed the United States in the abstract to recognizing Filipino independence at some future date, expanding the franchise for Filipino men, and turning the upper chamber of the Filipino legislature, previously an appointed commission, into an elected body.[2] Over the summer, Congress had passed a second Jones Act for Puerto Rico, which became law in 1917. The 1917 Jones Act granted Puerto Ricans U.S. citizenship, a status not granted to Filipinos, but did not resolve the question of future statehood or independence for the island. Instead, Puerto Rico retained its status as an "unincorporated territory" of the United States, that is, a territory not slated for future statehood. The 1917 Jones Act for Puerto Rico left in place universal male suffrage, and as with the Philippines transformed the Puerto Rican Senate into an elective body. Any decision to extend voting rights to women would be made, if at all, by the Puerto Rican legislature, and subject to veto by the U.S. colonial governor.[3]

Suffragists followed closely the congressional debates over these grants of increasing political independence to men in the Philippines and Puerto Rico.[4] The suffragists who boldly interrupted Wilson that December had chosen their moment with care, waiting for the precise instant in which the president turned his attention to the Puerto Rican question to let loose their banner.[5] In March 1914, during Wilson's first term, the Senate had debated and defeated a woman suffrage amendment to the federal Constitution for the first time since 1887. In 1915, when the House took up the question of women's federal enfranchisement for the first time in its history, it had similarly defeated the woman suffrage amendment.[6] Suffragists were intent on juxtaposing national legislation that expanded political autonomy in the Philippines and Puerto Rico against Congress's failure to pass a woman suffrage amendment for U.S women. By all accounts, their radical act achieved its purpose. By the end of the day, suffragists' exploits had become front-page news across the country.[7]

The women who went to the Capitol that day were members of the newly formed Woman's Party (WP), under the leadership of Alice Paul, who at thirty-one was well on her way to becoming known as one of the most militant women in the U.S. suffrage movement.[8] In 1913, as head of the NAWSA's Congressional Committee, Paul and Lucy Burns, a U.S. suffragist whom Paul had met in London while learning the tactics of militant British suffragettes, had organized a suffrage parade that took place in D.C. on the day before Wilson's first inauguration. The parade of more than 5,000 women was able to make its way through the streets of D.C. only with the aid of local police and the Pennsylvania National Guard.[9] Paul was determined to harness the growing energies of women across the states into a renewed push for a woman suffrage amendment, and in the 1914 midterm elections Paul and members of the Congressional Union, the name given to the NAWSA's newly revitalized Congressional Committee, campaigned against Democratic candidates in the nine states where women voted.[10] In 1914 Paul's efforts to "punish the party in power," a strategy adopted wholesale from the British suffrage movement, failed, but it marked a new style of confrontational activism and suffrage militancy that by 1916 included interrupting Wilson's annual message to Congress, and one year later picketing the White House in the midst of war.

Not all suffragists were happy about the type of publicity that the suffrage movement received in 1914 when Paul campaigned against the Democrats, or in 1916 when Woman's Party activists disrupted Wilson. In 1913 the NAWSA leadership had sought to curb Paul's militancy, and by 1914 the Congressional Union severed formal ties with the NAWSA. By 1916, when Paul's fellow Swarthmore graduate Mabel Vernon and nine other activists unrolled their suffrage banner during Wilson's speech, the Congressional Union had become the Woman's Party, a rival woman suffrage organization that was devoted first and foremost to the passage of a national woman suffrage amendment and that competed with the NAWSA for loyalty and support.

Since 1904, under NAWSA president Anna Howard Shaw, much of the life of the suffrage movement had taken place in the states, although between 1896 and 1910 no new states fully enfranchised women. The victories in California, Washington, Oregon, Kansas, Montana, and Nevada between 1910 and 1916 were hard-won, labor-intensive, and matched by defeated referenda in Ohio, Wisconsin, Michigan, North Dakota, South Dakota, Nebraska, Missouri, New York, New Jersey, Pennsylvania, and Massachusetts.[11] In 1915, when Carrie Chapman Catt returned to the presidency of the NAWSA after an eleven-year hiatus, she, like Paul, hoped to put life back into a national woman suffrage amendment, but she did not approve of Paul's confrontational tactics. After all, the Republican Party had also failed to adopt a woman suffrage plank in 1912. Moreover, whereas Wilson, a Democrat, personally favored votes for women even if his party opposed a federal constitutional amendment, the Republican Taft administration had not. In 1916, with a war in Europe looming on the horizon, Catt thought that suffragists' best hope of success lay not with antagonizing the president but rather with persuasion.[12]

In 1916 debates over tactics and style divided Catt and Paul, but both shared a growing awareness of how renewed congressional attention to the political status of the Philippines and Puerto Rico might provide opportunities for suffragists at home. In 1899, when the NAWSA had petitioned Congress to keep the word "male" out of the new territorial constitution for Hawaii, its demand was largely ignored. In 1912, however, when Republican representative Frank Mondell of Wyoming offered a woman suffrage amendment to the new territorial constitution for Alaska, it succeeded in passing the House despite Democratic protests. For those suffragists with their eyes fixed firmly on Congress in 1912, the Alaska victory indicated that at least with regard to federal territory, the opposition to national woman suffrage legislation might be weakening.[13] This knowledge supported and reinforced Paul's conviction that the time was ripe to push for a national woman suffrage amendment. It also suggested that the NAWSA would do well to keep abreast of congressional discussions about the Philippines and Puerto Rico, as the U.S. colonial possessions might be the next site of woman suffrage victories.

As Catt was well aware from her participation in the International Woman Suffrage Alliance (IWSA), an organization she helped form in 1904 "to gain political equality for women in every civilized land," colonial legislatures were often much more favorably disposed toward women's ballots than the imperial legislative bodies that oversaw colonial dependencies.[14] In 1893 women had won the vote in the British colony of New Zealand, and in 1894 and 1899, the British colonies of South Australia and Western Australia followed suit. In 1902, the new commonwealth government of Australia extended the federal suffrage to all white women, and in 1916 women had gained the full franchise in the Canadian provinces of Alberta, Manitoba, and Saskatchewan.[15] In contrast to the expanded suffrage enjoyed by women across the empire, British women living in England in 1916 could vote only in local elections and only if they were married. U.S. suffragists read about the successes of woman suffrage movements in the British colonies in the *Woman's Journal*, and Catt acquired firsthand knowledge of the potential for suffrage victories in the U.S. territories and colonies when she visited Hawaii and the Philippines during a round-the-world tour she conducted for the IWSA in 1911 and 1912. In both Hawaii and the Philippines, Catt was warmly received by local women's groups that included both native and foreign-born women.[16] Catt did not visit Puerto Rico, but had she done so, she would have encountered a growing woman suffrage movement that included women from both the laboring and upper classes.[17]

The revival of the push for the federal woman suffrage amendment in the 1910s coincided with the election of a Democratic president whose party was determined to sever U.S. colonial connections in the Philippines and reconfigure them in Puerto Rico. As historians of the suffrage movement are well aware, suffrage victories in individual states during the first decades of the twentieth century, and a war fought to make the world safe for democracy, contributed to a political climate in which suffragists hoped to advance their cause at the national level. Almost completely unknown, however, is that debates over new government bills for the U.S. colonial possessions also contributed to the suffrage victory by providing a way to discuss the question of woman suffrage that lifted it out of the states' rights framework that the opponents of woman suffrage had long used to send the woman question back to the states. When legislators made arguments for Filipino independence and extending U.S. citizenship to the inhabitants of Puerto Rico, the national press was filled with speeches about the individual right to self-government and self-sovereignty that had been largely absent from congressional discourse in the era of Jim Crow. And as they had done in the case of Utah, Wyoming, and Hawaii, suffragists took advantage of these discussions to raise the question of votes for women to the level of national debate.

By the second decade of the twentieth century, suffragists' efforts to insert the question of votes for women into congressional discussions about the right to self-government among the inhabitants of U.S. federal territories had a long history that stretched back to the 1870s and the debates over the proper type of government for D.C., voting rights in Utah Territory, Indian citizenship, and the territorial constitution for Hawaii. Despite the familiarity of this strategy, something important had changed. More than a decade of U.S. colonial rule had demonstrated the differences between the U.S. colonies of Puerto Rico and the Philippines, on the one hand, and U.S. territories such as Wyoming, Utah, and Washington, on the other hand. These were differences that had not been clear at the moment of acquiring Puerto Rico and the Philippines. Colonies were perpetual territories, unlikely ever to become states. This knowledge meant that by about 1912 the states' rights opposition to woman suffrage foundered, although it did not immediately sink, when suffragists once again attached woman suffrage amendments to the governing bills for these U.S. colonies.

By 1919, when the Senate finally ratified the woman suffrage constitutional amendment—the Nineteenth Amendment to the U.S. Constitution—Puerto Rican women had become citizens of the United States, yet the Nineteenth Amendment did not enfranchise Puerto Rican women. As inhabitants of an unincorporated territory, Puerto Rican women had civil and political rights that flowed directly from congressional action, and not from constitutional provision. The liminal status of Puerto Rico as a territory not on a path toward statehood has made it difficult to account for the story of Puerto Rican women's suffrage within the traditional narrative frame of U.S. history. That is not to say that the history of Puerto Rican women's struggle for suffrage has not been chronicled, but rather, that it has not been incorporated into the history of the U.S. woman suffrage movement and has been largely understood as part of the separate national, or rather territorial, history of Puerto Rico.[18] The disbanding of the NAWSA in 1920 and its transformation into the League of Women Voters have also contributed to the tendency to date the end of the U.S. woman suffrage movement to 1920, although attention to the continued disfranchisement of black women after its passage, and their struggles to claim the protections of the Nineteenth Amendment for themselves, has long rendered this date suspect as the proper end point for the history of the U.S. woman suffrage movement.[19]

The story of the National Woman's Party's (NWP) limited but continued engagement with the question of Puerto Rican woman suffrage through the 1920s and the congressional debates over Puerto Rican woman's suffrage in 1928 and 1929 are part of the larger history of Pan-American women's international organizing. These congressional debates are also an important episode in the history of the U.S. woman suffrage movement because they mark the moment when political rights for women became a contested feature of U.S. colonial rule. Like U.S. women in the 1870s who went to the polls to test the meaning of the Fourteenth and Fifteenth Amendments, Puerto Rican women in the 1920s went to the polls and attempted to vote, claiming that they had been enfranchised under the Nineteenth Amendment. And just as the legislative and judicial responses to suffragists' New Departure in the 1870s helped to define women's relationship to the state at a moment of national Reconstruction as well as the larger meaning of citizenship in the new Union, the responses to this Puerto Rican women's "New Departure" helped to define the meaning of U.S. colonial citizenship in the 1920s.

COLONIAL GOVERNMENT AND WOMAN SUFFRAGE: AMENDING THE JONES BILLS IN 1914 AND 1916

In May 1902, when the last of the Filipino insurgents surrendered after almost three years of war, the United States had a new empire and a new imperial president. The assassination of William McKinley in September 1901 put former New York governor Theodore Roosevelt into the White House. Celebrated as a hero for his military exploits during the Spanish-American War— Roosevelt had led a volunteer regiment of "Rough Riders" in the battle for San Juan Hill, Cuba—Roosevelt possessed an imperialist vision grounded in the belief that military ventures were a crucial site for the development of a "manly" character distinguished by the strength, courage, and fraternalism forged in battle.[20] To Roosevelt, U.S. imperialism and the challenge of governing colonies were opportunities to reinvigorate an American manhood dangerously weakened by the growing prosperity of urban life.

To the extent that Roosevelt believed that imperial projects provided important twentieth-century venues for the development of vital manhood, equally important was the corollary idea that a strong state required women's essential domesticity. In his writings and speeches Roosevelt emphasized that women's primary duty to the state was as "mothers of the race," a phrase that emphasized the special contributions of white women's maternity to the national vitality. Writing to Susan B. Anthony in 1898, Roosevelt agreed that women were "in many cases oppressed," but in contrast to suffragists, Roosevelt felt that "the trouble is in [woman's] own attitude, which laws cannot alter."[21] In the face of demands for women's political equality, Roosevelt urged women to turn their energies back to the domestic sphere.[22]

Despite Roosevelt's belief that imperial ventures were a site for the development of a revitalized American manhood, and that facing down the challenges of colonial rule would at once build men's character and contribute to the health and vitality of the nation, his first administration was beset by scandals over prostitution in the Philippines. As part of their campaign to prevent the Army regulation of vice in the U.S. colonial Philippines, members of the WCTU had petitioned President McKinley in 1900 to investigate reports by U.S. missionaries of official military inspections of Filipina prostitutes in the brothels frequented by U.S. soldiers.[23] The NAWSA joined with the WCTU in condemning the military inspections of Filipina prostitutes and attempted to link the problem of vice in the Philippines to the NAWSA's demand for woman suffrage. NAWSA resolutions for 1902 protested "the government regulation of vice in our new possessions" and urged that because Congress was now engaged in the process of making laws for a new civil government for the Philippines, it should "grant the native women whatever rights it confers on native men."[24] In 1899, the enfranchisement of Hawaiian women had been considered necessary for their protection, given the "uncivilized" character of Hawaiian men. In 1902, suffragists ascribed "uncivilized" behavior in the Philippines to the behavior of U.S. soldiers and claimed that enfranchised women at home would help Roosevelt face down this "element of savagery in Army circles" and facilitate the president's efforts to "roll back this tidal wave of barbarism."[25]

In 1902 U.S. suffragists' demand for the vote on behalf of native women in the Philippines was grounded in the belief that women represented the "civilized" element of society. By the turn of the century, this view had a long history among suffragists dating back at least as far as Blackwell's 1869 article in the *Woman's Journal* urging Congress to enfranchise Indian women on the same terms as Indian men. The 1902 Taft Commission report to Congress on the status of the Philippines helped popularize this view with respect to Filipina women. In 1900 McKinley had appointed William Howard Taft to head a commission charged with overseeing the transition from military to civil government in the Philippines. In his 1902 report to Congress, Taft recommended that Congress extend political rights to Filipina women before Filipino men because the women of the Philippines are the "backbone of the country; the active managers in general affairs; the home-makers; the shopkeepers; the providers for the families."[26] The Spanish archbishop for the Philippines agreed with Taft and urged Congress "that if it was intended to confer any political authority on the Filipinos, it should be conferred upon the female sex." Taft reportedly conveyed his thoughts to suffragist Harriet Potter Nourse during a private conversation in New York, and Nourse delightedly passed Taft's and Archbishop Nozelda's sentiments on to the NAWSA at their convention.[27]

Clemencia Lopez, the only Filipina woman to testify before Congress during its deliberations on the 1902 Philippine Organic Act creating a governing structure for the Philippines, did not agree that Congress should enfranchise

Filipina women on the same terms as Filipino men. It was not that she disputed Taft's characterization of Filipina women's virtues. Rather, as a member of a family of Filipino nationalists (her brother Sixto Lopez had been a member of the Philippine commission sent to the United States in 1898 to negotiate Philippine independence), Lopez disputed Congress's authority to legislate for the Philippines in the first place. Following her congressional appearance, Lopez attended a meeting of the New England Woman Suffrage Association (NEWSA), held in Boston, where she attempted to analogize the Philippine independence struggle to that of the woman suffrage question, telling members of the NEWSA "that we are both striving for much the same object—you for the right to take part in national life; we for the right to have a national life to take part in."[28] Despite the anti-imperial sympathies of individual suffragists, the NAWSA's formal demand that Congress enfranchise women in new U.S. colonial possessions served to legitimate the U.S. imperial project and for the most part Lopez' words fell on deaf ears. Historian Ian Tyrrell has noted that in the case of the WCTU, their efforts "to reform the imperial structure" by preventing the army inspection of prostitutes "undermined the potential of a moral anti-imperialism."[29] This was true for suffragists as well. The NAWSA critique of regulated vice and Army violence in the Philippines did not translate into a policy that criticized the U.S. imperial venture as a whole, although individual suffragists did level such critique. Rather, it revived the principles underlying the Hawaiian appeal of 1899, that votes for native women in the colonies and U.S. women at home were necessary for women's protection from male "barbarism," which by 1902 included U.S. soldiers overseas.

The 1902 Philippine Organic Act did not enfranchise Filipina women, and with governing laws now in place for the both the Philippines and Puerto Rico, the NAWSA strategy of demanding woman suffrage in the new U.S. possessions came to a halt. Over the next ten years, the NAWSA largely abandoned its commitment to a federal woman suffrage amendment as well. In the context of both empire and Jim Crow, national legislation authorizing women's ballots had very little hope of passage. In 1903 the Supreme Court's decision in *Giles v. Harris* closed the door on federal constitutional challenges to state constitutions that disfranchised black voters.[30] That same year, in *Hawaii v. Mankichi*, the Supreme Court decided that the Sixth Amendment did not apply in Hawaii when that territory was "unincorporated," that is, during the years between annexation in 1897 and the formal creation of a territorial constitution in 1899.[31] By limiting the application of the constitution in "unincorporated territories," a term devised in 1901 to describe the status of the territories acquired from Spain under the Treaty of Paris (including Puerto Rico and the Philippines), the Supreme Court's decision contributed to the notion of U.S. citizenship as distinctly "Anglo-Saxon."[32] This view was reinforced by the disfranchising constitutions across the states. A woman suffrage amendment that prohibited state disfranchisement on the basis of sex threatened this status quo because it depended on the premise that there already existed a national right to vote.

It was precisely this connection between woman suffrage and nationally guaranteed voting rights that kept black suffragists especially interested in federal suffrage legislation between 1900 and 1912. During these years, the National Association of Colored Women (NACW) remained one of the only organizations with its eye on a federal woman suffrage amendment. The NACW also made connections between woman suffrage and rolling back the tide of U.S. "barbarism," although its attention was directed less at the behavior of U.S. soldiers in Puerto Rico and the Philippines than at the lynching of black men and women within U.S. borders.

Alice Paul's return to the United States and her push for a federal woman suffrage amendment coincided with renewed national attention to the status of the Philippines and Puerto Rico. In the Philippines, the Nationalist Party had held a majority in the Assembly since the first general election in 1907, and by the time Wilson took office, Nationalist Party members were agitating for a date after which the Philippines would obtain complete independence from the United States.[33] The situation in Puerto Rico was somewhat different. Until about 1910, the Unionist Party, which dominated the Puerto Rican Assembly since the Foraker Act first constituted that body in 1901, had pushed for U.S. statehood. But by 1910, with the fate of Puerto Rico still undecided, even Unionists began talking less about U.S. statehood and more about greater political independence for Puerto Rico.[34] The 1912 presidential election was waged over tax reform, prohibition, the rights of labor, black disfranchisement, and even woman suffrage, but it was also an election about the future status of the Philippines and Puerto Rico. Wilson won the election on a platform that condemned this "experiment in imperialism" as one that had "laid our nation open to the charge of abandonment of the fundamental doctrine of self-government." The platform promised "to recognize the independence of the Philippine Islands as soon as a stable government can be established."[35] Wilson personally believed that establishing stable government in the Philippines might take considerably longer than did other members of his party. In his first annual message to Congress in December 1913, Wilson urged Congress to pass a new Philippine bill that promised independence for the islands. At the time, NAWSA suffragists were in the capital for their forty-fifth annual meeting, and they had urged Wilson to mention woman suffrage in his speech. He chose not to do so, but he did speak favorably about extending the ballot in the Philippines as part of a push for Filipino self-government. The NAWSA's response demonstrates how suffragists used discussions of U.S. imperialism to forward the woman suffrage cause. The NAWSA promptly adopted a resolution castigating the president for his failure to "recommend the freedom of half the citizens of the civilized world" while at the same time recognizing "the necessity for the extension of the ballot to the Filipinos."[36]

During Wilson's first term, suffragists' efforts to push a national woman suffrage amendment through Congress overlapped with congressional efforts to legislate a Philippine independence bill, and once again, congressional discussion regarding the voting rights of the inhabitants of federal territories provided an opportunity for suffragists to advance their question. In October 1914, it was the Republican House minority leader James Robert Mann of Illinois who first offered a woman suffrage amendment to the Philippine government bill then under discussion. The year before, Mann's home state of Illinois became the first state east of the Mississippi to hold a successful statewide woman suffrage referendum, and after 1913 Illinois women were authorized to vote in presidential elections and municipal elections.[37]

Like previous woman suffrage amendments to governing bills for U.S. territories, the Mann Amendment requested that the new government bill for the Philippines authorize woman suffrage by striking out the word "male" before "citizen."[38] What made Mann's woman suffrage amendment to the Philippine governing bill different than those offered in the past, however, was Mann's deliberate employment of legal distinctions between colonies and states in making his case for the enfranchisement of Filipina women. As Mann explained in defense of his amendment, "We have not here any complication of jurisdiction of the Federal Government in reference to the qualification of voters in the States." "That question," Mann insisted, "cannot arise here, because here we are fixing qualifications of voters for the Philippines." Those representatives who claimed to "favor woman suffrage, either as an idea or as a concrete proposition," he therefore asserted, ought to vote for the amendment and cease hiding behind any states' rights doctrine that was clearly not applicable to the Philippines.[39] During the March 1914 Senate debate over the woman suffrage amendment to the federal Constitution, the opposition to woman suffrage had once again been couched in terms of state authority to regulate the franchise, although many opponents to the federal amendment claimed to favor woman suffrage. With congressional elections just a month away, and with the Congressional Union organizing against Democratic candidates in those states where women voted, Mann sought to back the opponents of woman suffrage into a corner. In this, he was aided by his Progressive colleague James Wesley Bryan of Washington, who was "sick of Democrats that say they are for woman suffrage but side step the question by saying it is a state issue." "You are going to declare here this afternoon either for it in truth, without any faking, without any nonsense, or you are going to declare against it," Bryan threatened. In case any of his colleagues mistook his threat as an empty one, Bryan announced that he had "phoned down to the woman-suffrage headquarters and advised them to come here and bring their tablets and to note what goes on where there is no roll call." One way or another, Bryan announced, "we are going to find out whether the Democratic Party stands for suffrage or against it."[40]

To a large extent, Mann's efforts to put Democrats on the spot regarding whether or not they supported woman suffrage were successful. As the *New York Times* reported, Mann's amendment to the Philippine bill stirred the "House to war" and engendered one of the most acrimonious debates in decades.[41] Although historians agree that suffragists' campaign to defeat Democratic candidates in the 1914 midterm elections failed, in the month prior to that election, their threat lent a certain amount of weight to Mann's and Bryan's endeavor to attach a woman suffrage amendment to the Philippine bill and to put Democrats on the defensive. What became immediately clear in the context of the House debate over the Mann Amendment was that congressmen were aware of the political strength that woman suffrage activists were beginning to wield whether or not they were enfranchised. Indeed, Democratic representative William Atkinson Jones, who was personally responsible for getting the Philippine bill through the House, accused Mann of attaching a woman suffrage amendment to the bill only to get his name off the Congressional Union blacklist.[42] Mann's name had appeared on the list when he opposed granting a license to the NAWSA suffrage parade in D.C. the year before. In his defense, Mann claimed he had opposed the parade only to prevent the women of the country from being subject to Democratic abuse. When the Mann amendment failed 58 to 84, the Congressional Union immediately turned the vote into a campaign issue. In "Freedom for the Filipinos," the Congressional Union paper *Woman Citizen* asked members of the Democratic Party in Congress "to pause a moment to reflect upon the incongruity of deliberately blocking the passage of a resolution submitting to the people of the country the question of the political freedom of women while at the same time they are aroused over the necessity of immediate action in extending the political freedom of [Filipino] men." The Congressional Union asked women voters "to show by their vote at the polls this November that a political party which refuses self-government to women while it extends it to the Filipino, cannot hope to keep the support of the woman's vote."[43] When the Philippine bill passed the House on October 24, 1914, without a woman suffrage amendment, the NAWSA agreed with the Congressional Union that this action had been particularly unfair to women.[44]

In May 1916 when the House turned its attention to the Jones bill for Puerto Rico, Mann once again sought to attach a woman suffrage amendment to the bill. In the year between Mann's amendment to the Jones bill for the Philippines and the 1916 House debate on the Jones bill for Puerto Rico, the House had debated and defeated a woman suffrage amendment to the federal constitution for the first time since 1887, and once again the debate had been framed in states' rights terms. Although the Jones bill for Puerto Rico, like the Jones bill for the Philippines, was proposed as an effort to resolve the question of Puerto Rico's final status, the terms of the bill did not ultimately speak to this question. Rather, the bill extended a measure of political autonomy to Puerto Rico by changing the lower house into an elected body. It also turned the citizens of Puerto Rico into U.S. citizens, thus tying Puerto Rico even more closely to the United States. In the context of Puerto Rico's ever more irregular status, it was unclear whether Mann's argument that the states' rights opposition need not apply to Puerto Rico would be more or less convincing. But the day that Mann introduced his amendment to the Jones bill for Puerto Rico, many Democrats were absent from the House, and the woman suffrage amendment passed with little opposition. Both Democrats and Republicans rectified this situation the following day, voting to rescind Mann's amendment. While the final Jones bill for Puerto Rico did not explicitly give that colony woman suffrage, neither did it use the word "male" in its qualifications for electors. Approved by Wilson on March 2, 1917, the Jones Act for Puerto Rico specified that the first election for the legislature would include all those qualified previously under the law, which meant men, but thereafter suffrage requirements would be left to Puerto Rico.

The Puerto Rican Jones Act was a quiet and not well-remarked victory for suffragists, yet it did represent a significant change in the congressional approach to woman suffrage before the passage of the Nineteenth Amendment. The Republican senator John Shafroth of Colorado was head of the Senate Committee on the Pacific Islands and Puerto Rico when the Jones bill passed the Senate, and NAWSA suffragists appealed to him for help later that year in introducing a bill into the Senate that would enable the territorial legislature of Hawaii to enfranchise women. Shafroth introduced that bill into the Senate in May 1917, and it passed the House in June 1918. In the 1916 presidential election, both the Democratic Party and the Republican Party had adopted woman suffrage planks, although the Democrats remained committed to woman suffrage through individual state action. In certain respects, the endorsement of Shafroth's Hawaiian bill was consistent with the notion that woman suffrage in Hawaii should be left to the people of Hawaii, just as woman suffrage in Mississippi should be left to the people of Mississippi. But in the context of the long history of Democratic opposition to woman suffrage experiments in the territories, the Hawaiian bill, like the Jones Act for Puerto Rico, marked two important national victories for woman suffrage that anticipated the Nineteenth Amendment. Suffragists celebrated the passage of the Hawaiian bill, but Alice Stone Blackwell, Henry Brown Blackwell's daughter, pointed out one of the more obvious ironies to suffragists who had followed the tortured congressional logic regarding woman suffrage in the territories since the nineteenth century. In 1918 it seemed likely that women in the Philippines and Puerto Rico might get the vote before women in many U.S. states. At the end of the day, women in Puerto Rico could be granted the vote by a simple act of the Puerto Rican legislature, whereas women in Hawaii needed the legislature to submit a referendum to the voters.

THE "NEW DEPARTURE" IN PUERTO RICO

In April 1920, just months before the ratification of the Nineteenth Amendment, the National Woman's Party paper *Suffragist* noted that while the new amendment would extend "a third of the way across the Pacific" and include the women of the Hawaiian Islands, the Nineteenth Amendment would not enfranchise women in the Philippines and Puerto Rico.[45] Puerto Rican suffragists were not so certain, and in August 1920, just after the ratification of the Nineteenth Amendment, the Puerto Rican suffragist Genera Pagán attempted to register to vote.[46] Pagán had resided in New York for a short time toward the close of World War I. It is unclear to what extent she came into contact with U.S. suffragists, but as a U.S. citizen living in New York when the Nineteenth Amendment passed the House and Senate in May and June 1919, she was entitled to vote in the state of New York, as were other U.S. women citizens. Puerto Rican legislators were no more certain than suffragists regarding the application of the Nineteenth Amendment to Puerto Rico, and the government of Puerto Rico appealed to the U.S. Bureau of Insular Affairs for clarification, which, in turn, looked to the office of the judge advocate general of the War Department for guidance.

The War Department was quite positive that the Nineteenth Amendment did not apply to Puerto Rico. As Judge Advocate General E. H. Crowder memorialized his colleagues at the Bureau of Insular Affairs, "In light of two decades of American rule in the tropics, it may be stated as an axiom of government of our dependent peoples that a prerequisite to efficiency is adherence to the doctrine of the non-applicability of the Constitution as a body of organic law to outlying possessions of the United States."[47] Crowder's opinion was not based solely on a "doctrine of efficiency," as he put it, but also on the actual text of the Nineteenth Amendment, which stated that "the right of citizens of the United States to vote shall not be denied or abridged by the United States or by any State on account of sex." Puerto Rico was not a state, but rather an "autonomous dependency" of the United States, and as such Crowder was confident that the applicability of the Constitution to Puerto Rico was a matter that required congressional action. In support of this view Crowder cited the Supreme Court's 1903 decision in *Hawaii v. Mankichi* to show that only "fundamental rights" become operational in colonial context. The Supreme Court had never positively defined an exhaustive list of fundamental rights; however, as Crowder noted, "American political history makes it clear that suffrage has never been regarded as a natural or fundamental right of the citizens." Indeed, Crowder continued, "Within the Union, [suffrage] is at the present time quite extensively restricted by education and property qualifications."[48] Crowder went on to cite among other cases the District of Columbia's Supreme Court decision in *Spencer v. Board of Registration*, which had emerged when Douglass accompanied suffragists to the polls in 1871, to show that "participation in the suffrage is not of right, but is granted by the state on a consideration of what is most for the interest of the state." The Nineteenth Amendment, he asserted, "has to do with something not a fundamental right in any sense," and as such did not apply in Puerto Rico.[49] Crowder's efforts to think through the question of Puerto Rican women's voting rights in terms both of the colonial relationship between the United States and Puerto Rico, and of U.S. voting rights within U.S. political history highlighted an important aspect of women's citizenship in the context of empire. In the case of voting rights, physical location in the colony of Puerto Rico trumped Puerto Rican women's status as U.S. citizens. If Pagán had remained in New York, she would have been enfranchised and entitled to vote in the state of New York or any other state under the terms of the Nineteenth Amendment, but by removing to Puerto Rico, she lost her right to vote because Puerto Rico's colonial status meant that Puerto Rico "need not be inhibited in its discriminations" as were other states.[50]

In 1924, a Puerto Rican suffragist again attempted to register to vote, and once again was denied on account of sex. This time, however, the Puerto Rican suffrage organization Liga Social Sufragista joined with the petitioner in appealing the case to the Puerto Rican Supreme Court. In its decision, that court echoed the opinion of the U.S. judge advocate general that the Nineteenth Amendment did not operate in Puerto Rico, and that voting was not a fundamental right of U.S. citizenship. The Puerto Rican Supreme Court added the case of *Minor v. Happersett* (1875) to the list of U.S. legal precedents which established that voting was not a natural right, but rather regulated in ways "peculiar to Anglo-Saxon jurisprudence."[51]

U.S. suffragists in the continental United States had not been aware of the decision of the judge advocate general with regard to the case of the Genera Pagán, and thus they missed the beginnings of what might be characterized as the Puerto Rican New Departure. But they followed the case of *Morales et al. v. Board of Registration* with great interest, and in 1925, when the Liga Social Sufragista of Puerto Rico requested affiliation with the NWP, NWP suffragists responded enthusiastically.[52] The NWP had introduced the equal rights amendment into Congress in 1923 as part of its plan to extend the Nineteenth Amendment's protection of women's voting rights to other areas of law in which U.S. women experienced discrimination on account of sex. In 1925, NWP activists considered the question of votes for women in Puerto Rico as part of their work for "equal rights for all women subject to the jurisdiction of the United States."[53] In May, NWP vice president Margaret Whittemore cabled Antonio Barcelo, the president of the Puerto Rican assembly, that the "National Woman's Party of United States is gravely concerned at continued disfranchisement of Porto Rican women citizens of the United States and call [*sic*] upon you to insert the word female wherever necessary in the election law to give Porto Rican women their right to vote by act of this legislature."[54] NWP activists also cabled the U.S. colonial governor, Horace Towner: "National Woman's Party uniting with Porto Rican women expect you as official United States representative to use all possible power to gain full immediate suffrage for women of Porto Rico in this legislative session."[55] In 1925, Towner was a well-known supporter of women's rights, who four years earlier had helped pass the Sheppard-Towner Act, which gave federal funds to provide for infant and maternal health. Towner responded favorably and agreed to push for woman suffrage in Puerto Rico as long as literacy tests were made a prerequisite for voting. Towner's position on literacy tests echoed the opinion of those members of the Puerto Rican legislature who favored woman suffrage.

While Puerto Rican suffragists pursued the question of votes for women in Puerto Rico, in February 1927, NWP suffragists with the aid of Connecticut Republican John Bingham introduced a woman suffrage amendment to the 1917 Puerto Rican Jones Act that had governed the territory for a decade.[56] Between the introduction of the NWP's Puerto Rican woman suffrage amendment in February 1927 and the April 1928 hearings before the Committee on Territories and Insular Possessions, NWP members met with delegates from the Puerto Rican legislature, including Antonio Barcelo and Jose Soto, the president of the Puerto Rican House, when they visited D.C. in June 1927. During this meeting at D.C.'s Roosevelt Hotel between NWP suffragists and Puerto Rican legislative delegates, NWP members announced that "if the legislature of Porto Rico did not give the vote to Porto Rican women on the same terms as men, the National Woman's Party would undertake to secure it for them by act of Congress."[57] Barcelo had already introduced a woman suffrage bill into the Puerto Rican legislature, but this bill included literacy requirements for the vote. Barcelo told the NWP that he "would greatly regret" their action, "as the extension of the franchise is a matter for Porto Rico itself to determine," and that Puerto Rican women "trusted their [own] legislature and would be unwilling to have Congress enfranchise them."[58] The NWP's Burnita Shelton Matthews was unimpressed by Barcelo's claim that the enfranchisement of Puerto Rican women was a question for Puerto Rico. After all, the successful struggle for a federal woman suffrage amendment within the United States had been waged precisely against this way of thinking, and the passage of the Nineteenth Amendment meant that theoretically the question of woman suffrage was no longer a local question for Mississippi, or Virginia, or Massachusetts to decide on its own. To Matthews, Barcelo's position was simply an attenuated version of the anti–woman suffrage, states' rights argument that suffragists had heard voiced in opposition to their cause for more than fifty years.

The issues raised at the June 1927 meeting were left unresolved, but they served as the outline for the discussions that took place at the formal hearings before Congress the following April. On April 25, 1928, the U.S. Senate Committee on Territories and Insular Possessions held hearings on Senate Bill 753, "to amend the organic act of Porto Rico so as to provide that the right to vote shall not be denied or abridged on account of sex."[59] Attending the hearing that day were several representatives of the NWP; Felix Cordova Davila, the resident nonvoting representative of the Puerto Rican legislature in Congress; the Puerto Rican suffragists Marta Robert, director of the San Juan Maternity Hospital, and Rosa Emanuelli, a San Juan schoolteacher. Also in attendance were two members of the U.S. patriot groups the Sentinels of the Republic, and the Woman Patriot Publishing Company. These two organizations stood opposed to the Fourteenth Amendment, the Nineteenth Amendment, and the equal rights amendment.[60] At this hearing, Marta Robert and Rosa Emanuelli made the case that since the U.S. Congress had authored the Puerto Rican Organic Act, Congress was the proper site for any changes to the governing structure of Puerto Rico. In this view, woman suffrage was considered less a technical aspect of local election law than as foundational to the structure of

U.S. citizenship itself. This was much the same argument that Stanton had made in 1870 when she asked Congress to include woman suffrage in its new government bill for D.C. Robert and Emanuelli felt certain that if the 1917 Jones Act had been passed after the Nineteenth Amendment, Puerto Rico's ability to limit the franchise to men would have become unconstitutional. They believed that it was simply an accident of history that the Jones bill for Puerto Rico preceded this foundational change in U.S. constitutional law. As a practical measure, Puerto Rican suffragists had been willing to accept the restricted franchise offered by Barcelo, but because the Puerto Rican House had rejected Barcelo's bill for literate woman suffrage, Puerto Rican suffragists wanted equal rights made part of the Puerto Rican Jones bill; hence their appeal to the U.S. Congress. As Robert pointed out, if a Puerto Rican woman moved to the continental U.S., within six months she would become a voter in the state in which she resided; "the only thing that prohibits us from going to Porto Rico and voting and exercising our electoral right is just a little injustice from our men when they make the electoral law in Porto Rico."[61] To Emanuelli, a congressional amendment to the Jones bill for Puerto Rico would be a statement that Puerto Rican women were as much U.S. citizens as other U.S. women, that "as American citizens we are in the same position as women in the United States."[62]

It was precisely this desire to see Puerto Rico as like other U.S. states that informed Commissioner Davila's opposition. Davila was extremely careful not to frame the case against a woman suffrage amendment to the Jones bill for Puerto Rico as an assertion of Puerto Rican nationalism, although despite his best efforts, this was an implicit part of the Puerto Rican legislature's opposition to the amendment. As Davila explained, he personally was "very strongly in favor of woman suffrage." When asked by Senator Millard Tydings whether or not this amendment would be considered an act of interference in the local affairs of Puerto Rico, Davila responded that "Congress should not legislate in Porto Rican local matters," although he conceded that Congress had the power to do so. "I am the official representative of the people of Porto Rico here," Davila explained to the committee, and while personally in favor of woman suffrage, he was compelled "to maintain the principle that the Porto Rican people only are entitled to handle this matter."[63] These were dangerous waters, and neither Davila nor Chairman Bingham was fully prepared to engage in a debate over Puerto Rico's final status through the question of woman suffrage. Apologizing for the turn that the hearings had taken, Bingham brought them to a close.

In December 1928, the U.S. House voted to amend the Jones bill for Puerto Rico so as to grant woman suffrage, and in January 1929, Bingham reintroduced the question in the Senate.[64] The hearings before the Committee on Territories and Insular Possessions had produced both a majority report in favor of enfranchising Puerto Rican women and a minority report against. On February 11, 1929, when the Senate took up the discussion, it looked likely that the Senate, like the House, would vote to amend the Puerto Rican Jones bill in favor of woman suffrage, although the debate rehearsed both sides of the question.[65] Historian Gladys Jiménez-Muños suggests that by the spring of 1929, male legislators in Puerto Rico could see the "writing on the wall."[66] Despite their resentment at what looked to be "yet another case of federal usurpation of island authority," on April 16, 1929, the Puerto Rican legislature anticipated any action by the U.S. Congress and enfranchised literate women in Puerto Rico.[67] This action by the Puerto Rican legislature may have forestalled the imposition of woman suffrage on the island as an overt act of colonial rule, but by 1929, woman suffrage had clearly become a contested issue in the emerging politics of Puerto Rican nationalism.

In 1912, when U.S. suffragists shifted their energies back to the federal woman suffrage amendment, congressional discussions over the government and status of the Philippines and Puerto Rico were crucial to their ability to raise the question of votes for women at the national level in the age of Jim Crow. When suffragists and their allies attempted to attach woman suffrage amendments to the Jones bills for the Philippines and Puerto Rico, they were employing a strategy that dated back to the 1870s and the formative years of the U.S. woman suffrage movement. But in the context of U.S. empire, attaching woman suffrage amendments to the governing bills for U.S. territory helped suffragists and their legislative allies squash the states' right framework that had circumscribed suffragists' activities for decades. If the nineteenth-century U.S. women's movement had long succeeded in making the case that "domesticity" was crucial to the advancement of civilization and the success of American democracy, by 1929, suffragists were on the verge of making women's voting rights an integral part of U.S. colonial policy. Puerto Rican men's decision to enfranchise literate women forestalled this event in the short term, but the outlines for how woman suffrage might become a contested issue in the politics of nationalism were already beginning to emerge.

EPILOGUE

In 1890, when the anti–woman suffrage senator George Graham Vest of Mississippi protested Congress's decision to admit Wyoming Territory and its women voters into the Union, he claimed that he was being asked "to overturn our Anglo-Saxon civilization and to build up a new one upon the idea of woman suffrage."[1] To Vest, woman suffrage posed a threat to "Anglo-Saxon civilization" because suffragists wanted to break down the barriers between men's and women's proper spheres, and Vest believed that in civilized societies politics was a masculine space reserved for Anglo-Saxon men. By 1928, when Frank Towner, the U.S. colonial governor of Puerto Rico, lent his support to National Woman's Party activists as they endeavored to push Congress to enfranchise Puerto Rican women, woman suffrage was well on its way to becoming a benchmark of progress and the successful expansion of democratic values in the context of U.S. empire.

Mina Roces has demonstrated how this story was played out in a similar fashion in the Philippines during the 1930s. In 1933, the all male Filipino assembly, like the Puerto Rican legislature before it, reluctantly voted to enfranchise Filipina women. The U.S. colonial governor of the Philippines supported woman suffrage as one way of establishing the readiness of the Philippines for independent self-government. Unfortunately for Filipina suffragists, this pro-woman suffrage measure was only one section of a larger Administrative Code for the Philippines that ultimately did not pass the U.S. Congress. As a result, in 1935 when the Tydings-McDuffie Act laid out a plan for Filipino independence from the United States, Filipina suffragists were put in the position of trying to convince legislators all over again to vote for woman suffrage. As Roces explains, "For Filipino women, supporting the nationalist project meant lobbying for a government that would disenfranchise them as women."[2] Like Puerto Rican suffragists before them, Filipina activists discovered that votes for women might come to them more quickly in the context of U.S. colonial rule than under a new nationalist government. In the Filipino case, conceding the right to legislate women's political rights to local legislative bodies, rather than enforcing woman suffrage, softened the bite of imperial power relations by serving as a bargaining chip for reasserting some degree of political independence for men.

At different moments across the late nineteenth and early twentieth centuries, U.S. suffragists discovered that U.S. expansion had the potential to raise the woman question in Congress. Turning western territories into new states and governing territorial acquisitions accrued through the war with Spain, put the question of voting rights on the national agenda. For suffragists who came of age during Reconstruction, U.S. expansion and empire thus provided an important intellectual and political context for lifting the woman suffrage question out of the states' rights framework that had structured thinking about the woman question since the Civil War.

U.S. imperial ventures provided many activist women with the opportunity to link themselves with the project of exporting the Anglo-Saxon civilizing mission overseas and creating a public role for themselves as agents of American culture on a global stage. But even more importantly, expansion provided a forum in which suffragists could transform cultural arguments for women's power into more specific demands for women's votes. The process of creating new territorial constitutions, whether in the continental west or overseas, forced national conversations about the meaning and content of national citizenship and between 1870 and 1930, many U.S. suffragists intended to make voting rights crucial to the definition of American citizenship.

In 1920, suffragists were only partially successful. The Nineteenth Amendment failed to turn Puerto Rican women citizens into voters and it did not protect the voting rights of African American women citizens at home. But if suffragists failed to make suffrage and citizenship synonymous terms they did succeed in adding political rights for women to the list of markers symbolizing the achievement of "civilization" on a global stage. In the negotiation of global power relations across the twentieth century and into the present, political rights for women continue to function as a marker of success for experiments in expanding democracy. Conversely, conceding the right to legislate women's political rights to local legislative bodies often serves to soften the bite of imperial power relations and remains an important bargaining chip for reasserting some degree of political independence for men.

NOTES

CHAPTER 1: U.S. EXPANSION AND THE WOMAN QUESTION, 1870–1929

1. Julia Ward Howe celebrated her eightieth birthday on May 27, 1899. Blackwell's remarks were published in a special issue of the *Woman's Journal* brought out on that date to celebrate the event. Henry Brown Blackwell, *Woman's Journal*, 27 May 1899; Laura Elizabeth Howe Richards, Maud Howe Elliott, and Florence Howe Hall *Julia Ward Howe, 1819–1910* (Boston: Houghton Mifflin, 1925), 357. A draft of Blackwell's remarks can be found in his papers with a slight variation; "We were all annexationists then." Henry Brown Blackwell, 1873 [1899], Blackwell Family Papers, Library of Congress, Manuscript Division [BFP, LCMD]. Someone other than Henry Brown Blackwell misdated this unpublished manuscript at 1873.

2. The Samana Bay Company was incorporated in December 1872. Henry Brown Blackwell wrote his brother George that he and Samuel Howe had each contracted for $5,000 dollars of company stock. Henry Brown Blackwell to George Blackwell, 14 December 1872, Blackwell Family Papers, MC-411, Schlesinger Library, Radcliffe Institute [BFS-411]. After the Samana Bay Company failed in 1874, Samuel Gridley Howe recorded his own version of these events in a sixty-seven-page account written, he told Blackwell, as a "duty to historical truth, to the interests of Santo Domingo, and to my own good name." Samuel Gridley Howe to Henry Brown Blackwell, 6 September 1874, Howe Papers, Hayes Research Library, Perkins School, Watertown, MA [Perkins]; Samuel Gridley Howe, "My Experiences in Santo Domingo," 1874, Howe Papers, Perkins. See also "Santo Domingo and Samana Bay," in Harold Schwartz, *Samuel Gridley Howe: Social Reformer, 1801–1876* (Cambridge, MA: Harvard University Press, 1956), 291–320.

3. Henry Brown Blackwell, *Woman's Journal*, 27 May 1899.

4. "As a loyal American citizen, believing in our 'self-evident truths,' my sympathies are with the so-called 'insurgents' who are now compelled to regard our fleet and army as invaders." Henry Brown Blackwell, "The Philippines for the Filipinos," *Woman's Journal*, 14 January 1899.

5. Allison L. Sneider, "The Impact of Empire on the North American Woman Suffrage Movement: Suffrage Racism in an Imperial Context," *UCLA Historical Journal* 14 (1994): 14–32; Kristin Hoganson, "'As Badly Off as the Filipinos': U.S. Women's Suffragists and the Imperial Issue at the Turn of the Twentieth Century," *Journal of Women's History* 13 (2001): 9–33.

6. Henry Brown Blackwell, *Woman's Journal*, 27 May 1899.

7. Ibid.

8. U.S. Congress, Senate, Committee on Territories and Insular Possessions, *Woman Suffrage in Puerto Rico, Hearing on S. 753*, 70th Cong., 1st sess., 25 April 1928. See also Gladys M. Jiménez-Muñoz, "Deconstructing Colonialist Discourse: Links between the Women's Suffrage Movement in the United States and Puerto Rico," *Phoebe: An Interdisciplinary Journal of Feminist Scholarship, Theory, and Aesthetics* 5 (1993): 9–34; Gladys M. Jiménez-Muñoz, "Literacy, Class, and Sexuality in the Debate on Women's Suffrage in Puerto Rico during the 1920s," in Félix V. Matos Rodríguez and Linda C. Delgado, eds., *Puerto Rican Women's History: New Perspectives* (Armonk, NY: Sharpe, 1998), 143–70; Isabel Picó, "The History of Women's Struggle for Equality in Puerto Rico," in Edna Acosta-Belén, ed., *The Puerto Rican Woman: Perspectives on Culture, History, and Society*, 2nd ed. (New York: Praeger, 1986), 46–58.

9. George Graham Vest, *Congressional Record*, 51st Cong., 1st sess., 26 March 1890, 2671.

10. A good introduction to the long history of U.S. "imperial democracy" is Michael Ignatieff, "Who Are Americans to Think That Freedom Is Theirs to Spread?" *New York Times Magazine*, 26 June 2005. See also Ernest R. May, *Imperial Democracy: The Emergence of America as a Great Power* (New York: Harcourt, Brace and World, 1961); William Appleman Williams, *The Contours of American History* (Cleveland, Ohio: World Publishing, 1961); William Appleman Williams, *Empire as a Way of Life: An Essay on the Causes and Character of America's Present Predicament along with a Few Thoughts about an Alternative* (New York: Oxford University Press, 1980).

11. Important exceptions to this rule in the U.S. case include Sandra Stanley Holton, " 'To Educate Women into Rebellion': Elizabeth Cady Stanton and the Creation of a Transatlantic Network of Radical Suffragists," *American Historical Review* 99 (1994): 1112–36; Rosalyn Terborg-Penn, "Enfranchising Women of Color: Woman Suffragists as Agents of Imperialism," in Ruth Roach Pierson and Nupur Chaudhuri, eds., *Nation, Empire, Colony: Historicizing Gender and Race* (Bloomington: Indiana University Press, 1998), 41–56; Ellen Carol DuBois, "Woman Suffrage around the World: Three Phases of Suffragist Internationalism," in Caroline Daley and Melanie Nolan, eds., *Suffrage and Beyond: International Feminist Perspectives* (New York: New York University Press, 1994), 252–74; Ellen Carol DuBois, "Woman Suffrage and the Left: An International Socialist-Feminist Perspective," *New Left Review* 186 (1991): 20–45; Leila J. Rupp, *Worlds of Women: The Making of an International Women's Movement* (Princeton, NJ: Princeton University Press, 1997); Leila Rupp, "Constructing Internationalism: The Case of the Transnational Women's Organizations, 1888–1945," *American Historical Review* 99 (1994): 1571–1600; Hoganson, " 'As Badly Off as the Filipinos,' " 9–33; Sneider, "Impact of Empire on the North American Woman Suffrage Movement," 14–32; Jiménez-Muñoz, "Deconstructing Colonialist Discourse."

12. "All persons born or naturalized in the United States and subject to the jurisdiction thereof, are citizens of the United States and of the State wherein they reside. No State shall make or enforce any law which shall abridge the privileges or immunities

of citizens of the United States; nor shall any State deprive any person of life, liberty, or property, without due process of law; nor deny to any person within its jurisdiction the equal protection of the law." Article 14, Section 1, *Constitution of the United States of America* (adopted 1868); "The right of citizens of the United States to vote shall not be denied or abridged by the United States or by any State on account of race, color, or previous condition of servitude." Article 15, Section 1, *Constitution of the United States of America* (adopted 1870).

13. On the founding of the American Woman Suffrage Association and the National American Woman Suffrage Association, see Eleanor Flexner, *Century of Struggle: The Woman's Rights Movement in the United States*, rev. ed. (1959; Cambridge, MA: Belknap Press, 1975); Aileen S. Kraditor, *The Ideas of the Woman Suffrage Movement, 1890–1920* (New York: Columbia University Press, 1965); Ellen Carol DuBois, *Feminism and Suffrage: The Emergence of an Independent Women's Movement in America, 1848–1869* (Ithaca, NY: Cornell University Press, 1978); Rosalyn Terborg-Penn, *African American Women in the Struggle for the Vote, 1850–1920* (Bloomington: Indiana University Press, 1998); Ann D. Gordon, "Woman Suffrage (Not Universal Suffrage) by Federal Amendment," in Marjorie Spruill Wheeler, ed., *Votes for Women! The Woman Suffrage Movement in Tennessee, the South, and the Nation* (Knoxville: University of Tennessee Press, 1995), 3–24.

14. See, for example, Anna Garlin Spencer, "Duty to the Women of Our New Possessions," (1899), Elizabeth Cady Stanton, Susan B. Anthony, Matilda Joslyn Gage, and Ida Husted Harper, eds., *History of Woman Suffrage*, 6 vols. (1881–1922; reprint, New York: Arno Press, 1969) [*HWS*], 4:328–31.

15. Jean Fagan Yellin, *Women and Sisters: The Antislavery Feminists in American Culture* (New Haven, CT: Yale University Press, 1989); Michael D. Pierson, *Free Hearts and Free Homes: Gender and American Anti-slavery Politics* (Chapel Hill: University of North Carolina Press, 2003); Gerda Lerner, *The Feminist Thought of Sarah Grimké* (New York: Oxford University Press, 1998); Shirley J. Yee, *Black Women Abolitionists: A Study in Activism 1828–1860* (Knoxville: University of Tennessee Press, 1992).

16. *Minor v. Happersett*, 21 Wallace 162 (1875).

17. An important overview of restrictive franchise legislation across the states is Alexander Keyssar, *The Right to Vote: The Contested History of Democracy in the United States* (New York: Basic Books, 2000). See also Michael McGerr, *The Decline of Popular Politics: The American North, 1865–1928* (New York: Oxford University Press, 1986); Robert Wiebe, *Self-Rule: A Cultural History of American Democracy* (Chicago: University of Chicago Press, 1995).

18. See, for example, Christopher Lasch, "The Anti-imperialists, the Philippines, and the Inequality of Man," *Journal of Southern History* 24 (1958): 319–31; Robert L. Beisner, *Twelve against Empire: The Anti-imperialists, 1898–1900* (New York: McGraw-Hill, 1968); Richard Welch Jr., *Response to Imperialism: The United States and the Philippine-American War, 1899–1902* (Chapel Hill: University of North Carolina Press, 1979).

19. Federal authority to govern territory in the continental West began with the Ordinance of 1774, which set up temporary measures for congressional oversight of western lands ceded to the United States by individual colonies under the Articles

of Confederation. The Northwest Ordinance (1787) set the terms for the future settlement and admission of territories as new states. Article 4, Section 3 of the U.S. Constitution gave Congress the power to "dispose of and make all needful rules and regulations respecting the territory or other property belonging to the Unites States," and to admit new states into the Union. Throughout the nineteenth century, Congress admitted new states into the Union based on the terms set forth in the 1787 ordinance. See Gary Lawson and Guy Seidman, *The Constitution of Empire: Territorial Expansion and American Legal History* (New Haven, CT: Yale University Press, 2004).

20. See, for example, Reginald Horsman, *Race and Manifest Destiny: The Origins of American Racial Anglo-Saxonism* (Cambridge, MA: Harvard University Press, 1981); Gretchen Murphy, *Hemispheric Imaginings: The Monroe Doctrine and Narratives of U.S. Empire* (Durham, NC: Duke University Press, 2005).

21. Henry Brown Blackwell to Charles Sumner, 20 November 1871, BFP, LCMD.

22. On women's citizenship as a contested category for woman's rights activists, see Candice Lewis Bredbenner, *A Nationality of Her Own: Women, Marriage, and the Law of Citizenship* (Berkeley and Los Angeles: University of California Press, 1998); Linda Kerber, *No Constitutional Right to Be Ladies: Women and the Obligations of Citizenship* (New York: Hill and Wang, 1998); Nancy Isenberg, *Sex and Citizenship in Antebellum America* (Chapel Hill: University of North Carolina Press, 1998); Rogers Smith, " 'One United People': Second-Class Female Citizenship and the American Quest for Community," *Yale Journal of Law and the Humanities* 1 (1989): 229–73; Lori Ginzberg, *Untidy Origins: A Story of Woman's Rights in Antebellum New York* (Chapel Hill: University of North Carolina Press, 2005).

23. Carrie Chapman Catt, "Our New Responsibilities," *Woman's Journal*, 1 October 1898.

24. The general outline of Henry Brown Blackwell's involvement in Santo Domingo appears in Leslie Wheeler, ed., *Loving Warriors: Selected Letters of Lucy Stone and Henry B. Blackwell, 1853 to 1893* (New York: Dial Press, 1981), 235–37; Andrea Moore Kerr, *Lucy Stone: Speaking Out for Equality* (New Brunswick, NJ: Rutgers University Press, 1992), 162, 170; Samuel Gridley Howe to Henry Brown Blackwell, 6 September 1874, Howe Papers, Perkins; Samuel Gridley Howe, "My Experiences in Santo Domingo," 1874, Howe Papers, Perkins; "Santo Domingo and Samana Bay," 291–320.

25. John L. Comaroff and Jean Comaroff's effort to systemize the multiple meanings of "colonialism" across a range of disciplinary practices is an extraordinarily useful introduction to the difficulty of defining this term in the abstract. See John L. Comaroff and Jean Comaroff, *Of Revelation and Revolution: The Dialectics of Modernity on a South African Frontier*, vol. 2 (Chicago: University of Chicago Press, 1997), 15–29. See also Ann Laura Stoler and Fredrick Cooper, "Between Metropole and Colony: Rethinking a Research Agenda," in Ann Laura Stoler and Fredrick Cooper, eds., *Tensions of Empire: Colonial Cultures in a Bourgeois World* (Berkeley and Los Angeles: University of California Press, 1997), 1–56.

26. Christina Duffy Burnett and Burke Marshall, "Between the Foreign and the Domestic: The Doctrine of Territorial Incorporation, Invented and Reinvented," in

Christina Duffy Burnett and Burke Marshall, eds., *Foreign in a Domestic Sense: Puerto Rico, American Expansion, and the Constitution* (Durham, NC: Duke University Press, 2001), 13.

27. Kraditor, *Ideas of the Woman Suffrage Movement*; Rosalyn Terborg-Penn, "Discrimination against Afro-American Women in the Woman's Movement, 1830–1920," in Sharon Harley and Rosalyn Terborg-Penn, eds., *The Afro-American Woman: Struggles and Images* (Port Washington, NY: Kennikat Press, 1978); Suzanne Lebsock, "Woman Suffrage and White Supremacy: A Virginia Case Study," in Nancy A. Hewitt and Suzanne Lebsock, eds., *Visible Women: New Essays on American Activism* (Urbana: University of Illinois Press, 1993); Glenda Elizabeth Gilmore, *Gender and Jim Crow: Women and the Politics of White Supremacy in North Carolina, 1896–1920* (Chapel Hill: University of North Carolina Press, 1996); Sarah Hunter Graham, *Woman Suffrage and the New Democracy* (New Haven, CT: Yale University Press, 1996).

28. Gordon, "Woman Suffrage (Not Universal Suffrage) by Federal Amendment," 3.

29. See, for example, Suzanne M. Marilley, *Woman Suffrage and the Origins of Liberal Feminism in the United States, 1820–1920* (Cambridge, MA: Harvard University Press, 1996).

30. Louise Newman, *White Women's Rights: The Racial Origins of Feminism in the United States* (New York: Oxford University Press, 1999).

31. Ibid., 8.

32. Kevin K. Gaines, *Uplifting the Race: Black Leadership, Politics, and Culture in the Twentieth Century* (Chapel Hill: University of North Carolina Press, 1996); Nell Irvin Painter, *Standing at Armageddon: The United States 1877–1919* (New York: Norton, 1987); Stephanie J. Shaw, *What a Woman Ought to Be and Do: Black Professional Women Workers during the Jim Crow Era* (Chicago: University of Chicago Press, 1996); Paula Giddings, *When and Where I Enter: The Impact of Black Women on Race and Sex in America* (New York: Bantam Books, 1984).

33. Joan Jacobs Brumberg, "Zenanas and Girlless Villages: The Ethnology of American Evangelical Women, 1870–1910," *Journal of American History* 69 (1982): 347–71.

34. "Women Are for Peace," *Washington Post*, 16 February 1899; Susan B. Anthony to Clara Colby, 24 January 1899, Clara Beckwith Colby Collection, Huntington Library, CA, in Patricia G. Holland and Ann D. Gordon, eds., *Papers of Elizabeth Cady Stanton and Susan B. Anthony* (Wilmington, DE: Scholarly Resources, 1991, microfilm) [ECS/SBA Film] ser. 3.

35. This is a voluminous literature, but see, for example, Ann Laura Stoler, *Carnal Knowledge and Imperial Power: Race and the Intimate in Colonial Rule* (Berkeley and Los Angeles: University of California Press, 2002); Lora Wildenthal, *German Women for Empire, 1884–1945* (Durham, NC: Duke University Press, 2001); Catherine Hall, *Civilising Subjects: Metropole and Colony in the English Imagination, 1830–1867* (New York: Oxford University Press, 2002).

36. Antoinette Burton, *Burdens of History: British Feminists, Indian Women, and Imperial Culture, 1865–1915* (Chapel Hill: University of North Carolina Press, 1994); Catherine Hall, "The Nation Within and Without," in Catherine Hall, Keith McClelland, and Jane Rendall, *Defining the Victorian Nation: Class, Race, Gender and the Reform Act of 1867*

(Cambridge: Cambridge University Press, 2000), 179–233; Jane Rendall, "The Citizenship of Women and the Reform Act of 1867," in Hall, McClelland, and Rendall, *Defining the Victorian Nation*, 119–78; Jane Rendall, "Citizenship, Culture, and Civilization: The Languages of British Suffragists, 1866–1874," in Caroline Daley and Melanie Noland, eds., *Suffrage and Beyond: International Feminist Perspectives* (New York: New York University Press, 1994), 127–50; Patricia Grimshaw, "Women's Suffrage in New Zealand Revisited: Writing from the Margins," in Daley and Nolan, *Suffrage and Beyond*, 25–41; Raewyn Dalziel, "Presenting the Enfranchisement of New Zealand Women," in Daley and Nolan, *Suffrage and Beyond*, 42–66; Laura Nym Mayhall, "The South African War and the Origins of Suffrage Militancy in Britain," in Ian Christopher Fletcher, Laura Nym Mayhall, and Phillipa Levine, eds., *Women's Suffrage in the British Empire: Citizenship, Nation, and Race* (London: Routledge, 2000), 3–17; Ian Christopher Fletcher, " 'Women of the Nations, Unite!': Transnational Suffragism in the United Kingdom, 1912–1914," in Fletcher, Mayhall, and Levine, *Women's Suffrage in the British Empire*, 103–20; Mrinalini Sinha, "Suffragism and Internationalism: The Enfranchisement of British and Indian Women under an Imperial State," in Fletcher, Mayhall, and Levine, *Women's Suffrage in the British Empire*, 224–40.

37. Burton, *Burdens of History*, 10.

38. Paul A. Kramer, "The Darkness That Enters the Home: The Politics of Prostitution during the Philippine-American War," in Ann Laura Stoler, ed., *Haunted by Empire: Geographies of Intimacy in North American History* (Durham, NC: Duke University Press, 2006), 366–404; Ian Tyrrell, *Woman's World/Woman's Empire: The Woman's Christian Temperance Union in International Perspective, 1800–1930* (Chapel Hill: University of North Carolina Press, 1991), 200–227.

39. Catherine Hall, Keith McClelland, and Jane Rendall, *Defining the Victorian Nation: Class, Race, Gender and the Reform Act of 1867* (Cambridge: Cambridge University Press, 2000).

40. Ibid., 5.

41. Kristin Hoganson, *Fighting for American Manhood: How Gender Politics Provoked the Spanish-American and Philippine-American Wars* (New Haven, CT: Yale University Press, 1998); Mary Renda, *Taking Haiti: Military Occupation and the Culture of U.S. Imperialism* (Chapel Hill: University of North Carolina Press, 2001); Laura Briggs, *Reproducing Empire: Race, Sex, Science and U.S. Imperialism in Puerto Rico* (Berkeley and Los Angeles: University of California Press, 2002).

42. In a series of legal cases decided between 1901 and 1922, known collectively as the *Insular Cases*, the U.S. Supreme Court formulated a constitutional doctrine by which the United States could acquire and govern territory without the consent of the inhabitants and without the intention of turning this territory into new states. See Efrén Rivera Ramos, "Deconstructing Colonialism: The 'Unincorporated Territory' as a Category of Domination," in Burnett and Marshall, *Foreign in a Domestic Sense*, 104–20; Rogers Smith, *Civic Ideals: Conflicting Visions of Citizenship in U.S. History* (New Haven, CT: Yale University Press, 1997).

43. Sarah Barringer Gordon, *The Mormon Question: Polygamy and Constitutional Conflict in Nineteenth-Century America* (Chapel Hill: University of North Carolina Press, 2002);

Ellen Carol DuBois, "Taking the Law into Our Own Hands: *Bradwell, Minor,* and Suffrage Militance in the 1870s," in Nancy Hewitt and Suzanne Lebsock eds., *Visible Women: New Essays on American Activism* (Urbana: University of Illinois Press, 1993); Nancy Cott, *Public Vows: A History of Marriage and the Nation* (Cambridge, MA: Harvard University Press, 2000). See also Kerber, *No Constitutional Right to Be Ladies.*

CHAPTER 2: RECONSTRUCTION AND ANNEXATION

1. "Treaty Celebrated between the United States of America and the Dominican Republic, for the Incorporation of the Second with the First, 29 November 1869," Sen. Ex. Doc. No. 17, 41st Cong., 3rd sess., 16 January 1871.

2. Allan Nevins, *Hamilton Fish: The Inner History of the Grant Administration,* 2 vols., rev. ed. (1936; New York: Frederick Ungar Publishing Co., 1957); William S. McFeely, *Grant: A Biography* (New York: Norton, 1981); Robert Beisner, "Thirty Years before Manila: E. L. Godkin, Carl Schurz, and Anti-imperialism in the Gilded Age," *Historian* 30 (1968): 561–77; Harold T. Pinkett, "Efforts to Annex Santo Domingo to the United States, 1866–1871," *Journal of Negro History* 26 (1941): 12–45; Jeannette P. Nichols, "The United States Congress and Imperialism, 1861–1897," *Journal of Economic History* 21 (1961): 526–38; Eric Foner, *Reconstruction: America's Unfinished Revolution, 1863–1877* (New York: Harper and Row, 1988). 494–99; Charles C. Tansill, *The United States and Santo Domingo, 1798–1873: A Chapter in Caribbean Diplomacy* (Baltimore: Johns Hopkins University Press, 1938); Melvin M. Knight, *The Americans in Santo Domingo* (New York: Vanguard Press, 1928).

3. David Donald, *Charles Sumner and the Rights of Man* (New York: Knopf, 1970); Beverly Wilson Palmer, ed., *The Selected Letters of Charles Sumner, 1811–1874* (Boston: Northeastern University Press, 1990); Robert Beisner, *Twelve against Empire: The Anti-imperialists, 1898–1900* (New York: McGraw-Hill, 1968); Beisner, *From the Old Diplomacy to the New, 1865–1900* (Chicago: Harlan Davidson, 1986).

4. "Annexation of St. Domingo," *Daily National Republican* (Washington, DC), 26 January 1871.

5. Hearing, House and Senate Committees on the District of Columbia, 22 January 1870, *HWS* 2:411–18; "Woman Suffrage at Washington," *New York Tribune,* 24 January 1870, ECS/SBA Film ser. 3; "The Reception of the Delegates of the Woman Convention by the Committee of the District of Columbia," *Press* (Philadelphia), 24 January 1870, ECS/SBA Film ser. 3; "The Women and Congress," *World* (New York), 23 January 1870, ECS/SBA Film ser. 3; *National Republican* (Washington), 24 January 1870, ECS/SBA Film ser. 3; "Woman Suffrage," *Daily Morning Chronicle* (Washington, DC), 24 January 1870, ECS/SBA Film ser. 3. On January 26, 1869, Susan B. Anthony was granted a hearing before the Senate Committee on the District of Columbia by Senator Harlan, *HWS* 2:363.

6. On the gender-based ideology of postwar Republicanism, see Rebecca Edwards, *Angels in the Machinery: Gender and American Party Politics from the Civil War to the Progressive Era* (New York: Oxford University Press, 1997); Elsa Barkley Brown, "To Catch

the Vision of Freedom: Reconstructing Southern Black Women's Political History, 1865–1880," in Ann D. Gordon and Bettye Collier-Thomas, eds., *African American Women and the Vote, 1837–1965* (Amherst: University of Massachusetts Press, 1997), 66–99. On the Republican Party as a home for women partisans, see Melanie Gustafson, *Women and the Republican Party, 1854–1924* (Urbana: University of Illinois Press, 2001), Lisa Gail Materson, "Respectable Partisans: African American Women in Electoral Politics, 1877–1936" (Ph.D. diss., UCLA, 2000).

7. "Woman Suffrage at Washington," *New York Tribune*, 24 January 1870; "The Women and Congress," *World* (New York), 23 January 1870; "Female Suffrage for the District," *National Republican* (Washington, DC), 24 January 1870, ECS/SBA Film ser. 3.

8. Fannie Howland, *Hartford Courant*, 22 January 1870, reprinted in *HWS* 2:416–18.

9. Elizabeth Cady Stanton to Gerrit Smith, 25 January 1870, Smith Papers, Syracuse University Libraries, Syracuse, NY, in Ann D. Gordon, ed., *The Selected Papers of Elizabeth Cady Stanton and Susan B. Anthony: Against an Aristocracy of Sex, 1866 to 1873*, vol. 2 [ECS/ SBA Papers 2] (New Brunswick, NJ: Rutgers University Press, 2000), 299–300. "Woman Suffrage at Washington," *New York Tribune*, 24 January 1870, ECS/SBA Film ser. 3. Stanton had good cause for complaint; the *Tribune*'s New York correspondent described the suffragists as "dowdy" and as "outraged lingerers" but gave scant attention to their arguments. "The Reception of the Delegates of the Woman Convention by the Committee of the District of Columbia," *Press* (Philadelphia), 24 January 1870, ECS/SBA Film ser. 3; Emily Edson Briggs, *The Olivia Letters: Being Some History of Washington City for Forty Years as Told by the Letters of a Newspaper Correspondent* (New York: Neale, 1906), 157–63.

10. Elizabeth Cady Stanton and Susan B. Anthony are the subjects of numerous biographies. A wonderful introduction to their lives and work, and to the antebellum suffrage cohort generally, is Ann D. Gordon, ed., *The Selected Papers of Elizabeth Cady Stanton and Susan B. Anthony, vol. 1, In the School of Anti-slavery, 1840–1866* (New Brunswick, NJ: Rutgers University Press, 1997) [ECS/SBA Papers 1]. See also Lois Banner, *Elizabeth Cady Stanton: A Radical for Woman's Rights* (Boston: Little, Brown and Company, 1980); Kathleen Barry, *Susan B. Anthony: A Biography of a Singular Feminist* (New York: New York University Press, 1988); Elizabeth Griffith, *In Her Own Right: The Life of Elizabeth Cady Stanton* (New York: Oxford University Press, 1984); Lynn Sherr, *Failure Is Impossible: Susan B. Anthony in Her Own Words* (New York: Random House, 1995); Jeanne Boydston, *The Limits of Sisterhood: The Beecher Sisters on Women's Rights and Woman's Sphere* (Chapel Hill: University of North Carolina Press, 1988); Barbara Anne White, *The Beecher Sisters* (New Haven, CT: Yale University Press 2003).

11. See, for example, Robert J. Kaczorowski, "To Begin the Nation Anew: Congress, Citizenship, and Civil Rights after the Civil War," *American Historical Review* 92 (1987): 45–68; Richard L. Aynes, "Unintended Consequences of the Fourteenth Amendment," and Mary J. Farmer and Donald G. Nieman, "Race, Class, Gender, and the Unintended Consequences of the Fifteenth Amendment," both in David E. Kyvig, ed., *Unintended Consequences of Constitutional Amendment* (Athens: University of Georgia Press, 2000), 110–40, 141–63; Rogers M. Smith, *Civic Ideals: Conflicting Visions of Citizenship in U.S. History* (New Haven, CT: Yale University Press, 1997), 308–18.

12. Chattel slavery represented a liminal category between alien and citizen. In ante-bellum law the citizenship status of free blacks was ambiguous and varied from state to state until 1857, when the U.S. Supreme Court affirmatively denied black citizenship. *Scott v. Sanford*, 19 Howard 393 (U.S. 1857). See James H. Kettner, *The Development of American Citizenship, 1608–1870* (Chapel Hill: University of North Carolina Press, 1978), 300–33.

13. "Representatives shall be apportioned among the several States according to their respective numbers, counting the whole number of persons in each State, excluding Indians not taxed. But when the right to vote at any election for the choice of electors for President and Vice-President of the United States, Representatives in Congress, the Executive and Judicial officers of a State, or the members of the Legislature thereof, is denied to any of the male inhabitants of such State, being twenty-one years of age, and citizens of the United States, or in any way abridged, except for participation in rebellion, or other crime, the basis of representation therein shall be reduced in the proportion which the number of such male citizens shall bear to the whole number of male citizens twenty-one years of age in such State." *Constitution of the United States*, Amendment Fourteen, Section 2 (Aadopted 1868).

14. Ellen Carol DuBois, Feminism and Suffrage: The Emergence of an Independent Women's Movement in America, 1848–1869 (Ithaca, NY: Cornell University Press, 1978); Andrea Moore Kerr, Lucy Stone: Speaking Out for Equality (New Brunswick, NJ: Rutgers University Press, 1992); Rosalyn Terborg-Penn, African American Women in the Struggle for the Vote, 1850–1920 (Bloomington: Indiana University Press, 1998), 24–35.

15. "The right of citizens of the United States to vote shall not be denied or abridged by the United States or by any State on account of race, color, or previous condition of servitude." *Constitution of the United States*, Amendment Fifteen, Section 1 (Adopted 1870).

16. Frederick Douglass, "Woman Suffrage," *New York World*, 19 November 1868, as quoted in DuBois, *Feminism and Suffrage*, 165–66. The complete sentence from which Stanton's quote is taken reads, "So long as there is a disfranchised class, and that class the women of the nation, 'a man's government' is worse than 'a white man's government,' because in proportion as you multiply the tyrants, you make the condition of the subjects more hopeless and degraded." Stanton, "Manhood Suffrage," *Revolution*, 24 December 1868, ECS/SBA Papers 2: 195.

17. On the founding of the *Woman's Journal*, see Kerr, *Lucy Stone*, 145–49.

18. Anthony to Isabella Beecher Hooker, 10 January 1870, Isabella Hooker Collection, Harriet Beecher Stowe Center, Hartford, CN, ECS/SBA Papers 2:291–93.

19. Eleanor Flexner, *Century of Struggle* (1975), 155.

20. See Allan Johnston, Surviving Freedom: The Black Community of Washington, D.C., 1860–1880 (New York: Garland, 1993), 101–12.

21. John Clagett Proctor and Edwin Melvin Williams, "The Mayoral Period, 1802–71," in John Clagett Proctor, ed., *Washington Past and Present* (New York: Lewis Historical Pub. Co., 1930), 78–129; W. B. Bryan, *A History of the National Capital, 1815–1878* (New York: Macmillan, 1916), 546; Robert Goldman, *Reconstruction and Black Suffrage: Losing the Vote in Reese and Cruikshank* (Lawrence: University Press of Kansas, 2001), 11–12;

Alexander Keyssar, *The Right to Vote: The Contested History of Democracy in the United States* (New York: Basic Books, 2000), 87–92.

22. These six states were New Hampshire, Rhode Island, Vermont, Maine, New York, and Massachusetts. See Table A.4, in Keyssar, *The Right to Vote,* 337–341.

23. Constance McLaughlin Green, *Washington: Village and Capital, 1800–1878* (Princeton, NJ: Princeton University Press, 1962); Bryan, *History of the National Capital.*

24. Arnold H. Liebowitz, "United States Federalism: The States and the Territories," *American University Law Review* 28 (1979): 449–82; Robert F. Berkhofer Jr., "The Northwest Ordinance and the Principle of Territorial Evolution," in John Porter Bloom, ed., *The American Territorial System* (Athens: Ohio University Press, 1973), 45–55.

25. In March 1869, Indiana Republican George Julian introduced H.R. 68; "the right of suffrage in all the Territories of the United States, now or here-after to be organized, shall be based upon citizenship." H.R. 68, 41st Cong., 1st. sess., 15 March 1869.

26. *HWS* 2:102–51; Flexner, *Century of Struggle,* 151

27. *HWS* 2:104.

28. *New York Tribune,* 12 December 1866, reprinted in *HWS* 2:103.

29. *Congressional Record,* 39th Cong., 2nd sess., 12 December 1866, 84.

30. *New York Tribune,* 12 March 1866, reprinted in John W. Blassingame and John McKivigan, eds., *The Frederick Douglass Papers,* ser. 1, vol. 4., 1860–80 (New Haven, CT: Yale University Press, 1991), 119–23.

31. 27 January 1870, *New Era* (Washington, DC).

32. *HWS* 2:413.

33. Ibid.

34. "Universal Franchise!" 20 January 1870, *National Republican* (Washington, DC).

35. "The Blindness of Prejudice," *New National Era,* 27 January 1870.

36. The most careful accounting of individual black women's attendance at AWSA and NWSA conventions in the 1870s is found in Terborg-Penn, *African American Women in the Struggle for the Vote;* Rosalyn Terborg-Penn, "Discrimination against Afro-American Women in the Woman's Movement, 1830–1920," in Sharon Harley and Rosalyn Terborg-Penn, eds., *The Afro-American Woman: Struggles and Images* (Port Washington, NY: Kennikat Press, 1978), 17–27.

37. Jane Rhodes, Mary Ann Shadd Cary: The Black Press and Protest in the Nineteenth Century (Bloomington: Indiana University Press, 1998), 193.

38. *HWS* 2:413

39. Ibid.

40. Ibid.

41. Francis Minor to *The Revolution,* 14 October 1869, in *HWS* 2:407–9.

42. Ibid.

43. *HWS* 2:411.

44. On property and sex qualifications for the vote by state, see Keyssar, *The Right to Vote,* 325–402. On women voters in New Jersey, see Judith A. Klinghoffer and Lois Elkis, "'The Petticoat Electors': Women's Suffrage in New Jersey, 1776–1807," *Journal of the Early Republic* 12 (1992): 159–93.

45. Ellen Carol DuBois, "Taking the Law into Our Own Hands: *Bradwell, Minor,* and Suffrage Militance in the 1870s," in Nancy Hewitt and Suzanne Lebsock, eds., *Visible Women: New Essays on American Activism* (Urbana: University of Illinois Press, 1990): 19–40; DuBois, " 'Outgrowing the Compact of the Fathers': Equal Rights, Woman Suffrage, and the United States Constitution, 1820–1878," *Journal of American History* 74 (1987): 836–62.

46. Patricia Lucie, "On Being a Free Person and a Citizen by Constitutional Amendment," *Journal of American Studies* 12 (1978): 343–58.

47. *HWS* 2:407–8.

48. Donald, *Charles Sumner and the Rights of Man,* 282.

49. "Woman Suffrage at Washington," *New York Tribune,* 24 January 1870.

50. "Treaty Celebrated between the United States of America and the Dominican Republic, 29 November 1869"; "Convention Celebrated between the United States of America and the Dominican Republic for a Lease of the Bay and Peninsula of Samana, 29 November 1869" S. Ex. Doc. No. 17, 41st Cong., 3rd sess., 16 January 1871, 101–2.

51. U. S. Grant to the Senate of the United States, "Urging the Ratification of the Treaty with Santo Domingo," 31 May 1870, in Edward McPherson, *The Political History of the United States during the Period of Reconstruction* (Washington, DC: Chapman, 1880), 541–42.

52. Ibid.

53. On the Monroe Doctrine, see Ernest R. May, *The Making of the Monroe Doctrine* (Cambridge, MA: Belknap Press, 1975). As a prescription for expansive U.S. foreign policy across the nineteenth century, see William Appleman Williams, *The Tragedy of American Diplomacy* (New York: Dell, 1972); Williams, *The Contours of American History* (Cleveland, OH: World Publishing, 1961); and, more recently, Gretchen Murphy, *Hemispheric Imaginings: The Monroe Doctrine and Narratives of U.S. Empire* (Durham, NC: Duke University Press, 2004).

54. See Tansill, *The United States and Santo Domingo;* and Frank Moya Pons, "The Land Question in Haiti and Santo Domingo: The Sociopolitical Context of the Transition from Slavery to Free Labor, 1801–1843," in Manuel Moreno Fraginals, Frank Moya Pons, and Stanley L. Engerman, eds., *Between Slavery and Free Labor: The Spanish-Speaking Caribbean in the Nineteenth Century* (Baltimore: Johns Hopkins University Press, 1985), 181–214.

55. U. S. Grant to the Senate of the United States, "Urging the Ratification of the Treaty with Santo Domingo," 541–42.

56. Ibid.; Ulysses S. Grant, "President Grant's Second Annual Message," 5 December 1870, in Edward McPherson, ed., *Hand-Book of Politics, 1872–1876,* Vol. 1 (1872; reprint, New York: Da Capo Press, 1972), 16–22.

57. Grant appealed personally to Sumner for support and initially believed that Sumner favored annexation. See McFeely, *Grant,* 332–55; Nevins, *Hamilton Fish,* 1:309–34; Donald, *Charles Sumner and the Rights of Man,* 433–53.

58. *New York Times,* 8 January 1870.

59. *New York Herald,* 9 January 1870.

60. On the 1868 Cuban revolution, see Ada Ferrer, *Insurgent Cuba: Race, Nation, and Revolution, 1868–1898* (Chapel Hill: University of North Carolina Press, 1999); Louis Perez Jr., *Cuba: Between Reform and Revolution* (New York: Oxford University Press, 1988). On U.S. attitudes toward the Cuban insurgents, see Walter LaFeber, *The New Empire: An Interpretation of American Expansion, 1860–1898* (Ithaca, NY: Cornell University Press, 1963); William Appleman Williams, *The Roots of the Modern American Empire: A Study of the Growth and Shaping of Social Consciousness in a Marketplace Society* (New York: Random House, 1969).

61. McFeeley, *Grant*, 320–31.

62. "What the Dominicans Say," *New York Tribune*, 10 January 1870; "San Domingo," *Herald* (New York), 11 January 1870; "Santo Domingo," *New York Tribune*, 22 January 1870; *Nation*, 31 March 1870; *Daily National Republican*, 17 January and 19 February 1870. See also William Javier Nelson, *Almost a Territory: America's Attempt to Annex the Dominican Republic* (Newark: University of Delaware Press, 1990); Sumner Welles, *The Dominican Republic, 1844–1924*, vol. 1 (Mamaronek, NY: Appel, 1966).

63. "The St. Domingo Bargain," *Nation*, 3 February 1870.

64. Ibid. On the racial composition of Dominica in the 1870s, see H. Hoetink, *The Dominican People, 1850–1900: Notes for a Historical Sociology* (Baltimore: Johns Hopkins University Press, 1982).

65. McCormick, *Congressional Globe*, 41st Cong., 3rd sess., 27 January 1871, 798.

66. On antebellum U.S. slaveholders' interest in Cuba, see Eric Foner, *Free Soil, Free Labor, Freemen: The Ideology of the Republican Party before the Civil War* (New York: Oxford University Press, 1979); Frederick Merk, *Manifest Destiny and Mission in American History: A Reinterpretation*, with the collaboration of Lois Bannister Merk (1963; reprint, Cambridge, MA: Harvard University Press, 1995), 202–14.

67. On antebellum opposition to expansion, see, for example, Michael F. Holt, *The Rise and Fall of the American Whig Party: Jacksonian Politics and the Onset of the Civil War* (New York: Oxford University Press, 1999), 602–3.

68. Eric Foner calls the racist critique of annexation "among the most striking features of the whole affair." Foner, *Reconstruction*, 496. See also Eric Love, *Race over Empire: Racism and U.S. Imperialism, 1865–1900* (Chapel Hill: University of North Carolina Press, 2004).

69. "The Proposed Treaties with Saint Domingo," *New Era*, 10 March 1870.

70. Ibid.; also see "Letters to the Editor," *New Era*, 24 February 1870; 28 April 1870.

71. "The Proposed Treaties with Saint Domingo"; also see "F. H. Grice to the Editor," *New Era*, 24 February 1870.

72. *New York Herald*, 16 March 1871; *Daily National Republican*, 17 March 1871. On Sumner and the annexation of Santo Domingo, see Donald, *Charles Sumner and the Rights of Man*, 438–44, 467–73.

73. Charles Sumner, "Annexation of Dominica," *Congressional Globe*, 41st Cong. 2nd sess., 21 December 1870, 229.

74. See Donald, *Charles Sumner and the Rights of Man*, 57, 356.

75. Charles Sumner to Samuel Gridley Howe, 3 August 1871, in Palmer, *Selected Letters of Charles Sumner*, 2:565–67; Harold Schwartz, *Samuel Gridley Howe: Social Reformer, 1801–1876* (Cambridge, MA: Harvard University Press, 1956), 310–12.

76. William Lloyd Garrison, "American Swagger and Manifest Destiny," *Independent* (New York), 27 April 1871; William Lloyd Garrison, "Santo Domingo Question," *Independent* (New York), 13 April 1871, "William Lloyd Garrison on Santo Domino," *Daily National Republican*, 17 April 1871; Charles Sumner to William Lloyd Garrison, 26 April 1871, in Palmer, *Selected Letters of Charles Sumner,* 2:551; Charles Sumner to Gerrit Smith, 30 December 1870, in Palmer, *Selected Letters of Charles Sumner,* 2:535.

77. Lydia Maria Child to Charles Sumner, 4 July 1870, Charles Sumner Correspondence (MS Am 1), Houghton Library, Harvard University; Lydia Maria Child, "Dominica and Hayti," *National Standard,* 28 January 1871.

78. Lydia Maria Child to Charles Sumner, 4 July 1870.

79. See Carolyn Karcher, *The First Woman in the Republic: A Cultural Biography of Lydia Maria Child* (Durham, NC: Duke University Press, 1994), 384–86.

80. Child, "Dominica and Hayti."

81. Child, "Dominica and Hayti."

82. Lydia Maria Child to Charles Sumner, 4 July 1870.

83. Ibid.

84. Ibid.; Child, "Dominica and Hayti"; Karcher, *First Woman in the Republic,* 562–63.

85. James Bayard, "Annexation of Dominica," *Congressional Globe,* 41st Cong., 2nd sess., 21 December 1870, 225–26; 225; Foner, *Reconstruction,* 494–97; "This matter is becoming a great shame and scandal; and the Senate owes it to the country, the President, and itself to settle the point at issue immediately and without further unseemly wrangling; for enough of bitterness and division within the Republican column has already been developed." "Washington," *New York Times,* 10 June 1870. Beverly Wilson Palmer cites two editorials in the *Boston Daily Advertiser* that were especially critical of Sumner. *Boston Daily Advertiser,* 23 December 1870, 2, and 28 December 1870, 2, in Palmer, *Selected Letters of Charles Sumner,* 2:535; see also "The Triumph of the Administration," *Daily National Republican,* 13 January 1871; Donald, *Charles Sumner and the Rights of Man,* 475–76.

86. United States, "An Act to Enforce the Rights of Citizens of the United States to Vote in the Several States of This Union, and for Other Purposes," George P. Sanger, ed., *Statutes at Large and Proclamations of the United States from December 1869 to March 1871,* vol. 16(Boston: Little, Brown, 1871), 140–46. The May 21, 1870, Enforcement Act was designed to enforce the Fifteenth Amendment and specified criminal acts that would trigger federal prosecution for those attempting to prevent individuals from voting. The 1870 Enforcement Act went beyond the Fifteenth Amendment by affirming a "positive right to vote." See Goldman, *Reconstruction and Black Suffrage,* 18, 17–20; Xi Wang, *The Trial of Democracy: Black Suffrage and Northern Republicans, 1860–1910* (Athens: University of Georgia Press, 1997), 57–68.

87. On Sumner's civil rights bill, see Donald, *Charles Sumner and the Rights of Man,* 531–35.

88. On Democratic opposition to the Enforcement Acts, see Goldman, *Reconstruction and Black Suffrage,* 12–22.

89. On the movement for union between the NWSA and AWSA in 1870, see Alice Stone Blackwell, *Lucy Stone: Pioneer of Woman's Rights,* (Boston: Little, Brown, 1930),

217–18. See also "Appeal for a Union of the Woman Suffrage Associations," 14 March 1870, ECS/SBA Papers 2:307–11.

90. H.R. 339, 41st Cong., 2nd sess., 6 April 1870.

91. Charles Sumner, "Naboth's Vineyard: Speech in the Senate on the Proposed Annexation of San Domingo to the United States, 21 December 1870," Charles Sumner, ed., *The Works of Charles Sumner*, Vol. 14 (Boston: Lee and Shepard, 1883), 89–131.

92. Tansill, *The United States and Santo Domingo*, 430–33; Sumner Welles, *Naboth's Vineyard: The Dominican Republic 1844–1924*, vol. 1 (Mamaroneck, NY: Appel, 1966), 397–99; Donald, *Charles Sumner and the Rights of Man*, 470–73.

93. Erich Eyck, *Bismarck and the German Empire* (1950; New York: Norton, 1968); Edward Crankshaw, *Bismarck* (London: Macmillan, 1981).

94. Frederick Douglass to Charles Sumner, 6 January 1871, Charles Sumner Correspondence (MS Am 1), Houghton Library, Harvard University.

95. This incident is recounted in Donald, *Charles Sumner and the Rights of Man*, 470–77; Charles Sumner to Frederick Douglass, 6 January 1871, cited in Donald, *Charles Sumner and the Rights of Man*, 477; Charles Sumner to Samuel Gridley Howe, 30 December 1870 as cited in Schwarz, *Samuel Gridley Howe*, 295; Charles Sumner to William Lloyd Garrison, 29 December 1870, in Palmer, *Selected Letters of Charles Sumner*, vol. 2, 534–35.

96. See Roy F. Nichols, "The Kansas-Nebraska Act: A Century of Historiography," in Joel Silbey, ed., *National Development and Sectional Crisis, 1815–1860* (New York: Random House, 1970), 195–218; Nicole Etcheson, *Bleeding Kansas: Contested Liberty in the Civil War Era* (Lawrence: University Press of Kansas, 2004).

97. Frederick Douglass, "Slavery, Freedom, and the Kansas-Nebraska Act," 30 October 1854, in John W. Blassingame, et al., eds., *The Frederick Douglass Papers*, ser. 1, vol. 2, 1847–54 (New Haven, CT: Yale University Press, 1979), 538–39; William McFeeley, *Frederick Douglass* (New York: Norton, 1991), 179.

98. Frederick Douglass, "San Domingo Treaty," *New Era*, 8 December 1870.

99. W.D. Harriman to Charles Sumner, 24 December 1870, Charles Sumner Correspondence (MS Am 1), Houghton Library, Harvard University.

100. Susan B. Anthony, *Diary*, 10 January 1871, Pocket Diary 1871, Susan B. Anthony Papers, LCMD, in ECS/SBA Papers 2:403.

101. See, for example, "San Domingo in the House," *Daily National Republican*, 10 January 1871; Anthony arrived in D.C. from New York and may also have seen the *Tribune's* account of the debate in Congress. *New York Tribune*, 10 January 1871. On the Woodhull announcement, see Isabella Beecher Hooker, "Woman Suffrage in Washington," *Independent* (New York), 26 January 1871; "Victoria Woodhull Memorial," and "San Domingo," *Woodhull and Claflin's Weekly*, 7 January 1871.

102. *HWS* 2:443–44; *Congressional Globe*, 41st Cong. 3rd sess., 21 December 1870.

103. Victoria C. Woodhull, "The Memorial of Victoria C. Woodhull," 19 December 1870, reprinted in *The Argument for Woman's Electoral Rights under Amendments XIV and XV of the Constitution of the United States: A Review of My Work at Washington, D.C. in 1870–1871* (London: G. Norman & Son, Printers, 1887), 32–33.

104. Hooker, "Woman Suffrage in Washington," is Hooker's account of first discovering the news of Woodhull's hearing; see also Barbara Goldsmith, *Other Powers: The Age of Suffrage, Spiritualism, and the Scandalous Victoria Woodhull* (New York: Knopf, 1988), 246–57.

105. Goldsmith, *Other Powers*; Johanna Johnston, *Mrs. Satan: The Incredible Saga of Victoria C. Woodhull* (New York: Putnam, 1967); Emanie Sachs *"The Terrible Siren": Victoria Woodhull* (1928; reprint, New York: Arno Press, 1972); Mary Gabriel, *Notorious Victoria: The Life of Victoria Woodhull, Uncensored* (Chapel Hill, NC: Algonquin Books of Chapel Hill, 1998).

106. Lois Beachy Underhill, *The Woman Who Ran for President: The Many Lives of Victoria Woodhull* (Bridgehampton, NY: Bridge Works, 1995), 67–69.

107. On *Woodhull and Claflin's Weekly*, see ibid., 86–93; Goldsmith, *Other Powers*, 212–14; Johnston, *Mrs. Satan*, 60–64; Sachs *"The Terrible Siren,"* 66–74.

108. Ann Braude, *Radical Spirits: Spiritualism and Women's Rights in Nineteenth-Century America* (Boston: Beacon, 1989), 6, 76–81.

109. Elizabeth Cady Stanton, "Speech on Free Love," ca. 1871, ECS/SBA Papers 2:395. On the critique of marriage in the antebellum woman's rights movement, see Nancy Isenberg, *Sex and Citizenship in Antebellum America* (Chapel Hill: University of North Carolina Press, 1998); Braude, *Radical Spirits*.

110. Braude, *Radical Spirits*; Ellen Carol DuBois, "Feminism and Free Love," 2001, http://www2.h-net.msu.edu/ women/papers/freelove.html.

111. "There is a wide spread combination undermining *the family state* & we need to protect all the *customs* as well as the laws that tend to sustain it." Catharine E. Beecher to Elizabeth Cady Stanton, 16 May 1870, ECS/SBA Papers 2:335–36; Griffith, *In Her Own Right*, 101–2; Ellen Carol DuBois, "The Nineteenth-Century Woman Suffrage Movement and the Analysis of Woman's Oppression (1978)," in Ellen Carol DuBois, ed., *Woman Suffrage and Women's Rights* (New York: New York University Press, 1998), 68–80.

112. "If we can only keep our platform free from controverted theological & social topics, such as caused the New York *Times* & *World* of Dec 8. to adopt the heading (so unfortunate for our cause) of 'Woman Suffrage & Free Love.'" Henry Brown Blackwell to Isabella Beecher Hooker, 16 December 1869, in Anne Throne Margolis, ed., *Isabella Beecher Hooker Project* [IBHP] (Hartford, CT: Stowe-Day Foundation, 1979), 120/D1–10; "Mrs. Woodhull's paper is avowedly free love in its tone & scarcely a number appears which does not have an attack on marriage. It remains to be seen whether the effort of the American Society to keep clear of that element is wise & prophetic." Henry Brown Blackwell to John Hooker, 28 January 1871, IBHP 121/A7-A10; see Kerr, *Lucy Stone*, 72, 111–12, 152–53.

113. L. T. Merrill, "General Benjamin F. Butler in Washington," in Maud Burr Morris, ed., *Records of the Columbia Historical Society of Washington, D.C.*, vol. 39 (Washington, DC: Columbia Historical Society, 1938), 71–100; Robert Holzman, *Stormy Ben Butler* (New York: Macmillan, 1954); Howard Nash, *Stormy Petrel: The Life and Times of General Benjamin F. Butler, 1818–1893* (Rutherford, NJ: Farleigh Dickinson University Press, 1969).

114. Benjamin F. Butler, *Autobiography and Personal Reminiscences of Major-General Benjamin F. Butler; Butler's Book* (Boston: Thayer, 1892), 418, as cited in Mary Ryan,

Women in Public: Between Banners and Ballots, 1825–1880 (Baltimore: Johns Hopkins University Press, 1990), 3; Robert Werlich, *"Beast" Butler: The Incredible Career of Major General Benjamin Franklin Butler* (Washington, DC: Quaker Press, 1962).

115. Nathan Weiss, "The Political Theory and Practice of General Benjamin Franklin Butler" (Ph.D. diss., New York University, 1961); Nevins, *Hamilton Fish*, vol. 1.

116. Some have speculated that in the winter of 1870–71, Butler and Woodhull were involved in an affair. See Underhill, *The Woman Who Ran for President*, 96–98.

117. As a moment of "popular constitutionalism," see DuBois, "Taking the Law into Our Own Hands," 119; Brown, "To Catch the Vision of Freedom" 66–99.

118. The most comprehensive list of women's attempts to register and to vote after the Civil War is Ann D. Gordon, "Women Who Went to the Polls, 1868–1873," Appendix C, ECS/SBA Papers 2:645–54.

119. *HWS* 2:586.

120. *Woman's Journal*, 29 April 1871; ECS/SBA Papers 2:648. Black women were in the forefront of the woman suffrage movement in South Carolina, and Charlotte "Lottie" Rollin, one of the most active women in South Carolina, became an ex officio member of the AWSA executive committee. Nonetheless, it is clear that the ideas of the New Departure circulated in South Carolina. Terborg-Penn, *African American Women in the Struggle for the Vote*, 44–45. There is some indication that the managers of the election who accepted these women's ballots were also black. Although they were found guilty in the U.S. District Court of South Carolina, this case was appealed to the U.S. Circuit Court in Charlestown. See *Woman's Journal*, 29 April 1871; *Revolution*, 20 April 1871.

121. Gordon, "Women Who Went to the Polls, 1868–1873," 645–54. See also Keyssar, *The Right to Vote*, 433n16.

122. Henry Brown Blackwell to John Hooker, 28 January 1871, IBHP 121/A7–10.

123. "Are Women Not Already Legally Enfranchised?" *Woman's Journal*, 26 February 1870.

124. Ibid.

125. Emily Edson Briggs, "Victoria C. Woodhull: Her Memorial to Congress on the Subject of Woman Suffrage, 11 January 1871," in *The Olivia Letters*, 229–35.

126. *Evening Star*, 11 January 1871; *Daily National Republican*, 11 January 1871.

127. It is a common misperception that Woodhull was the first to make these legal arguments. It is likely that the origins of this erroneous perception can be credited to Woodhull herself. See Victoria Woodhull, "Introduction," in *The Argument for Woman's Electoral Rights under Amendments XIV and XV of the Constitution of the United States: A Review of My Work at Washington, D.C. in 1870–1871* (London: G. Norman & Son, Printers, 1887), 1–7. Madeline Stern has credited Woodhull's associates Stephen Pearl Andrews and James Harvey Blood with helping her formulate the constitutional logic contained in the memorial. Madeline B. Stern, "Political Theory," in Stern, ed., *The Victoria Woodhull Reader* (Weston, MA: M&S Press, 1974), n.p.

128. "Constitutional Equality," 2 January 1871, in Victoria C. Woodhull, *The Argument for Woman's Electoral Rights*, 36, 37.

129. Ibid. See DuBois, "Taking the Law into Our Own Hands," 114–38.

130. *HWS* 2:456.

131. Ibid.

132. Ibid.

133. See Marylynn Salmon, *Women and the Law of Property in Early America* (Chapel Hill: University of North Carolina Press, 1986); Joan Hoff, *Law, Gender, and Injustice: A Legal History of U.S. Women* (New York: New York University Press, 1991); Isenberg, *Sex and Citizenship in Antebellum America*.

134. Linda Kerber, *No Constitutional Right to Be Ladies: Women and the Obligations of Citizenship* (New York: Hill and Wang, 1998), 37. See also Smith, *Civic Ideals*, 234.

135. In her report on the Woodhull hearing for the *Woman's Journal*, Catherine Stebbins outlined for readers Riddle's argument on marriage and servitude. *Woman's Journal*, 28 January 1871.

136. Kaczorowski, "To Begin the Nation Anew," 45–68; Michael Les Benedict, "Preserving Federalism: Reconstruction and the Waite Court," in Philip B. Kurland and Gerhard Casper, eds., *The Supreme Court Review* (Chicago: University of Chicago Press, 1979), 39–79.

137. *HWS* 2:447.

138. See, for example, Wang, *Trial of Democracy*, 39–48; Foner, *Reconstruction*, 446.

139. Briggs, *The Olivia Letters*, 236.

140. Donald, Charles Sumner and the Rights of Man, 474–88.

141. Carl Schurz, "Speech of Hon. Carl Schurz," *Appendix to the Congressional Globe*, 41st Cong., 3rd sess., 11 January 1871, 30.

142. Ibid.

143. Ibid., 26–27.

144. Ibid., 29.

145. Foner, *Reconstruction*, 454–59.

146. Schurz, "Speech of Hon. Carl Schurz," 29.

147. Ibid., 27.

148. Ibid., 30.

149. Ibid., 31.

150. *Scott v. Sandford* 60 U.S. (19 How. 1857), 446, as cited in Owen Fiss, *Oliver Wendell Holmes Devise: History of the Supreme Court of the United States*, vol. 8, *Troubled Beginnings of the Modern State, 1888–1910* (New York: Macmillan, 1993), 231–32.

151. Hamilton Fish to General Babcock (6 November 1869), S. Ex. Doc. No. 17, 41st Cong., 3rd sess., 16 January 1871, 80–82.

152. Schurz, "Speech of Hon. Carl Schurz," 30.

153. "After the Republican Party, What?" *Revolution*, 23 March 1871, reprinted in *New Era*, 6 April 1871.

154. "San Domingo," *Woodhull and Claflin's Weekly*, 31 December 1870, 7 January 1871; 21 January 1871.

155. "San Domingo," *Woodhull and Claflin's Weekly*, 31 December 1870.

156. "San Domingo," *Woodhull and Claflin's Weekly*, 21 January 1871.

157. *Woman's Journal,* 25 February 1871. He arrived on 8 February 1871; *Daily National Republican,* 27 February 1871.

158. Henry Brown Blackwell, "Santo Domingo as It Is," *Hearth and Home,* 11 March 1871.

159. See Kerr, *Lucy Stone,* 74–79.

160. Alice Stone Blackwell to Kitty Brown Blackwell, 5 February 1871, BFP, LCMD, as cited in Leslie Wheeler, ed., *Loving Warriors: Selected Letters of Lucy Stone and Henry B. Blackwell, 1853 to 1893* (New York: Dial Press, 1981), 235. Kerr also uses this quote but dates it 1 February 1871; see Kerr, *Lucy Stone,* 273, n.7.

161. As cited in Kerr, *Lucy Stone,* 273, n.10.

162. *Report of the Commission of Inquiry to Santo Domingo* (Washington, DC: Government Printing Office, 1871).

163. Schwartz, *Samuel Gridley Howe*; Laura Richards, ed., *Letters and Journals of Samuel Gridley Howe: The Servant of Humanity* (Boston: Estes, 1909).

164. Report of the Commission of Inquiry to Santo Domingo, 231–32; Tansill, *The United States and Santo Domingo,* 119–20, 120n.23.

165. Blackwell, "Santo Domingo as It Is"; Henry Brown Blackwell, "Our Santo Domingo Correspondence," *Hearth and Home,* 22 April 1871.

166. Henry Brown Blackwell to Charles Sumner, 20 November 1871, BFP, LCMD.

167. Blackwell, "Santo Domingo as It Is."

168. Ibid.

169. Henry Brown Blackwell, "Woman in Santo Domingo—No. 1," *Woman's Journal,* 15 April 1871.

170. Henry Brown Blackwell, "Woman in Santo Domingo—No. 2," *Woman's Journal,* 29 April 1871.

171. Ibid.

172. Ibid.

173. Ibid.

174. Joan Jacobs Brumberg, "Zenanas and Girlless Villages: The Ethnology of American Evangelical Women, 1870–1910," *Journal of American History* 69 (1982): 347–71.

175. Henry Brown Blackwell, "Indians and Women," *Woman's Journal,* 12 February 1870.

176. Ibid.

177. Ibid.

178. Ibid.

179. Ibid.

180. Ibid.

181. Henry Brown Blackwell, "Santo Domingo—The Case Stated," *Independent* (New York), 20 April 1871; Henry Brown Blackwell to Charles Sumner, 20 November 1871, BFP, LCMD.

182. Report of the Commission of Inquiry to Santo Domingo.

183. Welles, *Naboth's Vineyard,* 399–401; Nevins, *Hamilton Fish,* 2:498–501.

184. "The Right Color for a Steamboat Diner," *Daily National Republican,* 29 March 1871.

185. *HWS* 2:587; *HWS* 3:813; "D.C. Suffrage," *Woodhull and Claflin's Weekly*, 29 April 1871; "Woman Suffrage in Washington," *Woman's Journal*, 29 April 1871, 22 April 1871; *New Era*, 27 April 1871; *Revolution*, 27 April 1871; *Evening Star*, 19 April 1871, 20 April 1871, 22 April 1871.

186. One week earlier, several members of the group had attempted to register to vote and brought bouquets of flowers to city hall for any registrar that would add their name to the lists. "Descent of Female Suffragists on Board of Registration," *Evening Star*, 14 April 1871.

187. *HWS* 2:461–64.

188. Edward Bates, *What Constitutes Citizenship? The Rights of Citizens* (Hartford: L.E. Hunt, 1868): 9. See also, Edward Bates, "Citizenship," 29 November 1862, *Official Opinions of the Attorneys General of the United States*, 10 Vols. (Washington: R. Farnham, 1852–1870) 10: 382, 388.

189. Constance McLaughlin Green, *The Secret City: A History of Race Relations in the Nation's Capital* (Princeton, NJ: Princeton University Press, 1967), 104.

190. "Mr. Frederick Douglass on Santo Domingo," *Baltimore American*, 25 April 1871.

191. *New Era*, 27 April 1871.

192. Schwartz, *Samuel Gridley Howe*, 318.

193. *Minor v. Happersett*, 21 Wallace 162, United States Reports, vol. 88 (1906).

194. *HWS* 2:738.

195. Ibid., 738, 742.

CHAPTER 3: WESTERN EXPANSION AND THE POLITICS OF FEDERALISM

1. On the dispossession of the Iroquois, see Laurence M. Hauptman, *Conspiracy of Interests: Iroquois Dispossession and the Rise of New York State* (Syracuse, NY: Syracuse University Press, 1999); and Hauptman, *The Iroquois in the Civil War: From Battlefield to Reservation* (Syracuse, NY: Syracuse University Press, 1993).

2. S. No. 107, *Congressional Record*, 45th Cong., 1st sess., 23 October 1877, 135.

3. Matilda Joslyn Gage, "Indian Citizenship," *National Citizen and Ballot Box*, May 1878. The Iroquois were not the only tribe to protest Ingalls's bill. See Seminole Nation, "Remonstrance of the Seminole and Creek Delegates against the Passage of Senate Bill No. 107, to Enable Indians to Become citizens of the United States," Senate Misc. Doc. No. 18, 45th Cong., 2nd sess., 14 January 1878.

4. Gage, "Indian Citizenship."

5. See, for example, Joan Smyth Iversen, *The Antipolygamy Controversy in U.S. Women's Movements, 1880–1925: A Debate on the American Home* (New York: Garland, 1997).

6. Two notable exceptions are Sarah Barringer Gordon, " 'The Liberty of Self-Degradation: Polygamy, Woman Suffrage, and Consent in Nineteenth-Century America," *Journal of American History* 83 (1996): 815–47; Louise Newman, "Assimilating Primitives: The 'Indian Problem' as a 'Woman Question,' " in *White Women's Rights: The Racial Origins of Feminism in the United States* (New York: Oxford University Press, 1999), 116–31.

7. The lands allotted to individual Indians by the Dawes Act were to be held in trust by the federal government for twenty-five years, a fact that kept Indians living on allotted lands in a condition of semi-wardship, but the law represented a watershed in the history of U.S. Indian relations because of its promise of citizenship. "An Act to Provide for the Allotment of Lands in Severalty," 8 February 1887, chap. 119, sec. 6., *Statutes at Large of the United States* (Washington, DC: Government Printing Office, 1887).

8. The Edmunds-Tucker Act reflected a majority commitment to stop the spread of Mormon polygamy, but it was also a hugely controversial instance of federal intervention into state control over voting rights. Utah Territory may have been only a state in the making, but the Edmunds-Tucker Act reminded many of congressional efforts to adopt an activist stance vis-à-vis voting rights within the states and was opposed as a "second Reconstruction in the west." "An Act to Amend…in Reference to Bigamy," 3 March 1887, chap. 397., sec. 20, *Statutes at Large of the United States* (Washington, DC: Government Printing Office, 1887).

9. *Minor v. Happersett*, 21 Wallace (1875).

10. On the increased federal control over immigration and naturalization law in the nineteenth century as a consolidation of federal authority over the states, see Rogers M. Smith, *Civic Ideals: Conflicting Visions of Citizenship in U.S. History* (New Haven, CT: Yale University Press, 1997), 357–71.

11. Between 1860 and 1880, the population of U.S. citizens in the western states nearly doubled, from approximately 15,000 to 28,000. In 1880, the population in the eastern states was approximately 22,000. See Margaret Walsh, *The American West: Visions and Revisions* (New York: Cambridge University Press, 2005), 46–47.

12. In 1878, the western territories of the United States included Arizona Territory, Washington Territory, Idaho Territory, Dakota Territory, Montana Territory, Wyoming Territory, Utah Territory, Indian Territory, and New Mexico Territory.

13. "An Indian Victory," *New York Times*, 7 July 1876, cited in Robert G. Hays, *A Race at Bay: New York Times Editorials on "The Indian Problem," 1860–1900* (Carbondale: Southern Illinois University Press, 1997), 143.

14. Paul I. Wellman, *The Indian Wars of the West* (Garden City, NY: Doubleday, 193); Charles M. Robinson III, *The Plains Wars, 1757–1900* (New York: Routledge, 2003); Thurman Lee Hester Jr., *Political Principles and Indian Sovereignty* (New York: Routledge, 2001), 53–66.

15. John R. Wunder, "No More Treaties: The Resolution of 1871 and the Alteration of Indian Rights to Their Homelands," in Wunder, ed., *Native American Law and Colonialism, before 1776 to 1903* (New York: Garland, 1996), 195–212; Jeanette Wolfley, "Jim Crow, Indian Style: The Disenfranchisement of Native Americans," *American Indian Law Review* 16 (1990): 167–202; Jill E. Martin, " 'Neither Fish, Flesh, Fowl, Nor Good Red Herring': The Citizenship Status of American Indians, 1830–1924," in John E. Meyer, ed., *American Indians and U.S. Politics: A Companion Reader* (Westport, CT: Praeger, 2002), 51–72.

16. See *Cherokee Nation v. Georgia*, 30 U.S. (5 Pet.) 1 (1831): 16–17; *Worcester v. Georgia*, 31 U.S. (6 Pet.) 515 (1832).

17. Blue Clark, *Lone Wolf v. Hitchcock: Treaty Rights and Indian Law at the End of the Nineteenth Century* (Lincoln: University of Nebraska Press, 1994); Sidney L. Harring, *Crow Dog's Case: American Indian Sovereignty, Tribal Law, and United States Law in the Nineteenth Century* (New York: Cambridge University Press, 1994); U.S. Department of the Interior, *Handbook of Federal Indian Law* (Washington, DC: U.S. Government Printing Office, 1941); JeDon A. Emenhiser, "A Peculiar Covenant: American Indian Peoples and the U.S. Constitution," in John M. Meyer, ed., *American Indians and U.S. Politics: A Companion Reader* (Westport, CT: Praeger, 2002), 3–10.

18. U.S., *Statutes at Large* 16 (1971): 566, cited in Wunder, "No More Treaties," 195.

19. Seminole Nation, "Remonstrance of the Seminole and Creek Delegates."

20. *Woman's Journal*, 22 December 1877.

21. Ibid.

22. Ibid.

23. Kathy Brown, "The Anglo-Algonquian Gender Frontier," in Nancy Shoemaker, ed., *Negotiators of Change: Historical Perspectives on Native American Women* (New York: Routledge, 1995), 26–48.

24. See especially Richard Drinnon, *Facing West: The Metaphysics of Indian-Hating and Empire-Building* (Minneapolis: University of Minnesota Press, 1980); see Robert F. Berkhofer Jr., *The White Man's Indian* (New York: Knopf, 1978).

25. Gail H. Landsman, "The 'Other' as Political Symbol: Images of Indians in the Woman Suffrage Movement," *Ethnohistory* 39 (1992): 247–84; Jo Ann Woodsum, "Native American Women: An Update," in Jo Carrillo, ed., *Readings in American Indian Law: Recalling the Rhythm of Survival* (Philadelphia: Temple University Press, 1998), 226–34.

26. Lewis H. Morgan, *Ancient Society, or Researches in the Lines of Human Progress from Savagery through Barbarism to Civilization* (1877; reprint, Cambridge: Belknap Press, 1964).

27. Ibid., 320–26.

28. Carolyn L. Karcher, *The First Woman in the Republic: A Cultural Biography of Lydia Maria Child* (Durham, NC: Duke University Press, 1994), 8–10.

29. Ibid., 11–12, 22, 87–93, 107–10, 559.

30. Gage, "Indian Citizenship."

31. Ibid.

32. Matilda Joslyn Gage, "Prospectus," *National Citizen and Ballot Box*, July 1878.

33. Matilda Joslyn Gage, "Centralized Power vs. State Rights," *Woman's Campaign*, 17 January 1873.

34. Matilda Joslyn Gage, "United States Rights and State Rights," *National Citizen and Ballot Box*, May 1878.

35. Ibid.

36. Ibid.

37. Ibid.

38. Ibid.

39. *United States v. Elm*, 24 December 1877, 25 Fed, No. 15, 408

40. Ibid.; Smith, *Civic Ideals*, 393–95.

41. *United States v. Elm*, 408.

42. *United States v. Anthony*, 24 Fed. Cas. (C.C.N.D.N.Y., 1873), 829–33.

43. Joan Hoff, *Law, Gender, and Injustice: A Legal History of U.S. Women* (New York: New York University Press, 1992), 152–61.

44. John Hooker, "Is the Family the Basis of the State?" *National Citizen and Ballot Box*, May 1879.

45. Ibid.

46. National Woman Suffrage Association, *Declaration of Rights of the Women of the United States*, 4 July 1876 (n.p., n.d.), in Ann D. Gordon, ed., *The Selected Papers of Elizabeth Cady Stanton and Susan B. Anthony: National Protection for National Citizens, 1873 to 1880*, vol. 3 [ECS/SBA Papers 3] (New Brunswick, NJ: Rutgers University Press, 2003), 234–41.

47. Susan B. Anthony, "Letter from Kansas City," *Woodhull and Claflin's Weekly*, 25 February 1871.

48. Cited in Ann D. Gordon, "Woman Suffrage (Not Universal Suffrage) by Federal Amendment," in Marjorie Spruill Wheeler, ed., *Votes for Women! The Woman Suffrage Movement in Tennessee, the South, and the Nation* (Knoxville: University of Tennessee Press, 1995), 6.

49. Cited in Eleanor Flexner, *Century of Struggle: The Woman's Rights Movement in the United States*, rev. ed. (Cambridge, MA: Belknap Press, 1975), 176.

50. Elizabeth Cady Stanton, "Woman Suffrage Organizations," *Golden Age,* December 1871.

51. Elizabeth Cady Stanton, " 'National Protection for National Citizens': Speech by Elizabeth Cady Stanton to the Senate Committee on Privileges and Elections," 11 January 1878, ECS/SBA. 359.

52. Ibid., 355–56.

53. Gordon, "Woman Suffrage (Not Universal Suffrage) by Federal Amendment," 8.

54. Steven Kantrowitz, *Ben Tillman and the Reconstruction of White Supremacy* (Chapel Hill: University of North Carolina Press, 2000), 3.

55. Eric Foner, *Reconstruction: America's Unfinished Revolution, 1863–1877* (New York: Harper & Row, 1988), 422–23; Robert W. Cherny, *American Politics in the Gilded Age, 1868–1900* (Wheeling, IL: Harland Davidson, 1997), 57. The establishment of redemption governments required actively overcoming the challenge of cross-race political coalitions that coalesced in the Independent and Greenback parties, and in the 1890s in the Populist Party. See, for example, Jane Dailey, *Before Jim Crow: The Politics of Race in Postemancipation Virginia* (Chapel Hill: University of North Carolina Press, 2000).

56. Elizabeth Boynton Harbert, "Arguments in Behalf of a Sixteenth Amendment to the Constitution," January 1878, Suffrage—Subject Collection, Sophia Smith Collection, Smith College Library, Amherst, MA, 21.

57. Elizabeth Cady Stanton, "Address," Eleventh National Woman's Rights Convention, 10 May 1866, *Concise History of Woman Suffrage*, 230, cited in Gordon, "Woman Suffrage (Not Universal Suffrage) by Federal Amendment," 6; ECS/SBA 1:587.

58. The best example of this type of generational explanation for racism in the suffrage movement can be found in Aileen S. Kraditor, *The Ideas of the Woman Suffrage Movement, 1890–1920* (New York: Columbia University Press, 1965).

59. Stanton, " 'National Protection for National Citizens'," 359.

60. Roslyn Terborg-Penn, *African American Women in the Struggle for the Vote, 1850–1920* (Bloomington: Indiana University Press, 1998), 110; *HWS* 3:74.

61. Elizabeth Cady Stanton to Matilda Joslyn Gage, June 1877, *Ballot Box*.

62. Jane Rhodes, *Mary Ann Shadd Cary: The Black Press and Protest in the Nineteenth Century* (Bloomington: Indiana University Press, 1998), 199–203.

63. Cherny, *American Politics in the Gilded Age*, 41–42.

64. Kirk H. Porter and Donald B. Johnson, comps., *National Party Platforms, 1840–1956* (Urbana: University of Illinois Press, 1956), 27.

65. "An Act to punish and prevent the Practice of Polygamy in the Territories of the United States and other Places, and disapproving and annulling certain Acts of the Legislative Assembly of the Territory of Utah," *United States Statutes at Large*, 37th Cong., 2nd Sess., 1 July 1862, Chp. 126, 501–502. On the Morrill Act as Republican legislation, see Edward Leo Lyman, *Political Deliverance: The Mormon Quest for Utah Statehood* (Urbana: University of Illinois Press, 1986), 11–13.

66. Lyman, *Political Deliverance*, 20–21.

67. On the federal efforts to revise marriage law in Utah Territory as a "sea change" in federal relations, see Sarah Barringer Gordon, *The Mormon Question: Polygamy and Constitutional Conflict in Nineteenth-Century America* (Chapel Hill: University of North Carolina Press, 2002), 122.

68. Cited in Iversen, *Antipolygamy Controversy in U.S. Women's Movements*, 22. Thomas G. Alexander, "An Experiment in Progressive Legislation: The Granting of Woman Suffrage in Utah in 1870," *Utah Historical Quarterly* 38 (1970): 24.

69. Elizabeth Cady Stanton, *Eighty Years and More: Reminiscences, 1815–1897* (1898; reprint, Boston: Northeastern University Pres, 1993), 284.

70. Emmeline B. Wells, "Home Again," *Woman's Exponent,* 1 June 1886, 4, cited in Iversen, *Antipolygamy Controversy in U.S. Women's Movements*, 62.

71. H.R. 3101, *Congressional Record*, 44th Cong., 1st sess., 10 April 1876, 2357; Lyman, *Political Deliverance*, 16–17, Gordon, *Mormon Question*, 111–112.

72. National Woman Suffrage Association, *Declaration of Rights of the Women of the United States by the National Woman Suffrage Association, 4 July 1876* (n.p., n.d.), in ECS/SBA Papers 3: 237.

73. Iversen, *Antipolygamy Controversy in U.S. Women's Movements*, 33.

74. *HWS* 3:129–30; Susan B. Anthony to Matilda Joslyn Gage, ca. 18 January 1879, in *National Citizen and Ballot Box*, February 1879, ECS/SBA Papers 3:432–33.

75. Elizabeth Cady Stanton and Susan B. Anthony, "Stand by the Republican Party," 30 July 1884, Elizabeth Boynton Harbert Collection, Huntington Library, San Marino, CA, B. 17, F. 12.

76. Lyman, *Political Deliverance*, 22–23.

77. Richard E. Welch Jr., *George Frisbee Hoar and the Half-Breed Republicans* (Cambridge, MA: Harvard University Press, 1971); Frederick H. Gillett, *George Frisbie Hoar* (Boston: Houghton Mifflin, 1934).

78. Clara Colby, *Woman's Tribune*, 1 March 1884.

79. Elizabeth Cady Stanton, "Meeting of the National Woman Suffrage Association, 21 January 1885," *Woman's Tribune*, March 1885, in Ann D. Gordon, ed., *The Selectd Papers of Elizabeth Cady Stanton and Susan B. Anthony: When Clowns Make Laws for Queens, 1880 to 1887*, vol. 4 [ECS/SBA Papers 4] (New Brunswick, NJ: Rutgers University Press, 2006), 396.

80. Clara Colby, *Woman's Tribune*, 1 March 1884.

81. Matilda Joslyn Gage, "United States Rights vs. State Rights," *National Citizen and Ballot Box*, February 1879.

82. *HWS* 3:128.

83. Clara Colby, *Woman's Tribune,* February 1886.

84. Lucy Stone, *Woman's Journal*, 9 January 1886.

85. Cherny, *American Politics in the Gilded Age*, 75–76.

86. Frederick Douglass, 16 April 1885, in *The Frederick Douglass Papers* [FDP], 5 vols., John W. Blassingame and John R. McKivigan, eds. (New Haven, CT: Yale University Press, 1979–1991), 5:178, cited in Xi Wang, *The Trial of Democracy: Black Suffrage and Northern Republicans, 1860–1910* (Athens: University of Georgia Press, 1997), 206.

87. Susan B. Anthony to Elizabeth Cady Stanton, 27, 29 January 1884, Susan B. Anthony Papers, University of Rochester Library, Rochester, NY, in ECS/SBA Papers 4:323, 324, 325, 326. See also Elizabeth Cady Stanton to Frederick Douglass, 27 January 1884, 27 May 1884, Fredrick Douglass Papers, LCMD, ECS/SBA 3:353–56, Frederick Douglass to Elizabeth Cady Stanton, 30 May 1884, Elizabeth Cady Stanton Papers, DLC, ECS/SBA Papers 3:356–57.

88. George Frisbee Hoar, *Congressional Record*, 49th Cong, 1st sess. (5 January 1886), 406.

89. George Edmunds, *Congressional Record*, 49th Cong. 1st sess., 5 January 1886, 406.

90. Derrell C. Roberts, *Joseph E. Brown and the Politics of Reconstruction* (Tuscaloosa, AL: University of Alabama Press, 1973).

91. Joseph Brown, *Woman's Journal*, 1 May 1886.

92. See Gordon, *Mormon Question*, 151.

93. Roberts, *Joseph E. Brown and the Politics of Reconstruction*, 70.

94. James Beck, "Admission of Washington Territory," *Woman's Journal*, 1 May 1886.

95. James Eustis, *Congressional Record*, 49th Cong., 1st sess., 18 April 1886, 3259.

96. Gordon, *Mormon Question*, 14, 144.

97. Mathew Butler, "Admission of Washington Territory," *Woman's Journal*, 1 May 1886.

98. Ibid.

99. James Beck, *New York Tribune*, 13 August 1875, cited in Morton Keller, *Affairs of State: Public Life in Late Nineteenth Century America* (Cambridge, MA: Belknap Press, 1977), 252–53.

100. Henry Moore Teller, "Admission of Washington Territory," *Woman's Journal*, 1 May 1886.

101. Ibid.

102. Ibid.

103. Rebecca Edwards, *Angels in the Machinery: Gender in American Party Politics from the Civil War to the Progressive Era* (New York: Oxford University Press, 1997).

104. Ibid., 6.

105. *HWS* 4:47, 85.

106. Ibid., 47–52.

107. Susan B. Anthony to Elizabeth Boynton Harbert, 3 June 1886, Elizabeth Boynton Harbert Collection, Huntington Library, CA.

108. Ibid.

109. *HWS* 4:86–93.

110. Elizabeth Cady Stanton, "Letter from Mrs. Stanton to the National Convention," *Woman's Tribune*, March 1887.

111. On women's disfranchisement in Washington Territory, see *HWS* 4:967–79; Sandra F. VanBurkleo, *"Belonging to the World": Women's Rights and American Constitutional Culture* (New York: Oxford University Press, 2001), 184–87.

112. Clara Colby, *Woman's Tribune*, 17 December 1887; Ingalls was the only Republican to "put his vote with the enemy" and support the Eustis Amendment disfranchising Washington women; Susan B. Anthony to Elizabeth Boynton Harbert, 3 June 1886.

113. On the legal history of Indians as federal wards after citizenship, see, N. D. Houghton, "The Legal Status of Indian Suffrage in the United States," *California Law Review* 19 (1931): 507–20.

114. Women voted in local school elections and some municipal elections before Wyoming's admission. Alex Keyssar, *The Right to Vote: The Contested History of Democracy in the United States* (New York: Basic Books, 2000), Table A.18; Kirk Porter, *A History of Suffrage in the United States* (1918; reprint, New York: Greenwood Press, 1969), 243–45.

115. Orville Platt, *Congressional Record*, 51st Cong., 1st sess., 25 June 1890, 6490.

116. Francis Jackson Garrison to Susan B. Anthony, March 1890, Ida Husted Harper Papers, Huntington Library, CA.

117. George Thomas Barnes, *Congressional Record*, 51st Cong., 1st. sess., 26 March 1890, 2671.

CHAPTER 4: IMPERIAL EXPANSION AND THE PROBLEM OF HAWAII, 1898–1902

1. "War," underlined in original. Susan B. Anthony to Rachel G. Foster Avery, 17 April 1898, Anthony-Avery Papers, University of Rochester, ECS/SBA Film ser. 3.

2. On the Senate vote, see Robert L. Beisner, *Twelve against Empire: The Anti-imperialists, 1898–1900* (New York: McGraw-Hill, 1968), 146; McKinley requested a war resolution from Congress on April 11, 1898. On the House vote, see Brian P. Damiani, *Advocates of Empire: William McKinley, the Senate and American Expansion, 1898–1899* (New York: Garland, 1987), 16.

3. Susan B. Anthony quoted in "Do Women Still Favor War? The Question Is Answered by Many of the Peace-Loving Sex," *Tribune* (New York), 31 July 1898.

4. Susan B. Anthony to Elizabeth Smith Miller, 30 May 1898, Smith Family Papers, New York Public Library, ECS/SBA Film ser. 3.

5. John L. Offner's *An Unwanted War: The Diplomacy of the United States and Spain over Cuba, 1895–1898* (Chapel Hill: University of North Carolina Press, 1992) provides an excellent discussion of key moments leading up to U.S. intervention. A good introduction

to popular perceptions of the war is Joseph E. Wisan, *The Cuban Crisis as Reflected in the New York Press (1895–1898)* (New York: Columbia University Press, 1934).

6. Susan B. Anthony to Elizabeth Smith Miller, 30 May 1898.

7. George F. Hoar, *Congressional Record.*, 55th Cong., 2nd sess., 11 April 1898, 4040–41, quoted in Frederick H. Gillett, *George Frisbie Hoar* (Boston: Houghton Mifflin, 1934), 203.

8. Susan B. Anthony to Rachel G. Foster Avery, 22 April 1898, Anthony-Avery Papers, University of Rochester, ECS/SBA Film ser. 3.

9. Ibid.

10. On the military history of the war, see David F. Trask, *The War with Spain in 1898* (New York: Macmillan, 1981).

11. George F. Hoar, *Congressional Record*, 55th Cong., 2nd sess., 11 April 1898, 4040–41, quoted in Gillett, *George Frisbie Hoar*, 203.

12. See, for example, Sally Engle Merry, *Colonizing Hawai'i: The Cultural Power of Law* (Princeton, NJ: Princeton University Press, 2000); Patricia Grimshaw, *Paths of Duty: American Missionary Wives in Nineteenth-Century Hawaii* (Honolulu: University of Hawaii Press, 1989).

13. A good introduction to U.S. expansionist sentiment toward Hawaii is Frederick Merk, *Manifest Destiny and Mission in American History: A Reinterpretation*, with the collaboration of Lois Bannister Merk (1963; reprint, Cambridge, MA: Harvard University Press, 1995), 232–37; Thomas J. McCormick, *China Market: America's Quest for Informal Empire, 1893–1901* (New York: Random House, 1967).

14. Beisner, *Twelve against Empire*, 23.

15. Philip S. Foner, *The Spanish-Cuban War and the Birth of American Imperialism, 1895–1902*, vol. 1 (New York: Monthly Review Press, 1972); Richard Hofstadter, "Racism and Imperialism," in *Social Darwinism in American Thought* (Boston: Beacon Press, 1944); Christopher Lasch, "The Anti-imperialists, the Philippines, and the Inequality of Man," *Journal of Southern History* 24 (1958): 319–31; Mathew Frye Jacobson, *Barbarian Virtues: The United States Encounters Foreign Peoples at Home and Abroad, 1876–1917* (New York: Hill and Wang, 2000); Walter LaFeber, *The New Empire: An Interpretation of American Expansionism, 1860–1898* (Ithaca, NY: Cornell University Press, 1963). On racial anti-imperialism and the annexation of Hawaii, see Eric T. L. Love, *Race over Empire: Racism and U.S. Imperialism, 1865–1900* (Chapel Hill: University of North Carolina Press, 2004).

16. On the emerging legal and constitutional questions raised by overseas expansion, see Sanford Levinson, "Installing the *Insular Cases* into the Canon of Constitutional Law," in Christina Duffy Burnett and Burke Marshall, eds., *Foreign in a Domestic Sense: Puerto Rico, American Expansion and the Constitution* (Durham, NC: Duke University Press, 2001), 121–39; Rogers M. Smith, *Civic Ideals: Conflicting Visions of Citizenship in U.S. History* (New Haven, CT: Yale University Press, 1997), 429–39.

17. "Treaty of Peace between the United States and the Kingdom of Spain," *United States Statutes at Large*, 30 (1899).

18. See Kristin Hoganson, "'As Badly Off as the Filipinos': U.S. Women's Suffragists and the Imperial Issue at the Turn of the Twentieth Century," *Journal of Women's History* 13 (2001): 9–33; Allison L. Sneider, "The Impact of Empire on the North American Woman

Suffrage Movement: Suffrage Racism in an Imperial Context," *UCLA Historical Journal* 14 (1994): 14–32.

19. Susan B. Anthony to Ida Husted Harper, 7 December 1898, Ida Husted Harper Collection, Woman Suffrage Scrapbook 1, LCMD, ECS/SBA Film ser. 3.

20. National American Woman Suffrage Association, "Memorial to Congress on Behalf of the Women of Hawaii," *Woman's Tribune*, 28 January 1899; *Woman's Journal*, 11 February 1899.

21. Henry Brown Blackwell, "The War with Spain," *Woman's Journal*, 16 April 1898.

22. Ibid.

23. William Lloyd Garrison, "Women and War," *Woman's Journal*, 30 April 1898.

24. Helen Adelaide Shaw, "A Challenge to the War Remonstrants," *Woman's Journal*, 11 June 1898; Florence Burleigh, "Mr. Garrison Partly Right," *Woman's Journal*, 28 May 1898.

25. Burleigh, "Mr. Garrison Partly Right."

26. Elizabeth Cady Stanton to Theodore Weld Stanton, 13 May 1898; Elizabeth Cady Stanton, "Opinion on the War," *True Republic*, 8 June 1898.

27. "Do Women Still Favor the War? The Question Answered by Many of the Peace Loving Sex," *Tribune* (New York), 31 July 1898.

28. See, for example, Karen J. Blair, *The Clubwoman as Feminist: True Womanhood Redefined, 1868–1914* (New York: Holmes and Meier, 1980); Anne Scott, *Natural Allies: Women's Associations in American History* (Urbana: University of Illinois Press, 1991).

29. Ellen M. Henrotin, "Women and Cuba," *Woman's Journal*, 16 April 1898.

30. "Do Women Still Favor the War?"

31. Ibid.

32. Ibid.

33. "The Negro Needs Freedom as Much as the Cuban," *Bee* (Washington), 5 March 1898, cited in George P. Marks III, *The Black Press Views American Imperialism, 1898–1900* (New York: Arno Press, 1971), 13.

34. Glenda Gilmore, *Gender and Jim Crow: Women and the Politics of White Supremacy in North Carolina, 1896–1920* (Chapel Hill: University of North Carolina Press, 1996), 78–82; Glenda Gilmore, "Black Militia in the Spanish-American/Cuban War," in Benjamin R. Beede, ed., *The War of 1898 and U.S. Interventions, 1898–1934: An Encyclopedia* (New York: Garland, 1994), 2:53–54. Kristin Hoganson has demonstrated the precise ways that anxieties over white masculinity informed much of the pro-war sentiment pushing the United States to war, and, indeed, that the debate over war reflected deep conflicts over men's and women's changing social roles. White men's political anxieties and arguments for the war were frequently grounded in the necessity of seizing this opportunity to invigorate U.S. manhood and represented a backlash against the ways in which activist women had become an increasingly visible and vital force in U.S. political life. In contrast, black men's masculinity was threatened less by the political achievements of black women than by white efforts to define masculinity in racial terms. See Kristin L. Hoganson, *Fighting for American Manhood: How Gender Politics Provoked the Spanish-American and Philippine American Wars* (New Haven, CT: Yale University Press, 1998).

35. On black feminism and anti-imperialism, see Hazel V. Carby, " 'On the Threshold of the Woman's Era': Lynching, Empire, and Sexuality in Black Feminist Theory," *Critical Inquiry* 12 (1985): 262–77; Nancy Hewitt, *Southern Discomfort: Women's Activism in Tampa, Florida 1880s–1920s* (Urbana: University of Illinois Press, 2001), 109; Patricia Schecter, *Ida B. Wells-Barnett and American Reform, 1880–1930* (Chapel Hill: University of North Carolina Press, 2001), 116.

36. Laura Elizabeth Howe Richards, Maud Howe Elliott, and Florence Howe Hall, *Julia Ward Howe, 1819–1910* (Boston: Houghton Mifflin, 1925), 328.

37. Kathi Kern, *Mrs. Stanton's Bible* (Ithaca, NY: Cornell University Press, 2001); Elizabeth Cady Stanton, *The Woman's Bible* (1895; Boston: Northeastern University Press, 1993).

38. May Wright Sewall, ed., *Genesis of the International Council of Women and the Story of Its Growth, 1888–1893* (Indianapolis: n.p., 1914), 6.

39. Ibid.

40. Steven Buechler, "Elizabeth Boynton Harbert and the Woman Suffrage Movement, 1870–1896," *Signs* 13 (1987): 78–97; Buechler, *The Transformation of the Woman Suffrage Movement: The Case of Illinois, 1850–1920* (New Brunswick, NJ: Rutgers University Press, 1986); Carolyn De Swarte Gifford, "Frances Willard and the Woman's Christian Temperance Union's Conversion to Woman Suffrage," in Marjorie Spruill Wheeler, ed., *One Woman, One Vote: Rediscovering the Woman Suffrage Movement* (Troutdale, OR: New Sage Press, 1995), 117–33.

41. Sewall, *Genesis of the International Council of Women*, 8.

42. Susan B. Anthony to Elizabeth Smith Miller, 1 January 1888, Smith Family Papers, ECS/SBA Film ser. 3.

43. U.S. women's organizations represented at the first meeting of the ICW also included the National Temperance Hospital and Medical College Association, the Woman's Auxiliary Conference of the Unitarian Association, the Western Women's Unitarian Conference, the Women's Ministerial Conference, the Woman's Centenary Association of the Universalist Church, the Women's Relief Corps of the GAR, the American Red Cross Society, the Young Ladies Mutual Improvement Association, the Woman's National Indian Association, the American Woman Suffrage Association, the Western Association of Collegiate Alumnae, the Association for the Advancement of Women, the Women's Educational and Industrial Union, the Grange, the Moral Education Society, the Sociologic Society of American, the Universal Peace Union, and the Woman's National Press Association. National Woman Suffrage Association, *Report of the International Council of Women, 1888* (Washington, DC: Darby, 1888), 49–50.

44. Ibid., 215.

45. Ibid., 34.

46. May Wright Sewall to Elizabeth Boynton Harbert, 12 June 1880, Elizabeth Boynton Harbert Collection, Huntington Library, San Marino, CA.

47. On NAWSA strategy in the 1890s, see Ann D. Gordon, "Woman Suffrage (Not Universal Suffrage) by Federal Amendment," in Marjorie Spruill Wheeler, ed., *Votes for Women! The Woman Suffrage Movement in Tennessee, the South, and the Nation* (Knoxville: University of Tennessee Press, 1995), 3–24. See also Eleanor Flexner, *Century of Struggle:*

The Woman's Rights Movement in the United States, rev. ed. (Cambridge, MA: Belknap Press, 1975); Sara Hunter Graham, "The Suffrage Renaissance: A New Image for a New Century, 1896–1910," in Marjorie Spruill Wheeler, ed., *One Woman, One Vote: Rediscovering the Woman Suffrage Movement* (Troutdale, OR: New Sage Press, 1995): 157–78.

48. On black women's commitment to the federal amendment campaign, see Lisa Gail Materson, "Respectable Partisans: African American Women in Electoral Politics, 1877–1936" (Ph.D. diss., UCLA, 2000); Linda Marie Perkins, "Black Feminism and 'Race Uplift,' 1890–1900," *Radcliffe Institute Working Paper* (Cambridge, MA: Institute for Advanced Study, 1981); Charles Wesley, *The History of the National Association of Colored Women's Clubs: A Legacy of Service* (Washington, DC: National Association of Colored Women's Clubs, 1984); Evelyn Brooks Higginbotham, *Righteous Discontent: The Women's Movement in the Back Baptist Church, 1880–1920* (Cambridge, MA: Harvard University Press, 1993); Schecter, *Ida B. Wells-Barnett and American Reform*; Rosalyn Terborg-Penn, *African-American Women in the Struggle for the Vote, 1850–1920* (Bloomington: Indiana University Press, 1998).

49. Kate Gordon cited in Terborg-Penn, *African-American Women in the Struggle for the Vote*, 111.

50. Marjorie Spruill Wheeler, *New Women of the New South: The Leaders of the Woman Suffrage Movement in the Southern States* (New York: Oxford University Press, 1993), 102; 102–5. See also Elna C. Green, *Southern Strategies: Southern Women and the Woman Suffrage Question* (Chapel Hill: University of North Carolina Press, 1997).

51. Terborg-Penn, *African-American Women in the Struggle for the Vote*, 111.

52. Henry Brown Blackwell, "A Solution to the Southern Question," 15 October 1890, U.S. Suffrage-Subject Collection, Sophia Smith Collections, Smith College Library, Northampton, MA.

53. The physical organization of the World's Columbian Exhibition both constituted and reflected a racialized and gendered definition of civilization that fully excluded black men and women and marginalized white women. Women's exhibits were restricted to one building in the White City, the area of the fairgrounds dedicated to the achievements of American civilization. In turn, black women were restricted to one exhibit within the Woman's Building. Black men did not appear in the White City at all. Frederick Douglass and the Mississippi-born antilynching activist and journalist Ida B. Wells protested these exclusions of the "colored American." See Ida B. Wells, ed., *The Reason Why the Colored American Is Not in the Worlds' Columbian Exposition: The Afro-American's Contribution to Columbian Literature* (Chicago, 1893); Gail Bederman, *Manliness and Civilization: A Cultural History of Gender and Race in the United States, 1880–1917* (Chicago: University of Chicago Press, 1995), 31–41; Schecter, *Ida B. Wells-Barnett and American Reform*, 94–98.

54. Rebecca Edwards, *Angels in the Machinery: Gender in American Party Politics from the Civil War to the Progressive Era* (New York: Oxford University Press, 1997), 158.

55. Damiani, *Advocates of Empire*.

56. Beisner, *Twelve against Empire*, 18–34; Richard E. Welch Jr., *Response to Imperialism: The United States and the Philippine American War, 1899–1902* (Chapel Hill: University of North Carolina Press, 1979).

57. On the Anti-Imperial League, see Daniel B. Schirmer, *Republic or Empire: American Resistance to the Philippine War* (Cambridge, MA: Schenkman, 1972); Welch, *Response to Imperialism*.

58. William Lloyd Garrison, "War and Imperialism Fatal to Self Government," *Woman's Journal*, 27 August 1898.

59. Lauren L. Basson, "Fit for Annexation but Unfit to Vote? Debating Hawaiian Suffrage Qualifications at the Turn of the Twentieth Century," *Social Science History* 29 (2005): 575–98.

60. Garrison, "War and Imperialism Fatal to Self Government.".

61. Alex Keyssar, *The Right to Vote: The Contested History of Democracy in the United States* (New York: Basic Books, 2000), 115; Kirk H. Porter, *A History of Suffrage in the United States* (1918; reprint, New York: Greenwood Press, 1969); Xi Wang, *The Trial of Democracy: Black Suffrage and Northern Republicans, 1860–1910* (Athens: University of Georgia Press, 1997), 260–51.

62. Garrison, "War and Imperialism Fatal to Self Government."

63. Henry Brown Blackwell, "America, the Mother of Republics," *Woman's Journal*, 18 June 1898.

64. Ibid.

65. Ibid.

66. Ibid.

67. Ibid.

68. Ibid.

69. Henry Brown Blackwell, "Home Rule for the Philippines," *Woman's Journal*, 18 June 1898.

70. Ibid.

71. Henry Brown Blackwell, "Self Government v. Imperialism," *Woman's Journal*, 5 May 1898.

72. Henry Brown Blackwell, "Home Rule versus Imperialism," *Woman's Journal*, 9 July 1898.

73. Garrison, "War and Imperialism Fatal to Self Government."

74. Ibid.

75. Blackwell, "Home Rule versus Imperialism."

76. Ibid.

77. Ibid.

78. Ibid.

79. Henry Brown Blackwell, "Militant Republicanism," *Woman's Journal*, 6 August 1898; Henry Brown Blackwell, "Self-Government v. Imperialism," *Woman's Journal*, 5 November 1898.

80. Henry Brown Blackwell, "Home Rule for the Philippines," *Woman's Journal*, 18 June 1898.

81. May Wright Sewall, "Stand by American Principles," *Woman's Journal*, 24 September 1898.

82. S.E.B., "Our Duty to the Philippines," *Woman's Journal*, 9 September 1898.

83. Susan B. Anthony to Mary L. Gannett, 15 August 1898, W. C. Gannet Papers, University of Rochester, NY, ECS/SBA Film ser. 3.

84. Susan B. Anthony to Elizabeth Cady Stanton, 2 December 1898, Anthony Family Collection, Huntington Library, CA, ECS/SBA Film ser. 3.

85. Ibid.

86. Carrie Catt, "Our New Responsibilities," *Woman's Journal*, 1 October 1898.

87. Ibid.88.Ibid.

89. Ibid.

90. Ibid.

91. Elizabeth Cady Stanton to Theodore Weld Stanton, 27 June 1899, E. C. Stanton Papers, Theodore Stanton Collection, Douglass Library, Rutgers University, NJ, ECS/SBA Film ser. 3; see also Hoganson, "'As Badly Off as the Filipinos,'" 9–33; Sneider, "Impact of Empire on the North American Woman Suffrage Movement," 14–32.

92. Kern, *Mrs. Stanton's Bible*, 181–98.

93. Harriot Stanton Blatch, "Mrs. Stanton Blatch on Imperialism: The Manifest Destiny of Women," *Woman's Journal*, 29 October 1898.

94. Ellen Carol DuBois, *Harriot Stanton Blatch and the Winning of Woman Suffrage* (New Haven, CT: Yale University Press, 1997); on Josephine Butler and the campaign against the Contagious Disease Acts, see Antoinette Burton, *Burdens of History: British Feminists, Indian Women, and Imperial Culture, 1865–1915* (Chapel Hill: University of North Carolina Press, 1994); on Stanton's trip to England and her familiarity with British suffragists in the 1880s, see Elizabeth Cady Stanton, *Eighty Years and More: Reminiscences, 1815–1897* (1898; Boston: Northeastern University Press, 1993), 352–68.

95. Blatch, "Mrs. Stanton Blatch on Imperialism"; Burton, *Burdens of History*, 130–55.

96. Burton, *Burdens of History*, 130–55.

97. Blatch, "Mrs. Stanton Blatch on Imperialism.".

98. Blatch, "Mrs. Stanton Blatch on Imperialism."

99. Burton, *Burdens of History*.

100. Ian Tyrrell, *Woman's World / Woman's Empire: The Woman's Christian Temperance Union in International Perspective, 1880–1930* (Chapel Hill: University of North Carolina Press, 1991).

101. Hoganson, "'As Badly Off as the Filipinos,'" 9–33.

102. Susan B. Anthony to Ida Husted Harper, 7 December 1898, Ida Husted Harper Collection, Woman Suffrage Scrapbook 1, LCMD, ECS/SBA Film ser. 3.

103. Whitney T. Perkins, *Denial of Empire: The United States and Its Dependencies* (Leiden, Netherlands: Sythoff, 1962), 68.

104. "Report of the Hawaiian Commission Appointed in Pursuance of the Joint Resolution to Provide for Annexing the Hawaiian Islands to the United States," Senate Executive Document 16, 55th Cong., 3rd sess., 7 July 1898.

105. Susan B. Anthony to Ida Husted Harper, 7 December 1898.

106. Susan B. Anthony to Clara Colby, 17 December 1898, Clara Beckwick Colby Collection, Huntington Library, CA, ECS/SBA Film ser. 3.

107. Ibid.

108. Ibid.

109. Susan B. Anthony to Rachel Foster Avery, 17 December 1898, Anthony-Avery Papers, University of Rochester, Rochester, NY, ECS/SBA Film ser. 3.

110. Susan B. Anthony to Clara Beckwick Colby, 27 December 1898, Clara Beckwick Colby Collection, Huntington Library, CA, ECS/SBA Film ser. 3.

111. Susan B. Anthony and the National American Woman Suffrage Association Officers, "Memorial to Congress on Behalf of the Women of Hawaii," *Woman's Tribune*, 28 January 1899; "On Behalf of the Women of Hawaii," *Woman's Journal*, 11 February 1899.

112. Susan B. Anthony and the National American Woman Suffrage Association Officers, "Memorial to Congress on Behalf of the Women of Hawaii."

113. Ibid.

114. Ibid.

115. Ibid.

116. Basson, "Fit for Annexation but Unfit to Vote?" 575–98.

117. Beisner, *Twelve against Empire*, 53–83.

118. Ibid.; E. L. Godkin, *Nation*, 29 December 1870, cited in Beisner, *Twelve against Empire*, 72.

119. "D's" letter reprinted in Elizabeth Cady Stanton and Susan B. Anthony, "The Women of Hawaii: Woman Suffrage in Our New Possessions," *Woman's Journal*, 28 January 1899.

120. Ibid.

121. Ibid.

122. *Collier's Weekly*, 21 January 1899, 2–3.

123. Stanton, "The Women of Hawaii."

124. Susan B. Anthony, "Statement on Territorial Constitutions," *Sun*, 21 May 1899, ECS/SBA Film ser. 3.

125. Ibid.

126. Stanton, "The Women of Hawaii."

127. Rachel Foster Avery, ed., *Proceedings of the Thirty First Annual Convention of the National American Woman Suffrage Association, 1899* (Warren, OH: Perry, n.d.).

128. *HWS* 4:343.

129. Anna Garlin Spencer, "Our Duty to the Women of Our New Possessions," *HWS* 4:328–31.

130. Ibid., 325.

131. Ibid.

132. Ibid.

133. Ibid., 328–31.

134. Ibid.

135. Ibid.

136. Ibid., 331.

137. Ibid., 333.

138. Ibid.

139. Ibid., 332, 333.

140. Ibid., 342–43.

141. Henry Brown Blackwell, "The Philippines for the Filipinos," *Woman's Journal*, 14 January 1899; Henry Brown Blackwell, "Not Conquerors but Protectors," *Woman's Journal*, 1 April 1899; Henry Brown Blackwell, "A Warning to Imperialists," *Woman's Journal*, 29 July 1899; see also "A Philippine Symposium," *Woman's Journal*, 18 March 1899.

142. "Women vs. Imperialism," *Woman's Journal*, 3 June 1899.

143. Susan B. Anthony, "Interview on the War," *Democrat and Chronicle*, 15 May 1899, ECS/SBA Film, ser. 3.

144. Ishbel Aberdeen, ed., *International Council of Women Report of Transactions of the Second Quinquennial Meeting Held in London, July 1899* (London: Fisher Unwin, 1900), 153.

145. Ibid., 154.

146. Ibid.

147. Susan B. Anthony to Clara Colby, 24 January 1899, Clara Colby Collection, Huntington Library, CA, CS/SBA Film, ser. 3.

148. "Women Are for Peace," *Washington Post*, 16 February 1899.

149. Perkins, *Denial of Empire*.

150. Henry Brown Blackwell, "Domestic Imperialism," *Woman's Journal*, 15 November 1902.

151. Smith, *Civic Ideals*, 432; Rogers M. Smith, " 'One United People': Second-Class Female Citizenship and the American Quest for Community," *Yale Journal of Law and the Humanities* 1 (1989): 262. On *Downes v. Bidwell*, 182 U.S. 244 (1901), see especially Christina Duffy Burnett and Burke Marshall, "Between the Foreign and the Domestic: The Doctrine of Territorial Incorporation, Invented and Reinvented," Sanford Levinson, "Installing the *Insular Cases* into the Canon of Constitutional Law," and Rogers M. Smith, "The Bitter Roots of Puerto Rican Citizenship," all in Christina Duffy Burnett and Burke Marshall, eds., *Foreign in a Domestic Sense: Puerto Rico, American Expansion, and the Constitution* (Durham, NC: Duke University Press, 2001), 1–38; 121–39; 373–88.

152. Kevin K. Gaines, "Black Americans' Racial Uplift Ideology as 'Civilizing Mission': Pauline E. Hopkins on Race and Imperialism," in Amy Kaplan and Donald E. Pease, eds., *Cultures of United States Imperialism* (Durham, NC: Duke University Press, 1993), 433–53; Bederman, *Manliness and Civilization*; Sylvia M. Jacobs, "Give a Thought to Africa: Black Women Missionaries in Southern Africa," in Nupur Chaudhuri and Margaret Strobel, eds., *Western Women and Imperialism: Complicity and Resistance* (Bloomington: Indiana University Press, 1992), 207–30. In contrast to scholarship that documents African American women's efforts to claim space for themselves in the work of civilization, Hazel Carby had documented instances where African American women activists linked "internal and external colonization." See Carby, " 'On the Threshold of the Woman's Era,' " 265.

CHAPTER 5: GETTING SUFFRAGE IN AN AGE OF EMPIRE, 1914–1929

1. Inez Haynes Irwin, *The Story of the Woman's Party* (1921; reprint, New York: Harcourt, Brace, 1971), 181.

2. Under U.S. rule, voting in the Philippines had been limited to men over twenty-three who met a property qualification and could read or write in Spanish or English. The 1916 Jones Act extended voting to those who could read and write a native language. Whitney T. Perkins, *Denial of Empire: The United States and Its Dependencies* (Leiden, Netherlands: Sythoff, 1962), 221–29.

3. Ibid., 128–29.

4. See, for example, "What about Women?" *Woman's Journal*, 12 February 1916; "Senate Takes Up Philippine Bill," *Woman's Journal*, 15 January 1916; "Senators Tell Why Filipinos Need the Vote," *Woman's Journal*, 22 January 1916.

5. Irwin, *Story of the Woman's Party*, 181.

6. *Congressional Record*, 63rd Cong., 3rd sess., 12 January 1915.

7. Irwin, *Story of the Woman's Party*, 181.

8. Christine A. Lunardini, *From Equal Suffrage to Equal Rights: Alice Paul and the National Woman's Party, 1910–1928* (New York: New York University Press, 1986); Linda Ford, *Iron-Jawed Angels: The Suffrage Militancy of the National Woman's Party, 1912–1920* (Lanham, MD: University Press of America, 1991).

9. Eleanor Flexner, *Century of Struggle: The Woman's Rights Movement in the United States*, rev. ed. (Cambridge, MA: Belknap Press, 1979), 274–86; Ellen Carol DuBois, *Harriot Stanton Blatch and the Winning of Woman Suffrage* (New Haven, CT: Yale University Press, 1997), 187–96; Nancy F. Cott, *The Grounding of Modern Feminism* (New Haven, CT: Yale University Press, 1987), 54.

10. These were Wyoming, Colorado, Utah, Idaho, Arizona, Washington, California, Kansas, and Oregon.

11. For a brief overview of individual state campaigns, see *HWS* 6. See also Rebecca J. Mead, *How the Vote Was Won: Woman Suffrage in the Western United States, 1868–1914* (New York: New York University Press, 2004).

12. Robert Booth Fowler, *Carrie Catt: Feminist Politician* (Boston: Northeastern University Press, 1986); Mary Gray Peck, *Carrie Chapman Catt: A Biography* (New York: Wilson, 1944).

13. *New York Times*, 25 April 1913; *HWS* 6:713–15.

14. *HWS* 6:820. See also Leila J. Rupp, *Worlds of Women: The Making of an International Women's Movement* (Princeton, NJ: Princeton University Press, 1997); Harriet Hyman Alonso, *Peace as a Woman's Issue: A History of the U.S. Movement for World Peace and Women's Rights* (Syracuse, NY: Syracuse University Press, 1993).

15. Patricia Grimshaw, "Women's Suffrage in New Zealand Revisited: Writing from the Margins," in Caroline Daley and Melanie Nolan, eds., *Suffrage and Beyond: International Feminist Perspectives* (New York: New York University Press, 1994), 25–41; Raewyn Dalziel, "Presenting the Enfranchisement of New Zealand Women Abroad," in Daley and Nolan, eds., *Suffrage and Beyond*, 42–64.

16. *HWS* 6: 715–722.

17. On the Puerto Rican women's movement more generally, see Yamila Azize-Vargas, "The Emergence of Feminism in Puerto Rico, 1870–1930," in Vicki L. Ruiz and Ellen Carol DuBois, eds., *Unequal Sisters: A Multicultural Reader in U.S. Women's History*, 3rd ed. (New York: Routledge, 2000), 268–75; Edna Acosta-Belén, ed., *The Puerto Rican Woman*, 2nd ed. (New York: Praeger, 1986); Félix V. Matos Rodríguez, "Women's History in Puerto Rican Historiography," in Félix V. Matos Rodríguez and Linda Delgado, eds., *Puerto Rican Women's History: New Perspectives* (Armonk, NY: Sharpe, 1998), 9–37.

18. Gladys Jiménez-Muñoz, "Deconstructing Colonialist Discourse: Links between the Women's Suffrage Movement in the United States and Puerto Rico," *Phoebe: An Interdisciplinary Journal of Feminist Scholarship, Theory, and Aesthetics* 5 (1993): 9–34, is a notable exception to this tendency in the literature.

19. Ann D. Gordon, ed., *African-American Women and the Vote, 1837–1965* (Amherst: University of Massachusetts Press, 1997).

20. Kristin Hoganson, *Fighting for American Manhood: How Gender Politics Provoked the Spanish-American and Philippine-American Wars* (New Haven, CT: Yale University Press, 1998), 144.

21. Theodore Roosevelt to Susan B. Anthony, 12 December 1898, Ida Husted Harper Collection, Huntington Library, CA.

22. Hoganson, *Fighting for American Manhood*, 144–50.

23. Ian Tyrrell, *Woman's World / Woman's Empire: The Woman's Christian Temperance Union in International Perspective, 1880–1930* (Chapel Hill: University of North Carolina Press, 1991), 212–219; Laura Briggs, *Reproducing Empire: Race, Sex, Science and U.S. Imperialism in Puerto Rico* (Berkeley and Los Angeles: University of California Press, 2002), 32; Hoganson, *Fighting for American Manhood*, 187.

24. "NAWSA Resolutions," *Woman's Journal*, 22 February 1902.

25. "Massacre and Torture Justified," *Woman's Journal*, 3 May 1902.

26. "Women in the Philippines," *Woman's Journal*, 22 February 1902.

27. Ibid.

28. "Women of the Philippines," *Woman's Journal*, 7 June 1902. See also Hoganson, " 'As Badly Off as the Filipinos': U.S. Women's Suffragists and the Imperial Issue at the Turn of the Century," *Journal of Women's History* 13 (2001): 25.

29. Tyrrell, *Woman's World / Woman's Empire*, 218.

30. *Giles v. Harris*, 189 U.S. 475 (1903). See Rogers M. Smith, *Civic Ideals: Conflicting Visions of Citizenship in U.S. History* (New Haven, CT: Yale University Press, 1997), 452.

31. *Hawaii v. Mankichi*, 190 U.S. 197 (1903). See Smith, *Civic Ideals*, 437–38.

32. *Downes v. Bidwell*, 182 U.S. 244 (1901). See Smith, *Civic Ideals*, 435–37.

33. Michael Salman, *The Embarrassment of Slavery: Controversies over Bondage and Nationalism in the American Colonial Philippines* (Berkeley and Los Angeles: University of California Press, 2001), 151–52; Charles B. Elliott, *The Philippines to the End of the Commission Government* (Indianapolis: Bobbs, Merrill, 1917); Joseph Ralston Hayden, *The Philippines: A Study in National Development* (New York: Macmillan, 1942).

34. Gladys Jiménez-Muñoz, " 'A Storm Dressed in Skirts' " Ambivalence in the Debate on Women's Suffrage in Puerto Rico, 1927–1929" (Ph.D. diss., SUNY Binghamton, 1993).

35. "Democratic Party Platform," 1912.

36. "Suffragists Rap Wilson for Silence," *New York Times*, 3 December 1912.

37. *HWS* 6:145–65.

38. *Congressional Record*, 63rd Cong., 2nd sess., 10 October 1914, 16427.

39. Ibid., 16428.

40. Ibid., 16430.

41. *New York Times*, 11 October 1914.

42. William Atkinson Jones, *Congressional Record*, 63rd Cong., 2nd sess., 10 October 1914, 16434, 16439.

43. "Freedom for the Filipinos," *Woman Citizen*, 17 October 1914.

44. "Filipino Women and the Vote," *Woman's Journal*, 24 October 1914.

45. "Including the Women of Hawaii," *Suffragist*, April 1920.

46. Azize-Vargas, "Emergence of Feminism in Puerto Rico," 272.

47. E. H. Crowder to Chief, Bureau of Insular Affairs, 11 November 1920, War Department, Office of the Judge Advocate General, Civil JAG 014.35, enclosure at 5 May 1925, National Woman's Party Papers (Sanford, NC: Microfilming Corporation of America, 1981), Series I, Correspondence, Reel 29, December 1924–June 1925.

48. Ibid.

49. Ibid.

50. Ibid.

51. *Morales y Benet, Peticionarias v. La Junta Local de Inscripciones*, 25 April 1924, 1924 WL 5831 (P.R.).

52. "Woman's Party Aids Porto Rican Women," *Equal Rights*, 16 May 1925; "Porto Rican Women Wish to Affiliate," *Equal Rights*, 18 July 1925.

53. "Woman's Party Aids Porto Rican Women"; "Porto Rican Women Wish to Affiliate."

54. Margaret Whittemore to Antonio Barcelo, 5 May 1925, National Woman's Party Papers, Series 1, Correspondence, Reel 29, December 1924–June 1925.

55. Margaret Whittemore to Horace M. Towner, 5 May 1925, National Woman's Party Papers, Series 1, Correspondence, Reel 29, December 1924–June 1925.

56. "Puerto Rican Suffrage Bill Introduced," *Equal Rights*, 19 February 1927.

57. Katherine Fisher, "Votes for Porto Rican Women," *Equal Rights*, 11 June 1927, cited in U.S. Congress, Senate, Committee on Territories and Insular Possessions, *Woman Suffrage in Puerto Rico, Hearing on S. 753*, 70th Cong., 1st sess., 25 April 1928, 14.

58. Ibid., 14–15.

59. Ibid., 1.

60. "Woman's Party Aids Porto Rican Women"; "Porto Rican Women Wish to Affiliate."

61. U.S. Congress, Senate, Committee on Territories and Insular Possessions, *Woman Suffrage in Puerto Rico*, 4.

62. Ibid., 5–6.

63. Ibid., 20.

64. John Bingham, *Congressional Record*, 70th Cong., 2nd sess., 17 December 1928, 756.

65. "Porto Rican Bill Favorably Reported," *Equal Rights* 19 January 1929; "Senate Discusses Porto Rican Woman Suffrage," *Equal Rights* 23 February 1929.

66. Jiménez-Muñoz, "Deconstructing Colonialist Discourse," 12.

67. Ibid.

EPILOGUE

1. *Congressional Record*, 51st Cong., 1st sess., 25 June 1890, 6488.

2. Mina Roces, "Is the Suffragist an American Colonial Construct? Defining 'the Filipino Woman' in Colonial Philippines," in Louise Edwards and Mina Roces, eds., *Women's Suffrage in Asia: Gender, Nationalism and Democracy* (London: RoutledgeCurzon, 2004), 29–30.

BIBLIOGRAPHY

MANUSCRIPTS AND ARCHIVAL SOURCES

Anthony-Avery Papers. University of Rochester Library, Rochester, NY.

Anthony Family Collection. Huntington Library, San Marino, CA.

Blackwell Family Papers. Library of Congress, Manuscript Division, DC.

Blackwell Family Papers, MC-411. Schlesinger Library, Radcliffe College, Cambridge, MA.

Olympia Brown Papers. Schlesinger Library, Radcliffe College, Cambridge, MA.

Carrie Chapman Catt Papers. New York Public Library, NY.

Clara Beckwith Colby Collection. Huntington Library, San Marino, CA.

Matilda Joslyn Gage Papers. Schlesinger Library, Radcliffe College, Cambridge, MA.

Garrison Family Papers. Sophia Smith Collection, Smith College Library, Northampton, MA.

Elizabeth Boynton Harbert Collection. Huntington Library, San Marino, CA

Ida Husted Harper Collection. Huntington Library, San Marino, CA.

Ida Husted Harper. Woman Suffrage Scrapbook 1, Library of Congress Manuscript Division, DC.

Samuel Gridley Howe Papers. Hayes Research Library, Perkins School, Watertown, MA.

International Council of Women. Records, 1888–1959. Sophia Smith Collection, Smith College, Northampton, MA.

Alma Lutz Collection. Huntington Library, San Marino, CA.

National Council of Women of the United States. Records, 1888–1976. New York Public Library, NY.

Alice Park Collection. Huntington Library, San Marino, CA.

May Wright Sewall Papers. Marion County Public Library, Indianapolis, IN.

Anna Howard Shaw Papers (Woman's Rights Collection). Schlesinger Library, Radcliffe College, Cambridge, MA.

Elizabeth Cady Stanton. Theodore Stanton Collection, Douglass Library, Rutgers University, New Brunswick. NJ.

Charles Sumner. Correspondence. (MS Am 1), Houghton Library, Harvard University, Cambridge, MA.

Suffrage—Subject Collection, Sophia Smith Collection, Smith College Library, Northampton, MA.

PUBLISHED MANUSCRIPT AND ARCHIVAL COLLECTIONS

National Woman's Party Papers, 1913–1974. Sanford, N.C.: Microfilming Corporation of America, 1977–1979.

Records of the National Association of Colored Women's Clubs, 1895–1992, Part 1: Minutes of National Conventions, Publications, and President's Office Correspondence. Lillian Serece Williams and Randolph Boehm, eds. Bethesda, MD: University Publications of America, 1993–1994.

The Papers of Elizabeth Cady Stanton and Susan B. Anthony. Patricia G. Holland and Ann D. Gordon, eds. Wilmington, DE: Scholarly Resources, c1991.

The Isabella Beecher Hooker Project: A Microfiche Edition of Her Papers and Suffrage Related Correspondence Owned by the Stowe-Day Foundation. Anne Throne Margolis and Margaret Granville Mair, eds. Hartford, CT: The Foundation, 1979.

PERIODICALS

Arena (Boston, MA)
Baltimore American
Boston Daily Advertiser
Boston Investigator
Collier's Weekly (Springfield, OH)
Crisis (New York, NY)
Daily Inter Ocean (Chicago, IL)
Daily National Republican (Washington, DC)
Democrat and Chronicle (Rochester, NY)
Equal Rights (Washington, DC)
Evening Star (Washington, DC)
Golden Age (Boston, MA)
Hearth and Home (New York, NY)
Independent (New York, NY)
Nation *(New York, NY)*
National Citizen and Ballot Box (Syracuse, NY)
National Notes (Kansas City, MO)
National Standard (New York, NY)
New National Era (Washington, DC)
New York Herald
New York Times
New York Tribune
New York World
Revolution (New York, NY)
Suffragist (Washington, DC)
True Republic (Cleveland, OH)

Washington Post
Woman Citizen (New York, NY)
Woman's Campaign (Washington, DC)
Woman's Journal (Boston, MA)
Woman's Signal (London, England)
Woman's Tribune (Beatrice, NE)
Woodhull and Claflin's Weekly (New York, NY)

CASES

Cherokee Nation v. Georgia, 30 U.S. (5 Pet.) 1 (1831).
Downes v. Bidwell, 182 U.S. 244 (1901).
Giles v. Harris, 189 U.S. 475 (1903).
Hawaii v. Mankichi, 190 U.S. 197 (1903).
Minor v. Happersett, 21 Wallace 162 (1875).
Morales y Benet, Peticionarias v. La Junta Local de Inscripciones, 25 April 1924, 1924 WL 5831 (P.R.).
Scott v. Sanford, 19 Howard 393 (U.S. 1857).
United States v. Anthony, 24 Fed. Cas. (C.C.N.D.N.Y., 1873).
United States v. Elm, 24 December 1877, 25 Fed, No. 15.
Worcester v. Georgia, 31 U.S. (6 Pet.) 515 (1832).

GOVERNMENT DOCUMENTS

Congressional Globe, 1868–1873
Congressional Record, 1873–1935
House Executive Documents
Senate Executive Documents
House Misc. Documents
Senate Misc. Documents
United States. *Official Opinions of the Attorneys General of the United States.* Washington, D.C.: Government Printing Office, 1873-.
——. *Reports of the Taft Philippine Commission (June-November 1900).* Washington, DC: Government Printing Office, 1901.
——. *Report of the Commission of Inquiry to Santo Domingo.* Washington, DC: Government Printing Office, 1871.
——. *The Statutes at Large and Proclamations of the United States of America.* Boston: Little Brown, 1863–1869.
——. *The Statutes at Large and Proclamations of the United States of America.* Boston: Little Brown, 1871–1873.
——. *The Statutes at Large of the United States.* Washington, D.C.: Government Printing Office, 1875–1936.

United States. Congress. Senate. Committee on Territories and Insular Possessions. *Woman Suffrage in Puerto Rico: Hearing on S. 753.* 70th Cong., 1st sess., 25 April 1928.

——. Congress. Senate and House. Committees on the District of Columbia. 22 January 1870.

PUBLISHED SOURCES

Aberdeen, Ishbel, ed. *International Council of Women Report of Transactions of the Second Quinquennial Meeting Held in London, July 1899.* London: Fisher Unwin, 1900.

Acosta-Belén, Edna, ed. *The Puerto Rican Woman.* 2nd ed. New York: Praeger, 1986.

Alexander, Thomas G. "An Experiment in Progressive Legislation: The Granting of Woman Suffrage in Utah in 1870." *Utah Historical Quarterly* 38 (1970): 20–30.

Alonso, Harriet Hyman. *Peace as a Woman's Issue: A History of the U.S. Movement for World Peace and Women's Rights.* Syracuse, NY: Syracuse University Press, 1993.

Avery, Rachel Foster, ed. *Proceedings of the Thirty First Annual Convention of the National American Woman Suffrage Association, 1899.* Warren, OH: Perry, n.d.

Aynes, Richard L. "Unintended Consequences of the Fourteenth Amendment." In *Unintended Consequences of Constitutional Amendment,* ed. David E. Kyvig, 110–40. Athens: University of Georgia Press, 2000.

Azize-Vargas, Yamila. "The Emergence of Feminism in Puerto Rico, 1870–1930." In *Unequal Sisters: A Multicultural Reader in U.S. Women's History,* 3rd ed., ed. Vicki L. Ruiz and Ellen Carol DuBois, 268–75. New York: Routledge, 2000.

Banner, Lois. *Elizabeth Cady Stanton: A Radical for Woman's Rights.* Boston: Little Brown, and Company, 1980.

Barry, Kathleen. *Susan B. Anthony: A Biography of a Singular Feminist.* New York: New York University Press, 1988.

Basson, Lauren L. "Fit for Annexation but Unfit to Vote? Debating Hawaiian Suffrage Qualifications at the Turn of the Twentieth Century." *Social Science History* 29 (2005): 575–98.

Bates, Edward. *What Constitutes Citizenship? The Rights of Citizens.* Hartford: L. E. Hunt, 1868.

Bederman, Gail. *Manliness and Civilization: A Cultural History of Gender and Race in the United States, 1880–1917.* Chicago: University of Chicago Press, 1995.

Beisner, Robert L. *From the Old Diplomacy to the New, 1865–1900.* 1975. 2nd ed., Chicago: Harlan Davidson, 1986.

——. "Thirty Years before Manila: E. L. Godkin, Carl Schurz, and Anti-imperialism in the Gilded Age." *Historian* 30 (1968): 561–77.

——. *Twelve against Empire: The Anti-imperialists, 1898–1900.* New York: McGraw-Hill, 1968.

Benedict, Michael Les. "Preserving Federalism: Reconstruction and the Waite Court." In *The Supreme Court Review,* ed. Philip B. Kurland and Gerhard Casper, 39–79. Chicago: University of Chicago Press, 1979.

Berkhoffer, Robert F., Jr. "The Northwest Ordinance and the Principle of Territorial Evolution." In *The American Territorial System,* ed. John Porter Bloom, 45–55. Athens: Ohio University Press, 1973.

———. *The White Man's Indian.* New York: Knopf, 1978.

Billington, Ray Allen. *Westward Expansion: A History of the American Frontier.* 2d ed. New York: Macmillan, 1960.

Blackwell, Alice Stone. *Lucy Stone: Pioneer of Woman's Rights.* Boston: Little, Brown, 1930.

Blair, Karen J. *The Clubwoman as Feminist: True Womanhood Redefined, 1868–1914.* New York: Holmes and Meier, 1980.

Boydston, Jeanne. *The Limits of Sisterhood: The Beecher Sisters on Women's Rights and Woman's Sphere.* Chapel Hill: University of North Carolina Press, 1988.

Brammer, Leila R. *Excluded from Suffrage History: Matilda Joslyn Gage, Nineteenth-Century American Feminist.* Westport, CN: Greenwood Press, 2000.

Braude, Ann. *Radical Spirits: Spiritualism and Women's Rights in Nineteenth-Century America.* Boston: Beacon Press, 1989.

Bredbenner, Candice Lewis. *A Nationality of Her Own: Women, Marriage, and the Law of Citizenship.* Berkeley and Los Angeles: University of California Press, 1998.

Briggs, Emily Edson. *The Olivia Letters: Being Some History of Washington City for Forty Years as Told by the Letters of a Newspaper Correspondent.* New York: Neale, 1906.

Briggs, Laura. *Reproducing Empire: Race, Sex, Science and U.S. Imperialism in Puerto Rico.* Berkeley and Los Angeles: University of California Press, 2002.

Brown, Elsa Barkley. "To Catch the Vision of Freedom: Reconstructing Southern Black Women's Political History, 1865–1880." In *African American Women and the Vote, 1837–1965,* ed. Ann D. Gordon and Bettye Collier-Thomas, 66–99. Amherst: University of Massachusetts Press, 1997.

Brown, Kathy. "The Anglo-Algonquian Gender Frontier." In *Negotiators of Change: Historical Perspectives on Native American Women,* ed. Nancy Shoemaker, 26–48. New York: Routledge, 1995.

Brumberg, Joan Jacobs. "Zenanas and Girlless Villages: The Ethnology of American Evangelical Women, 1870–1910." *Journal of American History* 69 (1982): 347–71.

Bryan, W. B. *A History of the National Capital, 1815–1878.* New York: Macmillan, 1916.

Buechler, Steven. "Elizabeth Boynton Harbert and the Woman Suffrage Movement, 1876–1896." *Signs* 13 (1987): 78–97.

———. *The Transformation of the Woman Suffrage Movement: The Case of Illinois, 1850–1920.* New Brunswick, NJ: Rutgers University Press, 1986.

Bullock, Penelope L. *The Afro-American Periodical Press, 1838–1909.* Baton Rouge: Louisiana State University Press, 1981.

Burnett, Christina Duffy, and Burke Marshall. "Between the Foreign and the Domestic: The Doctrine of Territorial Incorporation, Invented and Reinvented." In *Foreign in a Domestic Sense: Puerto Rico, American Expansion, and the Constitution,* ed. Christina Duffy Burnett and Burke Marshall, 1–38. Durham, NC: Duke University Press, 2001.

Burnett, Christina Duffy, and Burke Marshall., eds. *Foreign in a Domestic Sense: Puerto Rico, American Expansion, and the Constitution*. Durham, NC: Duke University Press, 2001.

Burton, Antoinette. *Burdens of History: British Feminists, Indian Women, and Imperial Culture, 1865–1915*. Chapel Hill: University of North Carolina Press, 1994.

Carby, Hazel V. "'On the Threshold of the Woman's Era': Lynching, Empire, and Sexuality in Black Feminist Theory." *Critical Inquiry* 12 (1985): 262–77.

Cherny, Robert W. *American Politics in the Gilded Age, 1868–1900*. Wheeling, IL: Harland Davidson, 1997.

Child, Lydia Maria. Carolyn L. Karcher, ed., *Hobomok and Other Writings on Indians*. New Brunswick, NJ: Rutgers University Press, 1986.

Clark, Blue. *Lone Wolf v. Hitchcock: Treaty Rights and Indian Law at the End of the Nineteenth Century*. Lincoln: University of Nebraska Press, 1994.

Cohen, Felix S. *Handbook of Federal Indian Law*. Washington: Government Printing Office, 1942.

Comaroff, John L., and Jean Comaroff. *Of Revelation and Revolution: The Dialectics of Modernity on a South African Frontier*. Vol. 2. Chicago: University of Chicago Press, 1997.

Cott, Nancy F. *The Grounding of Modern Feminism*. New Haven, CT: Yale University Press, 1987.

———. *Public Vows: A History of Marriage and the Nation*. Cambridge, MA: Harvard University Press, 2000.

Crankshaw, Edward. *Bismarck*. London: Macmillan, 1981.

Dailey, Jane. *Before Jim Crow: The Politics of Race in Postemancipation Virginia*. Chapel Hill: University of North Carolina Press, 2000.

Dalziel, Raewyn. "Presenting the Enfranchisement of New Zealand Women." In *Suffrage and Beyond: International Feminist Perspectives*, ed. Caroline Daley and Melanie Nolan, 42–66. New York: New York University Press, 1994.

Damiani, Brian P. *Advocates of Empire: William McKinley, the Senate and American Expansion, 1898–1899*. New York: Garland, 1987.

De Santis, Vincent P. *Republicans Face the Southern Question: The New Departure Years, 1877–1897*. Baltimore: Johns Hopkins Press, 1959.

Donald, David. *Charles Sumner and the Rights of Man*. New York: Knopf, 1970.

Douglass, Frederick. *The Frederick Douglass Papers*. 5 Vols. John W. Blassingame and John McKivigan, eds. New Haven, CT: Yale University Press, 1979–1991.

———. *Frederick Douglass on Women's Rights*. Philip S. Foner, ed. Westport, CT: Greenwood Press, 1976.

Drinnon, Richard. *Facing West: The Metaphysics of Indian-Hating and Empire-Building*. Minneapolis: University of Minnesota Press, 1980.

DuBois, Ellen Carol. "Feminism and Free Love." 2001. http://www2.h-net.msu.edu/~women/papers/freelove.html.

———. *Feminism and Suffrage: The Emergence of an Independent Women's Movement in America, 1848–1869*. Ithaca, NY: Cornell University Press, 1978.

——. *Harriet Stanton Blatch and the Winning of Woman Suffrage*. New Haven, CT: Yale University Press, 1997.

——. "The Nineteenth-Century Woman Suffrage Movement and the Analysis of Woman's Oppression (1978)." In *Woman Suffrage and Women's Rights*. Ellen Carol DuBois, ed., 68–80. New York: New York University Press, 1998.

——. " 'Outgrowing the Compact of the Fathers': Equal Rights, Woman Suffrage, and the United States Constitution, 1820–1878." *Journal of American History* 74 (1987): 836–62.

——. "Taking the Law into Our Own Hands: *Bradwell, Minor*, and Suffrage Militance in the 1870s." In *Visible Women: New Essays on American Activism*, ed. Nancy Hewitt and Suzanne Lebsock. Urbana: University of Illinois Press, 1993.

——. "Woman Suffrage and the Left: An International Socialist-Feminist Perspective." *New Left Review* 186 (1991): 20–45.

——. "Woman Suffrage around the World: Three Phases of Suffragist Internationalism." In *Suffrage and Beyond: International Feminist Perspectives*, ed. Caroline Daley and Melanie Nolan, 252–74. New York: New York University Press, 1994.

Edwards, Rebecca. *Angels in the Machinery: Gender and American Party Politics from the Civil War to the Progressive Era*. New York: Oxford University Press, 1997.

Elliott, Charles B. *The Philippines to the End of the Commission Government*. Indianapolis, IN: Bobbs, Merrill, 1917.

Emenhiser, JeDon A. "A Peculiar Covenant: American Indian Peoples and the U.S. Constitution." In *American Indians and U.S. Politics: A Companion Reader*, ed. John M. Meyer, 3–10. Westport, CT: Praeger, 2002.

Etcheson, Nicole. *Bleeding Kansas: Contested Liberty in the Civil War Era*. Lawrence: University Press of Kansas, 2004.

Eyck, Erich. *Bismarck and the German Empire*. 1950. Reprint, New York: Norton, 1968.

Farmer, Mary J., and Donald G. Nieman. "Race, Class, Gender, and the Unintended Consequences of the Fifteenth Amendment." In *Unintended Consequences of Constitutional Amendment*, ed. David E. Kyvig, 141–63. Athens: University of Georgia Press, 2000.

Faulkner, Carol. *Women's Radical Reconstruction: The Freedmen's Aid Movement*. Philadelphia: University of Pennsylvania Press, 2004.

Ferrer, Ada. *Insurgent Cuba: Race, Nation, and Revolution, 1868–1898*. Chapel Hill: University of North Carolina Press, 1999.

Fiss, Owen. *Oliver Wendell Holmes Devise: History of the Supreme Court of the United States*. Vol. 3, *Troubled Beginnings of the Modern State, 1888–1910*. New York: Macmillan, 1933.

Fletcher, Ian Christopher. " 'Women of the Nations, Unite!': Transnational Suffragism in the United Kingdom, 1912–1914." In *Women's Suffrage in the British Empire: Citizenship, Nation, and Race*, ed. Ian Christopher Fletcher, Laura Nym Mayhall, and Phillipa Levine, 103–20. London: Routledge, 2000.

Flexner, Eleanor. *Century of Struggle: The Woman's Rights Movement in the United States*. 1959. Rev. ed., Cambridge, MA: Belknap Press, 1975.

Foner, Eric. *Free Soil, Free Labor, Freemen: The Ideology of the Republican Party before the Civil War*. New York: Oxford University Press, 1979.

———. *Reconstruction: America's Unfinished Revolution, 1863–1877*. New York: Harper and Row, 1988.

Foner, Philip S. *The Spanish-Cuban War and the Birth of American Imperialism, 1895–1902*. Vol. 1. New York: Monthly Review Press, 1972.

Ford, Linda. *Iron-Jawed Angels: The Suffrage Militancy of the National Women's Party, 1912–1920*. Lanham, MD: University Press of America, 1991.

Fowler, Robert Booth. *Carrie Catt: Feminist Politician*. Boston: Northeastern University Press, 1986.

Gabriel, Mary. *Notorious Victoria: The Life of Victoria Woodhull, Uncensored*. Chapel Hill, NC: Algonquin Books of Chapel Hill, 1998.

Gaines, Kevin K. "Black Americans' Racial Uplift Ideology as 'Civilizing Mission': Pauline E. Hopkins on Race and Imperialism." In *Cultures of United States Imperialism*, ed. Amy Kaplan and Donald E. Pease, 433–53. Durham, NC: Duke University Press, 1993.

———. *Uplifting the Race: Black Leadership, Politics, and Culture in the Twentieth Century*. Chapel Hill: University of North Carolina Press, 1996.

Gatewood, Willard B. *"Smoked Yankees" and the Struggle for Empire: Letters from Negro Soldiers, 1898–1902*. Urbana: University of Illinois Press, 1971.

———. *Black Americans and the White Man's Burden, 1898–1903*. Urbana: University of Illinois Press, 1975.

Giddings, Paula. *When and Where I Enter: The Impact of Black Women on Race and Sex in America*. New York: Bantam Books, 1984.

Gifford, Carolyn De Swarte. "Frances Willard and the Woman's Christian Temperance Union's Conversion to Woman Suffrage." In *One Woman, One Vote: Rediscovering the Woman Suffrage Movement*, ed. Marjorie Spruill Wheeler, 117–33. Troutdale, OR: New Sage Press, 1995.

Gillett, Frederick H. *George Frisbie Hoar*. Boston: Houghton Mifflin, 1934.

Gilmore, Glenda Elizabeth. "Black Militia in the Spanish-American/Cuban War." In *The War of 1898 and U.S. Interventions, 1898–1934: An Encyclopedia*, ed. Benjamin R. Beede, 2:53–54. New York: Garland, 1994.

———. *Gender and Jim Crow: Women and the Politics of White Supremacy in North Carolina, 1896–1920*. Chapel Hill: University of North Carolina Press, 1996.

Ginzberg, Lori. *Untidy Origins: A Story of Woman's Rights in Antebellum New York*. Chapel Hill: University of North Carolina Press, 2005.

Goldman, Robert. *Reconstruction and Black Suffrage: Losing the Vote in Reese and Cruikshank*. Lawrence: University Press of Kansas, 2001.

Goldsmith, Barbara. *Other Powers: The Age of Suffrage, Spiritualism, and the Scandalous Victoria Woodhull*. New York: Knopf, 1988.

Gordon, Ann D., ed. *African-American Women and the Vote, 1837–1965*. Amherst: University of Massachusetts Press, 1997.

———, ed. *The Selected Papers of Elizabeth Cady Stanton and Susan B. Anthony: In the School of Anti-slavery, 1840 to 1866*. Vol. 1. New Brunswick, NJ: Rutgers University Press, 1997.

——, ed. *The Selected Papers of Elizabeth Cady Stanton and Susan B. Anthony: Against an Aristocracy of Sex, 1866 to 1873.* Vol. 2. New Brunswick, NJ: Rutgers University Press, 2000.

——, ed. *The Selected Papers of Elizabeth Cady Stanton and Susan B. Anthony: National Protection for National Citizens, 1873 to 1880.* Vol. 3. New Brunswick, NJ: Rutgers University Press, 2003.

——, ed. *The Selected Papers of Elizabeth Cady Stanton and Susan B. Anthony: When Clowns Make Laws for Queens, 1880 to 1887.* Vol. 4. New Brunswick, NJ: Rutgers University Press, 2006.

——. "Woman Suffrage (Not Universal Suffrage) by Federal Amendment." In *Votes for Women! The Woman Suffrage Movement in Tennessee, the South, and the Nation,* ed. Marjorie Spruill Wheeler, 3–24. Knoxville: University of Tennessee Press, 1995.

Gordon, Sarah Barringer. "The Liberty of Self-degradation: Polygamy, Woman Suffrage, and Consent in Nineteenth-Century America." *Journal of American History* 83 (1996): 815–47.

——. *The Mormon Question: Polygamy and Constitutional Conflict in Nineteenth-Century America.* Chapel Hill: University of North Carolina Press, 2002.

Graff, Henry F. *American Imperialism and the Philippine Insurrection: Testimony Taken from Hearings on Affairs in the Philippine Islands before the Senate Committee on the Philippines, 1902.* Boston: Little Brown, 1969.

Graham, Sarah Hunter. "The Suffrage Renaissance: A New Image for a New Century, 1896–1910." In *One Woman, One Vote: Rediscovering the Woman Suffrage Movement,* ed. Marjorie Spruill Wheeler, 157–78. Troutdale, OR: New Sage Press, 1995.

——. *Woman Suffrage and the New Democracy.* New Haven, CT: Yale University Press, 1996.

Green, Constance McLaughlin. *The Secret City: A History of Race Relations in the Nation's Capital.* Princeton, NJ: Princeton University Press, 1967.

——. *Washington: Village and Capital, 1800–1878.* Princeton, NJ: Princeton University Press, 1962.

Green, Elna C. *Southern Strategies: Southern Women and the Woman Suffrage Question.* Chapel Hill: University of North Carolina Press, 1997.

Griffith, Elizabeth. *In Her Own Right: The Life of Elizabeth Cady Stanton.* New York: Oxford University Press, 1984.

Grimshaw, Patricia. *Paths of Duty: American Missionary Wives in Nineteenth-Century Hawaii.* Honolulu: University of Hawaii Press, 1989.

——. "Women's Suffrage in New Zealand Revisited: Writing from the Margins." In *Suffrage and Beyond: International Feminist Perspectives,* ed. Caroline Daley and Melanie Nolan, 25–41. New York: New York University Press, 1994.

Gustafson, Melanie. *Women and the Republican Party, 1854–1924.* Urbana: University of Illinois Press, 2001.

Hall, Catherine. *Civilising Subjects: Metropole and Colony in the English Imagination, 1830–1867.* New York: Oxford University Press, 2002.

——. "The Nation Within and Without." In *Defining the Victorian Nation: Class, Race, Gender and the Reform Act of 1867,* by Catherine Hall, Keith McClelland, and Jane Rendall, 179–233. Cambridge: Cambridge University Press, 2000.

Hall, Catherine, Keith McClelland, and Jane Rendall. *Defining the Victorian Nation: Class, Race, Gender and the Reform Act of 1867.* Cambridge: Cambridge University Press, 2000.

Harper, Ida Husted. *The Life and Work of Susan B. Anthony*. 3 vols. Indianapolis: Bowen-Merrill Company, 1899–1908.

———. *Woman Suffrage Throughout the World*. New York: North American Review Publishing Co., 1907.

———. *The World Movement for Woman Suffrage*. New York: National American Woman Suffrage Association, 1911.

Harper, Frances Ellen. Frances Smith Foster, ed. *A Brighter Coming Day: A Frances Ellen Watkins Harper Reader*. New York: Feminist Press at the City University of New York, 1990.

Harring, Sidney L. *Crow Dog's Case: American Indian Sovereignty, Tribal Law, and United States Law in the Nineteenth Century*. New York: Cambridge University Press, 1994.

Hauptman, Laurence M. *Conspiracy of Interests: Iroquois Dispossession and the Rise of New York State*. Syracuse, NY: Syracuse University Press, 1999.

———. *The Iroquois in the Civil War: From Battlefield to Reservation*. Syracuse, NY: Syracuse University Press, 1993.

Hayden, Joseph Ralston. *The Philippines: A Study in National Development*. New York: Macmillan, 1942.

Hays, Robert G. *A Race at Bay: New York Times Editorials on "The Indian Problem," 1860–1900*. Carbondale: Southern Illinois University Press, 1997.

Hester, Thurman Lee, Jr. *Political Principles and Indian Sovereignty*. New York: Routledge, 2001.

Hewitt, Nancy. *Southern Discomfort: Women's Activism in Tampa, Florida 1880s–1920s*. Urbana: University of Illinois Press, 2001.

Higginbotham, Evelyn Brooks. *Righteous Discontent: The Women's Movement in the Black Baptist Church, 1880–1920*. Cambridge, MA: Harvard University Press, 1993.

Hoar, George Frisbie. *Autobiography of Seventy Years*. New York: C. Scribner's Sons, 1903.

Hoetink, H. *The Dominican People, 1850–1900: Notes for a Historical Sociology*. Baltimore: Johns Hopkins University Press, 1982.

Hoff, Joan. *Law, Gender, and Injustice: A Legal History of U.S. Women*. New York: New York University Press, 1991.

Hofstadter, Richard. "Racism and Imperialism." In *Social Darwinism in American Thought*. Boston: Beacon Press, 1944.

Hoganson, Kristin. "'As Badly Off as the Filipinos': U.S. Women's Suffragists and the Imperial Issue at the Turn of the Twentieth Century." *Journal of Women's History* 13 (Summer 2001): 9–33.

———. *Fighting for American Manhood: How Gender Politics Provoked the Spanish-American and Philippine-American Wars*. New Haven, CT: Yale University Press, 1998.

Holland, Patricia G., and Ann D. Gordon, eds. *Papers of Elizabeth Cady Stanton and Susan B. Anthony*. Wilmington, DE: Scholarly Resources, 1991. Microfilm.

Holt, Michael F. *The Rise and Fall of the American Whig Party: Jacksonian Politics and the Onset of the Civil War*. New York: Oxford University Press, 1999.

Holton, Sandra Stanley. "'To Educate Women into Rebellion': Elizabeth Cady Stanton and the Creation of a Transatlantic Network of Radical Suffragists." *American Historical Review* 99 (1994): 1112–36.

Holzman, Robert. *Stormy Ben Butler*. New York: Macmillan, 1954.

Horsman, Reginald. *Race and Manifest Destiny: The Origins of American Racial Anglo-Saxonism*. Cambridge, MA: Harvard University Press, 1981.

Houghton, N. D. "The Legal Status of Indian Suffrage in the United States." *California Law Review* 19 (1931): 507–20.

Howe, Samuel Gridley. *Letters on the Proposed Annexation of Santo Domingo in Answer to Certain Charges in the Newspaper*. Boston: Wright and Porter, 1871.

——. Laura Elizabeth Howe Richards and F. B. Sanborn. *Letters and Journals of Samuel Gridley Howe*. Boston: D. Estes, 1906.

Ignatieff, Michael. "Who Are Americans to Think That Freedom Is Theirs to Spread?" *New York Times Magazine*, 26 June 2005.

Irwin, Inez Haynes. *The Story of the Woman's Party*. 1921. Reprint, New York: Harcourt Brace, 1971.

Isenberg, Nancy. *Sex and Citizenship in Antebellum America*. Chapel Hill: University of North Carolina Press, 1998.

Iversen, Joan Smyth. *The Antipolygamy Controversy in U.S. Women's Movements, 1880–1925: A Debate on the American Home*. New York: Garland, 1997.

Jacobs, Sylvia M. "Give a Thought to Africa: Black Women Missionaries in Southern Africa." In *Western Women and Imperialism: Complicity and Resistance*, ed. Nupur Chaudhuri and Margaret Strobel, 207–30. Bloomington: Indiana University Press, 1992.

Jacobson, Mathew Frye. *Barbarian Virtues: The United States Encounters Foreign Peoples at Home and Abroad, 1876–1917*. New York: Hill and Wang, 2000.

Jiménez-Muñoz, Gladys M. "Deconstructing Colonialist Discourse: Links between the Women's Suffrage Movement in the United States and Puerto Rico." *Phoebe: An Interdisciplinary Journal of Feminist Scholarship, Theory, and Aesthetics* 5 (Spring 1993): 9–34.

——. "Literacy, Class, and Sexuality in the Debate on Women's Suffrage in Puerto Rico during the 1920s." In *Puerto Rico Women's History: New Perspectives*, ed. Félix V. Matos Rodríguez and Linda C. Delgado, 143–70. Armonk, NY: Sharpe, 1998.

——. " 'A Storm Dressed in Skirts': Ambivalence in the Debate on Women's Suffrage in Puerto Rico, 1927–1929." Ph.D. diss., SUNY Binghamton, 1994.

Johnston, Allan. *Surviving Freedom: The Black Community of Washington, D.C., 1860–1880*. New York: Garland, 1993.

Johnston, Johanna. *Mrs. Satan: The Incredible Saga of Victoria C. Woodhull*. New York: Putnam, 1967.

Kaczorowski, Robert J. "To Begin the Nation Anew: Congress, Citizenship, and Civil Rights after the Civil War." *American Historical Review* 92 (1987): 45–68.

Kantrowitz, Steven. *Ben Tillman and the Reconstruction of White Supremacy*. Chapel Hill: University of North Carolina Press, 2000.

Karcher, Carolyn L. *The First Woman in the Republic: A Cultural Biography of Lydia Maria Child*. Durham, NC: Duke University Press, 1994.

Keller, Morton. *Affairs of State: Public Life in Late Nineteenth Century America*. Cambridge, MA: Belknap Press, 1977.

Kerber, Linda. *No Constitutional Right to Be Ladies: Women and the Obligations of Citizenship.* New York: Hill and Wang, 1998.

Kern, Kathi. *Mrs. Stanton's Bible.* Ithaca, NY: Cornell University Press, 2001.

Kerr, Andrea Moore. *Lucy Stone: Speaking Out for Equality.* New Brunswick, NJ: Rutgers University Press, 1992.

Kettner, James H. *The Development of American Citizenship, 1608–1870.* Chapel Hill: University of North Carolina Press, 1978.

Keyssar, Alexander. *The Right to Vote: The Contested History of Democracy in the United States.* New York: Basic Books, 2000.

Klinghoffer, Judith A., and Lois Elkin. "'The Petticoat Electors': Women's Suffrage in New Jersey." *Journal of the Early Republic* 12 (1992): 161–93.

Knight, Melvin M. *The Americans in Santo Domingo.* New York: Vanguard Press, 1928.

Kraditor, Aileen S. *The Ideas of the Woman Suffrage Movement, 1890–1920.* New York: Columbia University Press, 1965.

Kramer, Paul A. "The Darkness That Enters the Home: The Politics of Prostitution during the Philippine-American War." In *Haunted by Empire: Geographies of Intimacy in North American History,* ed. Ann Laura Stoler, 366–404. Durham, NC: Duke University Press, 2006.

LaFeber, Walter. *The New Empire: An Interpretation of American Expansion, 1860–1898.* Ithaca, NY: Cornell University Press, 1963.

Landsman, Gail H. "The 'Other' as Political Symbol: Images of Indians in the Woman Suffrage Movement." *Ethnohistory* 39 (1992): 247–84.

Lasch, Christopher. "The Anti-imperialists, the Philippines, and the Inequality of Man." *Journal of Southern History* 24 (1958): 319–31.

Lawson, Gary, and Guy Seidman. *The Constitution of Empire: Territorial Expansion and American Legal History.* New Haven, CT: Yale University Press, 2004.

Lebsock, Suzanne. "Woman Suffrage and White Supremacy: A Virginia Case Study." In *Visible Women: New Essays on American Activism,* ed. Nancy A. Hewitt and Suzanne Lebsock. Urbana: University of Illinois Press, 1993.

Lerner, Gerda. *The Feminist Thought of Sarah Grimké.* New York: Oxford University Press, 1998.

Levinson, Sanford. "Installing the *Insular Cases* into the Canon of Constitutional Law." In *Foreign in a Domestic Sense: Puerto Rico, American Expansion, and the Constitution,* ed. Christina Duffy Burnett and Burke Marshall, 121–39. Durham, NC: Duke University Press, 2001.

Liebowitz, Arnold H. "United States Federalism: The States and the Territories." *American University Law Review* 28 (1979): 449–82.

Love, Eric T. *Race over Empire: Racism and U.S. Imperialism, 1865–1900.* Chapel Hill: University of North Carolina Press, 2004.

Lucie, Patricia. "On Being a Free Person and a Citizen by Constitutional Amendment." *Journal of American Studies* 12 (1978): 343–58.

Lunardini, Christine A. *From Equal Suffrage to Equal Rights: Alice Paul and the National Woman's Party, 1910–1928.* New York: New York University Press, 1986.

Lyman, Edward Leo. *Political Deliverance: The Mormon Quest for Utah Statehood*. Urbana: University of Illinois Press, 1986.

Marilley, Suzanne M. *Woman Suffrage and the Origins of Liberal Feminism in the United States, 1820–1920*. Cambridge, MA: Harvard University Press, 1996.

Marks, George P., III. *The Black Press Views American Imperialism, 1898–1900*. New York: Arno Press, 1971.

Martin, Jill E. " 'Neither Fish, Flesh, Fowl, Nor Good Red Herring': The Citizenship Status of American Indians, 1830–1924." In *American Indians and U.S. Politics: A Companion Reader*, ed. John E. Meyer, 51–72. Westport, CT: Praeger, 2002.

Materson, Lisa Gail. "Gendered Political Space and the Church: African-American Women's Partisan Mobilization in the Midwest during the Late Nineteenth and Early Twentieth Centuries." Paper in author's possession. U.S. Women's History Invited Lecture Series, 1 December 2000, Rice University, Houston, TX.

———. "Respectable Partisans: African American Women in Electoral Politics, 1877–1936." Ph.D. diss., UCLA, 2000.

May, Ernest R. *Imperial Democracy: The Emergence of America as a Great Power*. New York: Harcourt, Brace and World, 1961.

———. *The Making of the Monroe Doctrine*. Cambridge, MA: Belknap Press, 1975.

Mayhall, Laura Nym. "The South African War and the Origins of Suffrage Militancy in Britain." In *Women's Suffrage in the British Empire: Citizenship, Nation, and Race*, ed. Ian Christopher Fletcher, Laura Nym Mayhall, and Phillipa Levine, 3–17. London: Routledge, 2000.

McCormick, Thomas J. *China Market: America's Quest for Informal Empire, 1893–1901*. New York: Random House, 1967.

McFeely, William S. *Frederick Douglass*. New York: Norton, 1991.

———. *Grant: A Biography*. New York: Norton, 1981.

McGerr, Michael. *The Decline of Popular Politics: The American North, 1865–1928*. New York: Oxford University Press, 1986.

McPherson, Edward, ed. *Hand-Book of Politics, 1872–1876*. Vol. 1. 1872. Reprint, New York: De Capo Press, 1972.

———. *The Political History of the United States during the Period of Reconstruction*. Washington, DC: Chapman, 1880.

Mead, Rebecca J. *How the Vote Was Won: Woman Suffrage in the Western United States, 1868–1914*. New York: New York University Press, 2004.

Merk, Frederick. *Manifest Destiny and Mission in American History: A Reinterpretation*. With the collaboration of Lois Bannister Merk. 1963. Reprint, Cambridge, MA: Harvard University Press, 1995.

Merrill, L. T. "General Benjamin F. Butler in Washington." In *Records of the Columbia Historical Society of Washington, D.C.,* vol. 39, ed. Maud Burr Morris, 71–100. Washington, DC: Columbia Historical Society, 1938.

Merry, Sally Engle. *Colonizing Hawai'i: The Cultural Power of Law*. Princeton, NJ: Princeton University Press, 2000.

Morgan, Lewis H. *Ancient Society, or Researches in the Lines of Human Progress from Savagery through Barbarism to Civilization.* 1877. Reprint, Cambridge, MA: Belknap Press, 1964.

Murphy, Gretchen. *Hemispheric Imaginings: The Monroe Doctrine and Narratives of U.S. Empire.* Durham, NC: Duke University Press, 2005.

Nash, Howard. *Stormy Petrel: The Life and Times of General Benjamin F. Butler, 1818–1893.* Rutherford, NJ: Farleigh Dickinson University Press, 1969.

National Woman Suffrage Association. *Report of the International Council of Women, 1888.* Washington, DC: Darby, 1888.

——. *Declaration of the Rights of Women of the United States by the National Woman Suffrage Association, 4 July 1876.* N.p., n.d.

Nelson, William Javier. *Almost a Territory: America's Attempt to Annex the Dominican Republic.* Newark: University of Delaware Press, 1990.

Nevins, Allan. *Hamilton Fish: The Inner History of the Grant Administration.* 2 vols. 1936. Rev. ed., New York: Frederick Ungar Publishing Co., 1957.

Newman, Louise. "Assimilating Primitives: The 'Indian Problem' as a 'Woman Question.'" In *White Women's Rights: The Racial Origins of Feminism in the United States,* 116–31. New York: Oxford University Press, 1999.

——. *White Women's Rights: The Racial Origins of Feminism in the United States.* New York: Oxford University Press, 1999.

Nichols, Jeannette P. "The United States Congress and Imperialism, 1861–1897." *Journal of Economic History* 21 (1961): 526–38.

Nichols, Roy F. "The Kansas-Nebraska Act: A Century of Historiography." In *National Development and Sectional Crisis, 1815–1860,* ed. Joel Silbey, 195–218. New York: Random House, 1970.

Offner, John L. *An Unwanted War: The Diplomacy of the United States and Spain over Cuba, 1895–1898.* Chapel Hill: University of North Carolina Press, 1992.

Painter, Nell Irvin. *Standing at Armageddon: The United States, 1877–1919.* New York: Norton, 1987.

Palmer, Beverly Wilson, ed. *The Selected Letters of Charles Sumner, 1811–1874.* Boston: Northeastern University Press, 1990.

Peck, Mary Gray. *Carrie Chapman Catt: A Biography.* New York: Wilson, 1944.

Perez, Louis, Jr. *Cuba: Between Reform and Revolution.* New York: Oxford University Press, 1988.

Perkins, Linda Marie. "Black Feminism and 'Race Uplift,' 1890–1900." *Radcliffe Institute Working Paper.* Cambridge, MA: Institute for Advanced Study, 1981.

Perkins, Whitney T. *Denial of Empire: The United States and Its Dependencies.* Leiden, Netherlands: Sythoff, 1962.

Picó, Isabel. "The History of Women's Struggle for Equality in Puerto Rico." In *The Puerto Rican Woman: Perspectives on Culture, History, and Society,* 2nd ed., ed. Edna Acosta-Belén, 46–58. New York: Praeger, 1986.

Pierson, Michael D. *Free Hearts and Free Homes: Gender and American Anti-slavery Politics.* Chapel Hill: University of North Carolina Press, 2003.

Pinkett, Harold T. "Efforts to Annex Santo Domingo to the United States, 1866–1871." *Journal of Negro History* 26 (1941): 12–45.

Pons, Frank Moya. "The Land Question in Haiti and Santo Domingo: The Sociopolitical Context of the Transition from Slavery to Free Labor, 1801–1843." In *Between Slavery and Free Labor: The Spanish-Speaking Caribbean in the Nineteenth Century*, ed. Manuel Moreno Fraginals, Frank Moya Pons, and Stanley L. Engerman, 181–214. Baltimore: Johns Hopkins University Press, 1985.

Porter, Kirk H. *A History of Suffrage in the United States*. 1918. Reprint, New York: Greenwood Press, 1969.

Porter, Kirk H., and Donald B. Johnson, comps. *National Party Platforms, 1840–1956*. Urbana: University of Illinois Press, 1956.

Proctor, John Clagett, and Edwin Melvin Williams. "The Mayoral Period, 1802–71." In *Washington Past and Present*, ed. John Clagett Proctor, 78–129. New York: Lewis Historical Pub. Co., 1930.

Rafael, Vincente L. *White Love: And Other Events in Filipino History*. Durham: Duke University Press, 2000.

Ramos, Efrén Rivera. "Deconstructing Colonialism: The 'Unincorporated Territory' as a Category of Domination." In *Foreign in a Domestic Sense: Puerto Rico, American Expansion, and the Constitution*, ed. Christina Duffy Burnett and Burke Marshall, 104–20. Durham, NC: Duke University Press, 2001.

Renda, Mary. *Taking Haiti: Military Occupation and the Culture of U.S. Imperialism*. Chapel Hill: University of North Carolina Press, 2001.

Rendall, Jane. "Citizenship, Culture, and Civilization: The Languages of British Suffragists, 1866–1874." In *Suffrage and Beyond: International Feminist Perspectives*, ed. Caroline Daley and Melanie Noland, 127–50. New York: New York University Press, 1994.

——. "The Citizenship of Women and the Reform Act of 1867." In Catherine Hall, Keith McClelland, and Jane Rendall, 119–78. Cambridge: Cambridge University Press, 2000.

Rhodes, Jane. *Mary Ann Shadd Cary: The Black Press and Protest in the Nineteenth Century*. Bloomington: Indiana University Press, 1998.

Richards, Laura, ed. *Letters and Journals of Samuel Gridley Howe: The Servant of Humanity*. Boston: Estes, 1909.

Richards, Laura Elizabeth Howe, Maud Howe Elliott, and Florence Howe Hall. *Julia Ward Howe, 1819–1910*. Boston: Houghton Mifflin, 1925.

Roberts, Derrell C. *Joseph E. Brown and the Politics of Reconstruction*. Tuscaloosa, AL: University of Alabama Press, 1973.

Robinson, Charles M., III. *The Plains Wars, 1757–1900*. New York: Routledge, 2003.

Roces, Mina. "Is the Suffragist an American Colonial Construct? Defining 'the Filipino Woman' in Colonial Philippines." In *Women's Suffrage in Asia: Gender, Nationalism and Democracy*, ed. Louise Edwards and Mina Roces, 24–58. London: RoutledgeCurzon, 2004.

Rodríguez, Félix V. Matos, "Women's History in Puerto Rican Historiography." In *Puerto Rican Women's History: New Perspectives*, ed. Félix V. Matos Rodríguez and Linda Delgado, 9–37. Armonk, NY: Sharpe, 1998.

Rupp, Leila J. "Constructing Internationalism: The Case of the Transnational Women's Organizations, 1888–1945." *American Historical Review* 99 (1994): 1571–1600.

———. *Worlds of Women: The Making of an International Women's Movement*. Princeton, NJ: Princeton University Press, 1997.

Ryan, Mary. *Women in Public: Between Banners and Ballots, 1825–1880*. Baltimore: John Hopkins University Press, 1990.

Sachs, Emanie. *"The Terrible Siren": Victoria Woodhull*. 1928. Reprint, New York: Arno Press, 1972.

Salman, Michael. *The Embarrassment of Slavery: Controversies over Bondage and Nationalism in the American Colonial Philippines*. Berkeley and Los Angeles: University of California Press, 2001.

Salmon, Marylynn. *Women and the Law of Property in Early America*. Chapel Hill: University of North Carolina Press, 1986.

Satter, Beryl. *Each Mind a Kingdom: American Women, Sexual Purity, and the New Thought Movement, 1875–1920*. Berkeley: University of California Press, 1999.

Schecter, Patricia. *Ida B. Wells-Barnett and American Reform, 1880–1930*. Chapel Hill: University of North Carolina Press, 2001.

Schirmer, Daniel B. *Republic or Empire: American Resistance to the Philippine War*. Cambridge, MA: Schenkman, 1972.

Schwartz, Harold. *Samuel Gridley Howe: Social Reformer, 1801–1876*. Cambridge, MA: Harvard University Press, 1956.

———. "Santo Domingo and Samana Bay." In *Samuel Gridley Howe: Social Reformer, 1801–1876*. Cambridge, MA: Harvard University Press, 1956.

Scott, Anne Firor. *Natural Allies: Women's Associations in American History*. Urbana: University of Illinois Press, 1991.

Sewall, May Wright, ed. *Genesis of the International Council of Women and the Story of Its Growth, 1888–1893*. Indianapolis: n.p., 1914.

Shaw, Stephanie J. *What a Woman Ought to Be and Do: Black Professional Women Workers during the Jim Crow Era*. Chicago: University of Chicago Press, 1996.

Sherr, Lynn. *Failure Is Impossible: Susan B. Anthony in Her Own Words*. New York: Random House, 1995.

Siegel, Reva B. "She the People: The Nineteenth Amendment, Sex Equality, Federalism, and the Family." *Harvard Law Review* 115, no. 4 (February 2002): 947–1046.

Sinha, Mrinalini. "Suffragism and Internationalism: The Enfranchisement of British and Indian Women under an Imperial State." In *Women's Suffrage in the British Empire: Citizenship, Nation, and Race*, ed. Ian Christopher Fletcher, Laura Nym Mayhall, and Phillipa Levine, 224–40. London: Routledge, 2000.

Smith, Rogers M. "The Bitter Roots of Puerto Rican Citizenship." In *Foreign in a Domestic Sense: Puerto Rico, American Expansion, and the Constitution*, ed. Christina Duffy Burnett and Burke Marshall, 373–88. Durham, NC: Duke University Press, 2001.

———. *Civic Ideals: Conflicting Visions of Citizenship in U.S. History*. New Haven, CT: Yale University Press, 1997.

——."'One United People': Second-Class Female Citizenship and the American Quest for Community." *Yale Journal of Law and the Humanities* 1 (1989): 229–73.

Sneider, Allison L. "The Impact of Empire on the North American Woman Suffrage Movement: Suffrage Racism in an Imperial Context." *UCLA Historical Journal* 14 (1994): 14–32.

Stanton, Elizabeth Cady. *Eighty Years and More: Reminiscences, 1815–1897*. 1898. Reprint, Boston: Northeastern University Press, 1993.

——. *The Woman's Bible*. 1895. Reprint, Boston: Northeastern University Press, 1993.

Stanton, Elizabeth Cady, Susan Brownell Anthony, Matilda Joslyn Gage, and Ida Husted Harper, eds. *History of Woman Suffrage*. 6 vols. 1881–1922. Reprint, New York: Arno Press, 1969.

Statutes at Large of the United States. Washington, DC: Government Printing Office, 1887.

Stern, Madeline B. "Political Theory." In *The Victoria Woodhull Reader*, n.p. Weston, MA: M&S, 1974.

Stoler, Ann Laura. *Carnal Knowledge and Imperial Power: Race and the Intimate in Colonial Rule*. Berkeley and Los Angeles: University of California Press, 2002.

Stoler, Ann Laura, and Fredrick Cooper. "Between Metropole and Colony: Rethinking a Research Agenda." In *Tensions of Empire: Colonial Cultures in a Bourgeois World*, ed. Ann Laura Stoler and Fredrick Cooper, 1–56. Berkeley and Los Angeles: University of California Press, 1997.

Stoner, Lynn K. *From the House to the Streets: The Cuban Woman's Movement for Legal Reform, 1898–1940*. Durham: Duke University Press, 1991.

Sumner, Charles. "Naboth's Vineyard: Speech in the Senate on the Proposed Annexation of San Domingo to the United States, 21 December 1870." In *The Works of Charles Sumner*, ed. Charles Sumner, vol. 14, 89–131. Boston: Lee and Shepard, 1870–1883.

Tansill, Charles C. *The United States and Santo Domingo, 1798–1873: A Chapter in Caribbean Diplomacy*. Baltimore: Johns Hopkins University Press, 1938.

Terborg-Penn, Rosalyn. *African American Women in the Struggle for the Vote, 1850–1920*. Bloomington: Indiana University Press, 1998.

——. "Discrimination against Afro-American Women in the Woman's Movement, 1830–1920." In *The Afro-American Woman: Struggles and Images*, ed. Sharon Harley and Rosalyn Terborg-Penn, 17–27. Port Washington, NY: Kennikat Press, 1978.

——. "Enfranchising Women of Color: Woman Suffragists as Agents of Imperialism." In *Nation, Empire, Colony: Historicizing Gender and Race*, ed. Ruth Roach Pierson and Nupur Chaudhuri, 41–56. Bloomington: Indiana University Press, 1998.

Trask, David F. *The War with Spain in 1898*. New York: Macmillan, 1981.

Tyrrell, Ian. *Woman's World/Woman's Empire: The Woman's Christian Temperance Union in International Perspective, 1800–1930*. Chapel Hill: University of North Carolina Press, 1991.

Underhill, Lois Beachy. *The Woman Who Ran for President: The Many Lives of Victoria Woodhull*. Bridgehampton, NY: Bridge Works, 1995.

U.S. Department of the Interior. *Handbook of Federal Indian Law*. Washington, DC: U.S. Government Printing Office, 1941.

VanBurkleo, Sandra F. *"Belonging to the World": Women's Rights and American Constitutional Culture*. New York: Oxford University Press, 2001.

Walsh, Margaret. *The American West: Visions and Revisions*. New York: Cambridge University Press, 2005.

Wang, Xi. *The Trial of Democracy: Black Suffrage and Northern Republicans, 1860–1910*. Athens: University of Georgia Press, 1997.

Weiss, Nathan. "The Political Theory and Practice of General Benjamin Franklin Butler." Ph.D. diss., New York University, 1961.

Welch, Richard E., Jr. *George Frisbee Hoar and the Half-Breed Republicans*. Cambridge, MA: Harvard University Press, 1971.

——. *Response to Imperialism: The United States and the Philippine-American War, 1899–1902*. Chapel Hill: University of North Carolina Press, 1979.

Welles, Sumner. *The Dominican Republic, 1844–1924*, vol. 1. Mamaronek, NY: Appel, 1966.

——. *Naboth's Vineyard: The Dominican Republic 1844–1924*, vol. 1. Mamaroneck, NY: Appel, 1966.

Wellman, Paul I. *The Indian Wars of the West*. Garden City, NY: Doubleday, 1993.

Wells, Ida B., ed. *The Reason Why the Colored American Is Not in the Worlds' Columbian Exposition: The Afro-American's Contribution to Columbian Literature*. Chicago, 1893.

Werlich, Robert. *"Beast" Butler: The Incredible Career of Major General Benjamin Franklin Butler*. Washington, DC: Quaker Press, 1962.

Wesley, Charles. *The History of the National Association of Colored Women's Clubs: A Legacy of Service*. Washington, DC: National Association of Colored Women's Clubs, 1984.

Wheeler, Leslie, ed. *Loving Warriors: Selected Letters of Lucy Stone and Henry B. Blackwell, 1853 to 1893*. New York: Dial Press, 1981.

Wheeler, Marjorie Spruill. *New Women of the New South: The Leaders of the Woman Suffrage Movement in the Southern States*. New York: Oxford University Press, 1993.

White, Barbara Anne. *The Beecher Sisters*. New Haven, CT: Yale University Press, 2003.

Wiebe, Robert. *Self-Rule: A Cultural History of American Democracy*. Chicago: University of Chicago Press, 1995.

Wildenthal, Lora. *German Women for Empire, 1884–1945*. Durham, NC: Duke University Press, 2001.

Williams, William Appleman. *The Contours of American History*. Cleveland, Ohio: World Publishing, 1961.

——. *Empire as a Way of Life: An Essay on the Causes and Character of America's Present Predicament along with a Few Thoughts about an Alternative*. New York: Oxford University Press, 1980.

——. *The Roots of the Modern American Empire: A Study of the Growth and Shaping of Social Consciousness in a Marketplace Society*. New York: Random House, 1969.

——. *The Tragedy of American Diplomacy*. New York: Dell, 1972.

Wisan, Joseph E. *The Cuban Crisis as Reflected in the New York Press (1895–1898)*. New York: Columbia University Press, 1934.

Wolfley, Jeanette. "Jim Crow, Indian Style: The Disenfranchisement of Native Americans." *American Indian Law Review* 16 (1990): 161–202.

Woodhull, Victoria. *The Argument for Woman's Electoral Rights under Amendments XIV and XV of the Constitution of the United States: A Review of My Work at Washington, D.C. in 1870–1871.* London: G. Norman & Son, Printers, 1887.

Woodsum, Jo Ann. "Native American Women: An Update." In *Readings in American Indian Law: Recalling the Rhythm of Survival,* ed. Jo Carrillo, 226–34. Philadelphia: Temple University Press, 1998.

Wunder, John R. "No More Treaties: The Resolution of 1871 and the Alteration of Indian Rights to Their Homelands." In *Native American Law and Colonialism, before 1776 to 1903,* ed. John R. Wunder, 195–212. New York: Garland, 1996.

Yee, Shirley J. *Black Women Abolitionists: A Study in Activism 1828–1860.* Knoxville: University of Tennessee Press, 1992.

Yellin, Jean Fagan. *Women and Sisters: The Antislavery Feminists in American Culture.* New Haven, CT: Yale University Press, 1989.

INDEX

Page numbers in **bold** represent maps.

CPSIA information can be obtained at www.ICGtesting.com
Printed in the USA
BVOW06s2231300815

415657BV00003B/11/P

9 780195 321173